ELVIS COSTELLO

Icons of Pop Music

Series Editors: Jill Halstead, Goldsmiths, University of London, and
Dave Laing, independent writer and broadcaster
Books in this series, designed for undergraduates and the general reader,
offer a critical profile of a key figure or group in twentieth-century pop
music. These short paperback volumes focus on the work rather than on
biography, and emphasize critical interpretation.

Published

The Velvet Underground
Richard Witts

Forthcoming

Bob Dylan
Keith Negus

Björk
Nicola Dibben

Elton John
Dave Laing

Joni Mitchell
Jill Halstead

ELVIS COSTELLO

DAI GRIFFITHS

INDIANA
University Press
Bloomington & Indianapolis

This book is a publication of

Indiana University Press
601 North Morton Street
Bloomington, Indiana 47404-3797 USA

http://iupress.indiana.edu

Telephone orders   800-842-6796
Fax orders   812-855-7931
Orders by e-mail iuporder@indiana.edu

First published in the United Kingdom by Equinox Publishing Ltd.

Manufactured in Great Britain

The author thanks Carcanet Press Ltd for permission to reproduce no. 242 from *A Bad Day for the Sung Dynasty* (1984) by Frank Kuppner.

Cataloging information is available from the Library of Congress.

ISBN   978-0-253-22006-6 (pbk.)

1 2 3 4 5 13 12 11 10 09 08

Contents

Tables

Appendices

Preface

If I were to claim that I'd been thinking about Elvis Costello for a long time, I'm sure the same could be said by many other music fans of a certain age. The first Costello album I acquired was *Armed Forces*, around the time it came out, a dodgy Portuguese pressing bought from Andy's in the market at Cambridge. I remember that *Imperial Bedroom* seemed to demand a different kind of listening so that, with *King Of America*, I was sufficiently intrigued to write a paper about 'Sleep Of The Just' which was presented at a conference organized by Allan Moore in Ealing in July 1992 and at a research seminar organized by Stan Hawkins in Oslo in September 1996.[1] As vinyl gave way in my collection, first to cassette (*King Of America* to *Mighty Like A Rose*), and thence to CD, I was a Costello record-collector of moderate devotion: albums, occasional singles, no bootlegs. I didn't often see him perform in concert, something likely to show through as the book progresses. A curious connection is that I contributed to the Meltdown Festival in London during Costello's year of curatorship (1995), co-leading a workshop on songwriting: at some point in the day Costello appeared to perform a song I like to think was 'Favourite Hour', accompanied by John Woolrich at the piano. His voice was about a yard away from where I sat, and a quite extraordinary thing; we shook hands, and off he went. By the time of *When I Was Cruel*, I was collecting Costello's records more from a sense of duty: my CD collection was burgeoning, inducing a more distracted type of listening, and one of the pleasures of this book has been to acquaint myself better with his recent work. I set out with the idea of presenting Costello's career as an ascent to the peak of *King Of America* and *Blood And Chocolate*, and the chapter on words still bears traces of that intention, but the reader will soon discover that the book claims Costello's more recent work to have extended and deepened tendencies found in the earlier work.

In planning the book, I was keen to avoid a chronological presentation, feeling that a thematic approach was due in Costello's case. The first chapter adopts the perspective of the past, in two ways. It examines the basic issue of what we refer to in talking about Elvis Costello's work, finding examples where this has been presented as a matter of contradiction. An interlude discusses Costello's "iconic" status by reference to his spectacles. Finally, Costello's various allusions to the music of the past offer a platform to consider the wide range of influences upon his work. The second chapter is a survey of Costello's music, with additional sections on recording and voice. The main survey is presented as a conundrum, whereby Costello fits uneasily into being described as a "popular" musician, having later produced works by the procedures of "classical" music. The chapter selects examples from the entire range of Costello's output, and supports its musical vocabulary with references to specific points in recordings so that, by listening to the recording, the reader will hear the point made. For my part, the musical detail is based primarily on listening and working out at the piano, although, where available, scores were also consulted. The section on Costello's recording talks about the producer Clive Langer, while the section on voice makes reference to his father, Ross MacManus, among many others. The third chapter is a discussion of the words of Costello's songs, and includes a brief review of his collected prose, the liner notes he produced for reissues of his recordings on CD. After a brief review of other authors on Costello's words, the chapter examines aspects of technique in songwriting, and discusses examples under the familiar division into political songs and songs of romance. In both cases, boundaries to the range of Costello's subject matter are suggested. The chapter selects from the range of Costello's output, but focuses on examples from *King Of America*, *Blood And Chocolate*, and *Spike*. The fourth and final chapter reviews Costello's reception, focusing on various chart summaries, and his musical influence on others. Selected readings of Costello from journalism and academia are reviewed as case studies.

Taken as a whole, the book comes close to realizing a view I have had in mind for some time, that in order to understand songs one needs to have studied only two famous textbooks: Walter Piston's *Harmony* and *The New Princeton Encyclopaedia of Poetry and Poetics* (Preminger and Brogan 1993).[2] I was led through Piston's book by Huw Thomas at Amman Valley

Comprehensive School, and owe everything to that initial guidance. I often refer to Paul Zollo's interviews with songwriters (Zollo 1997), an essential text for all students of songwriting. Writing about tonal music in this context, I am indebted to the work of Walter Everett, as well as to David Brackett and Allan Moore. Among many writers on Costello who have provided food for thought, Larry David Smith's book was provocative and Graeme Thomson's biography much consulted. I have fond memories of listening to Costello many years ago with David Roe and Alison Sharpe, and many friends have contributed ideas, among them David Hesmondhalgh, Lee Marshall, Keith Negus and Jason Toynbee. Simon Frith's work is a consistent presence, in helping to think clearly about musical authenticity, but much else besides.

I am grateful to various libraries: Oxford Brookes University, the Bodleian Library of Oxford University, the Music Faculty Library in Oxford, the Westgate Library in Oxford, and the National Sound Archive of the British Library in London. Many websites were useful: the Elvis Costello Information service was indispensable (Richard Groothuizen); the chart lists in the final chapter are indebted to rocklistmusic.com (Julian White); and other journalist sites were useful: rockcritics.com (Scott Woods and others), rocksbackpages.com (Barney Hoskyns and others) and robertchristgau.com (Robert Christgau). Martin Strong's discography was a dependable point of reference.

Oxford Brookes University funded teaching support from January to April 2007 which enabled me to complete the book and I am grateful to colleagues in the Music department, in the School of Arts and Humanities, for helping to cover my absence. The series editors Dave Laing and Jill Halstead were attentive and solicitous; so too was Sandra Margolies as copy-editor. Antonia King helped prepare the tables, while Dave Cradduck prepared the index.

I benefited from some calm periods in Normandy at the home of John and Edwina King, and in Ammanford, South Wales, at the home of my father, Lynn Griffiths. Home life in Oxford was assisted by two particular "fancy chicks", Matilda and Elizabeth, who kept us entertained and supplied with eggs throughout the time of research and writing. Antonia King has endured years of Costello on the stereo and piano, but has been at all times cheerful, supportive and inspiring, and it is to her that the book is dedicated.

Oxford, 2007

1 Past

Who or what is Elvis Costello?

> After 25 years, it seems rather urgent to find an answer to the question: Who (or what) exactly is Elvis Costello? The strange thing is that this question is not posed at all. Pop critics do not pose it, neither does the wider audience and his fans are the least surprised of all. (Bookmens 2004: 66)

Rene Bookmens's question – who (or what) exactly is Elvis Costello? – can be put another way: to whom or what do we refer when we talk about Elvis Costello?

There was the baby born in London on 25 August 1954: nine years after 1945 "a child is born", as the opening track of *When I Was Cruel* helpfully points out. He was christened Declan MacManus,[1] complicatedly brought into play as an authorial name during Costello's career. Costello is his mother's maiden name, also used by his father Ross MacManus,[2] and he changed his first name to "Elvis" in 1976 in reference to Elvis Presley. Costello has revelled in the many alternative names he could devise: the Little Hands of Concrete, the Emotional Toothpaste, Eamonn Singer, Napoleon Dynamite, one of the Coward Brothers, the Imposter. His backing band has been called Attractions, Confederates, Imposters, and the Rude Five. With names, Costello seems to be entertained less by consistency and more by instabilities, possibilities and inventions. The real constants in Costello's life are harder to list: same mother and father, of course, different wives (Mary, Cait and Diana), same children (son Matthew Costello appears on *All This Useless Beauty*). Homes in different cities: London, Liverpool, Dublin, New York.

If Elvis Costello the person keeps us on our toes, then surely his is a body of work, an *oeuvre*, in which Costello is the ... well, what is his *job*? "What do you do for a living, Dad?"

"Well, son, I forge in the smithy of my soul the uncreated conscience of my race."[3]

Talking to David Hepworth in 2003 Costello gives it a shot, and we mark by italics the jobs applied for:

"I'm a working *musician*. This is what I do. I say this without any embarrassment at all. I am an *artist*. I am vocationally an artist who happens to be a musician and I happen to make my livelihood at it. *I create works of imagination*. I had to come to terms with the fact that it doesn't fit in. Being gifted with words in rock and roll is not exactly difficult. It's not over-populated with geniuses. Put me in among a bunch of philosophers or serious literary people and I wouldn't seem so smart. I have a one-trick talent which is *to write songs*. I've understood it instinctively since I was tiny." (in Hepworth 2003: 69)

One job Costello doesn't apply for is poet, and everyone's a bit sceptical of using that word for the words of songwriters; Costello travels the long and winding road of "gifted with words in rock'n'roll". He's forgotten that he was a record producer, for Squeeze, the Specials and the Pogues, and that he was at times a film and television actor. Before becoming a professional musician, he had jobs like you and me: computer programmer, for example. Some occupations in Costello's list happen simultaneously: the musician may often multi-task, like a one-man band or church organist, using feet and hands, keyboards and stops. A working musician for sure but, as far as I know, Costello is always hired as a singer rather than an instrumentalist.[4] But he can do all sorts of musical tasks: playing guitar, piano, electronic gadgets; surely he could play a bass line and keep a steady drumbeat, and of course he writes: words, music, songs. The songs are works of fiction, imaginative or creative works: "I create works of imagination."

So, Costello is a musician and a writer of sorts. Moreover, he's been in the public eye a long time and may well be famous. Is that so? It depends whom you talk to.[5] Like most of us (*rentiers* aside), Costello has to make money, and this takes us into another area, his relationship to the music industry. The usual short-cut into understanding or representing this aspect is via the record label and, another multiplicity, Costello's recordings appear under several different labels, reflecting shifts in his and in the music industry's history. He first signed to the independent label Stiff in 1976, and in the UK his work remained for many years on small-scale labels: Stiff (eventually owned by ZTT), Radar, F-Beat and its offshoots Demon and Edsel. However, in 1977 he signed for the USA to the major label Columbia, eventually part of the Sony corporation. A switch to Warner in 1987 enabled his records to appear on Rhino and Rykodisc. Switching again in 1996 to PolyGram (later Universal) opened the door to several characterful labels, many of which had distinguished histories, now presented as niche markets: Deutsche Grammophon, Lost Highway, Def Jam, Verve and Mercury. Thus, having had dealings with three of the major corporations – Sony, Universal and Warner – Costello is a case-study of the shifts in the record industry of his time.[6] In addition, and at a more mundane level, one imagines that, as a record fan himself,[7] Costello might value the associations of some of the labels.

The story of his dealings with the music industry has been scripted largely by Costello himself, since people tend not to interview the managers, executives or the office staff, and there may well be other stories that have yet to be heard. For instance, Costello was managed for seventeen years by Jake Riviera, the *nom de plume* of Andrew Jakeman, co-founder of Stiff Records, but they parted company in 1994: who knows what Riviera might one day have to say about Costello?[8] When Costello protests about the iniquities of the music business, we recall Philip Larkin's question about Edward Thomas: "Couldn't he have worked in a bank?"[9] However, taking his cue from Costello, Larry David Smith reinforces the Romantic idea of artist-hero battling against nasty men in suits. "In a word, anti-institutional" he may be (Smith 2004: 235), but Costello has spent all his life dealing with them; Smith continues,

> Once Captain MacManus charts his musical course, Mr Costello braves whatever industry obstacles appear before him … The MacManus–Costello pairing makes for one artistically ambitious, commercially fearless team. It is every artist's dream, and every record company's nightmare … If given a choice between wearing a hair shirt for 100 years and succumbing to the demands of the record industry for one single, I believe both of these artists [Costello and Bob Dylan] would wind up scratching themselves to death (probably within the first ten

minutes). To them, an industrial edict is a note from hell. (*ibid.*: 233–4, 234, 256)

Moving away from Costello the person, earning a crust, we turn to Costello's works, and these make the complexities encountered so far seem like a walk in the park. First, there are the questions of what "the work" *is*, and *by* whom, which we'll have consistent cause to ponder as the book progresses. Costello's excellent bibliographer, James Perone, indicates an answer in his work list and index: Costello is the author of a sequence of works (arranged alphabetically by Perone), in four groups: instrumental pieces and songs by Costello alone, and instrumental pieces and songs written in collaboration with others. Thus, 'Dead Letter' on *The Juliet Letters* is *not* included by Perone, since it is entirely by Paul Cassidy, but he includes each individual track on the television soundtrack *GBH*, which was composed by both Costello and Richard Harvey. At Perone's time of writing the total was 381, up to and including *Extreme Honey* (1997) (Perone 1998: 175–91). Perhaps most significantly, for Perone, "work" means each individual song or piece, rather than the collections of songs as albums, however much we may be used to regarding the album as a defining category, for instance, in constituting the most notable events of Costello's musical career. By rough calculation, Perone's list would have reached, at the time of my writing, over 500 items.

Since albums gather together individual tracks, as well as being temporal objects in themselves, they introduce greater manageability of quantity: conceptually, however, with Costello, there are still several distinctions to be made. Most familiarly, there are (at time of writing) fifteen albums by Costello the rock musician, and you'd be right immediately to be suspicious of *that* confident job description: *My Aim Is True, This Year's Model, Armed Forces, Get Happy!!, Trust, Punch The Clock, Goodbye Cruel World, King Of America, Blood And Chocolate, Spike, Mighty Like A Rose, Brutal Youth, All This Useless Beauty, When I Was Cruel, The Delivery Man*. In addition, there were two collections of fugitive material, such as single releases not included on albums, B-sides, demos, live performances: *Ten Bloody Marys & Ten How's Your Fathers* and *Out Of Our Idiot*.[10] With the arrival of CD, most of the albums were reissued, most of them *twice*, including much "new" fugitive material, ever-expanding in nature, such as alternative versions of previously released tracks, rearrangements, radio sessions, and remixes. At a quantitative extreme, *Get Happy!!* increased from an original 20 tracks, ten per side, in 1980 to 30 at its first reissue in 1993, and to 50 at its second reissue in 2003. Original albums seem to have become gathering-points for several other works, reminiscent of the study books and scores issued by the publisher W. W. Norton that include the original work alongside other documents of varying kinds.[11] The additional material is nearly all by Costello, the exception being the second reissue programme which does occasionally include tracks from other people's records, doubtless dependent on copyright clearance (including examples by George Jones, Madness, Rob Wasserman).

There were, in addition, several compilations of tracks, sometimes "greatest hits" packages sure to include single releases; some compilations, such as *Girls Girls Girls*, and *Extreme Honey* to an extent, were presented more by way of thematic overview. The single releases were gathered together in 2003 as three box sets of CDs, although the singles tended to be tied into the current album release and, as a result, were later included in the extended versions of albums. The singles were often issued with promotional videos, and these were gathered together in 2005 as a DVD called *The Right Spectacle*. Certain songs were performed frequently in concert settings, and recordings of those performances have sometimes been officially issued (*El Mocambo*, 1978, in *The First 2½ Years*, and *Live In Memphis*, 2005 as a DVD), as well as forming the staple diet of bootleg recordings. My distinctions between works have assumed a particular national context, Britain in my case, and some records will have slightly different appearances or content in other countries.

Enough, already, to keep the discographer busy, and a possible start to answering Bookmens's question, but we have more to observe, in areas that will introduce fresh but significant insecurity over what to call Costello's job. With *The Juliet Letters*, he began a series of works where he wrote a musical score to be performed by musicians other than his regular accompanists, a different mode closer to what we might term composition, written by a *composer* as opposed to a *songwriter*. These include *North* and *Il Sogno*, the former being a real balance between the composed song-collection and the "rock" albums. In other words, *North* could just as easily have appeared in the list of albums, taking that to sixteen, but one difference between *North* and *When I Was Cruel*, for example, is that all the tracks on *North* end "dead", i.e., end musically, whereas the tracks on *When I Was Cruel* can fade, i.e., end technologically. *Il Sogno* really does point towards a different work history, in which the piece could in theory be staged or performed with no input from Costello, something that doesn't quite pertain to the songs, even assuming performances by the most fastidiously precise tribute band. *The Juliet Letters* is the same, but seems so far to have been marked by Costello's vocal: however, there is no reason why one or more of the songs could not become repertory pieces for singers, assuming they can find a string quartet as accompaniment.

Collaborations add further complexity: *Painted From Memory* consists entirely of songs written in collaboration with Burt Bacharach; *The River In Reverse* consists mostly of cover versions of songs by Allen Toussaint, as well as collaborative songs; the composition of *The Juliet Letters* was a collaboration with the Brodsky Quartet; both soundtrack albums (*GBH* and *Jake's Progress*) were collaborations with Richard Harvey and are made up of instrumental pieces. A small complication for the collaborative songs is whether both words and music are jointly written or whether one writer takes words, the other music. *The Juliet Letters* is easier, because the score specifies the creative contribution of each of the five individuals, at least in terms of words and music. *Painted From Memory* sees words and music shared in attribution, and discussion of that work could just as easily appear in a book on Bacharach, with the same issue of how much weight to accord to each individual author. Other individual songs may be credited to Costello and someone else, for instance, uxorious songs co-written with Cait O'Riordan, and more recently with Diana Krall; joint credits with, among others, Clive Langer, Paul McCartney, Jim Keltner and Jimmy Cliff. Prompted by considerations of collaboration, we begin to peer over the cliff towards the wide sea of creativity and wonder about contributions by members of bands, and, further into the nature of musical material, especially what constitutes its originality or its belonging to Costello.

We then reach the clearer areas of artisan musicianship: Costello's covers of songs by others where he's primarily a *singer*. The two main albums for these are *Almost Blue* and *Kojak Variety*, whose expanded editions add greatly to their content. However, covers appear throughout the records, sometimes on original albums ('I Wanna Be Loved', 'Don't Let Me Be Misunderstood'),[12] on the B-side of singles (Rodgers and Hart's 'My Funny

Valentine', Leon Payne's 'Psycho', Richard Thompson's 'Withered And Died'),
on *Ten Bloody Marys & Ten How's Your Fathers* and *Out Of Our Idiot* and
the expanded CD editions. In turn, his songs are covered by others. A
distinction could be made here between the "prospective" practice of writing
a song for someone else, whether or not Costello then records the song
himself, and the "retrospective" cover of a song already recorded by Costello.
There are cases of both: Costello wrote with Cait O'Riordan an album of
songs for Wendy James (*Now Ain't The Time For Your Tears*, 1993); and
Bespoke Songs, Lost Dogs, Detours And Rendezvous is a 1998 compilation
of "prospective" songs, some of which were in turn rendered ("retrospectively") by Costello himself, for instance, on *All This Useless Beauty*. The
more standard type of retrospective cover, of a song Costello has already
recorded, frequently appears, and there has been a tribute album made up
entirely of such covers.[13]

Consideration of Costello's output has clearly put paid to any expectation
of neatness. My job as critic surely involves making some sense of this by
what may seem like arbitrary selection and, while I shall refrain from pointing
out that Costello is, *unfortunately*, still alive, the future may yet confirm or
contradict any suggested narrative. William Empson had the notion that "life
involves maintaining oneself between contradictions that can't be resolved by
analysis".[14] With contradiction in mind, Simon Frith looked at Bruce
Springsteen's *Live* boxed collection of vinyl records, which so cluttered
record shops at Christmas 1986. He presented a sequence of contradictions
that revealed the constructed nature of rock authenticity, leaving it for dead
in a final rhetorical flourish.[15] Frith observed Springsteen to be: a millionaire
who dresses as a worker, someone who wears work clothes even when not
working, an employer doubling as employee, a 37-year-old teenager, a shy
exhibitionist, the superstar-as-friend, and someone whose most successful
"record" is "live". Springsteen's seven contradictions are applicable to other
recorded performers, and it is no surprise that commentators have discovered contradictions in Costello's case:

> The most striking difference between Costello on record and
> Costello in the flesh is that the contradictions of the persona
> stand out much more starkly under the lights: all at once, he
> communicates the arrogance of the next big thing and the fear

of the impostor who's sure he'll be shot before he gets through his third number. (Marcus 1993: 26)[16]

EC: the name conjures up a kaleidoscope of images. Punk. Poseur. Intellectual. Bank clerk. Wimp. Angry young man. Humanist. Racist. Anti-trendy. The new trend. Literate lyricist for the new music. Inaccessible source to the press. Valuable commodity to a large corporation. Famous for his scorn of the same. (Reese 1981: 23)

Extreme Honey also illustrates the problems his marketing men face: Elvis is too abrasive for Adult Contemporary, Americana, Country or Classic formats; too white for urban; too old for pop; too sensibly-dressed for alternative; too pop for classical; not ingratiating enough for a music business that has been taken over by TV. (Hepworth 2003: 67)

How riddled with infuriating contradictions his musical trajectory has been: bile versus tenderness, violence in tandem with craft, contempt for and fascination with America. (Hoskyns 1991)

Elvis Costello's music criticizes the culture of consumption as fully as it participates in it. (Thurschwell 1999: 288)

A man of many contradictions – a punk who has sung with George Jones, Tony Bennett and the Count Basie Orchestra, not to mention a string quartet; one who dismisses critics, yet has been known to comment on the performances of others in a manner not unlike a music critic; a writer best known for "revenge and guilt" who penned the absolutely beautiful ballad 'Sweet Pear'; an artist accused of being a racist because of comments he made that were purely meant to shock, yet an active foe of racist organizations and active participant in the "Rock Against Racism" concerts; a singer who has worn the eyeglass styles of Buddy Holly and John Lennon; and probably the most gifted, the most artistically acclaimed, and most prolific writer of popular song of his generation – these are all Elvis Costello. (Perone 1998: 12)

Larry David Smith is the most sustained of the fragmenters, positing his study on the idea of three distinct *personae*: Declan MacManus, for education and an exploratory attitude to musical genre, Elvis Costello for voice and attitude to the music industry, and an invention called Citizen Elvis for attitude to subject matter, or "heart, soul and intelligence" (Smith 2004: 233–4).[17] (It isn't clear which of them plays the guitar.) Allow me to suggest a few contradictions of my own. As I shall examine in a later chapter, Costello's attitude to confessional songwriting could be summed up by a question and answer: *Are Costello's songs truthful? He can't tell.* I agree with Thurschwell's statement above: Costello is a self-styled enemy of the music industry but also a textbook case of commodity fetishism. But the one that strikes me as uppermost goes something like this: Costello grants his listeners absolute autonomy but keeps telling them what to think. Costello always deflects criticism by reference to listener choice. Here, the reference to reproduction technology is typical, with the listener as judge or God: "If you are not in the mood for 'Playboy To A Man' then I'm sure you know how to work the pause or skip buttons on your CD player" (*Mighty Like A Rose* n03). Elsewhere, "It is for the listener to decide what they take away from it" (*Il Sogno* n04). At the same time, Costello is remarkable in the degree to which he converses with those autocratic listeners in their wigs and crowns. Christopher Ricks has an interesting line about Tennyson, to do with writing about a writer – "why am *I* attending to *Tennyson* instead of *his* attending to *me*" (Ricks 2003: 7) – but in Costello's case, the listener can feel flattered, amazed by the sheer amount of comment and attention Costello is prepared to offer. Rene Bookmens avoids contradiction, describing instead "'uncanny identities' that Costello inhabits in his musical journey through the postmodern decades of the 20th century"; he insists that "the differences are not real differences after all" (Bookmens 2004: 67), an apposite, contradictory point to end our extended answer to the question "Who is Elvis Costello?"

Interlude: Costello as an "icon of pop music"

The series in which this book appears is devoted to "icons of pop music", but Bookmens is clear: Costello "never reached the iconical status of a Bob Dylan or Bruce Springsteen" (Bookmens 2004: 67). I rather agree with this judgement, feeling that iconic status has something of the visual about it and that, in such fleeting terms, Costello still looks like the cover of *This Year's*

Model (1978), and that by musically progressing, he cannot be tied to an easily identifiable sonic label: were he to be run over by a bus, it would be 'Oliver's Army' (*Armed Forces*, 1979) that would be played in surprised and sombre tribute.[18] We shall soon arrive at Costello's music, but any life in the public eye demands some degree of attention to visual appearance.

The Right Spectacle is Costello's collection of promotional videos, the title punning between making a right spectacle of himself and choosing the right pair of spectacles. Graeme Thomson, whose biography uses images of spectacles to illustrate part and chapter divisions, recounts Jake Riviera's firm advice when the glasses were first adopted in 1977: "Don't fucking take them off!" (Thomson 2004: 80). An earlier pop icon, John Lennon, needed glasses to see, only to remove them for vanity, but his were dark and chunky, as worn by not one but two of the five Zombies. No longer a professional Beatle, Lennon did a lot for round steel-rimmed spectacles during the 1970s, and Paul McCartney has described the wearing of glasses as a similarity between Lennon and Costello: "They both got specs, so people with glasses, they've got a different sort of attitude to the world. Bit more of a pussy cat on the inside [he says "outside"] and more aggressive on the outside."[19] Morrissey's wearing fake glasses for effect on the inner sleeve of *Hatful Of Hollow* in 1984 may have signalled a change of fortune from avoidance to deliberate adoption.

Costello's visual appearance, on the covers of albums and singles, includes a decision about glasses, and these change over the years in approximate correspondence to the drift of his music. *My Aim Is True*, *This Year's Model* and *Get Happy!!* carry the enduring image: bookish, nerdy specs, assuring good visibility. They return with irony on *Spike* and clarity on *For The Stars*. The pair portrayed on the cover of *Trust* has the same shape, beneath quizzical eyebrows and tinted for the sun. *Punch The Clock*, like *The Juliet Letters*, has a light-framed, blonde model of glasses, indicating the dubious advice of style consultants in the 1980s, "the decade that music and good taste forgot" (*Punch The Clock* n03). *Almost Blue* is a good cover for specs experts, who'll know that glasses are taken off in that way only when things are serious and a headache is about to start, brought on by listening to too much country music. After this time, the specs jostle with other adornments of Costello's head: beards, moustaches, hats, crowns. *Il Sogno* and *North* have a new type: little oblong glasses, cool dad ageing snazzily.

Images of Elvis Costello invariably involve a decision about spectacles: this is from the period of *My Aim Is True* (1977).

Glasses are to be avoided by pop or rock icons. When Elvis Costello first appeared there were two great bespectacled singer-songwriters, Elton John from Britain and Randy Newman from America: they got away with it, possibly because they played the piano. Lumbered by the effort to be taken even remotely seriously, women had to stay well clear of glasses. Perhaps the unfettered face tapped into the sense of unfettered freedom that came with the terrain of the newly sensitive, authentic rock form. In that sense, Buddy Holly and Hank Marvin belonged to an earlier generation: when most of the Shadows did something quite as poppy and light-hearted as playing guitars in a row with synchronized kicks, who cared that one of them was a specco? Alongside the appropriation of the name Elvis, Costello's glasses were a sign of the time, comparable to the sunglasses worn by Graham Parker and John Cooper Clarke.

Costello joins Joni Mitchell (*par excellence*), Bob Dylan, John Squire of the Stone Roses, and many others, in having designed the visual appearance of his own sleeves: under the sobriquet of Eamonn Singer, Costello's artwork appears on *Blood And Chocolate*, *Goodbye Cruel World*, the single of 'Tokyo Storm Warning', and the "visual design" of *Brutal Youth*. I am not sure how much input he had on some of the other artwork, sensing his interest to be not quite as all-encompassing as Mitchell's, and he doesn't emerge from the British art school's decisive stake in visual correspondence.[20] He was lucky to work with "Barney Bubbles" (Colin Fulcher), who died in 1983.[21] Bubbles's cover for *Imperial Bedroom* is perhaps the most enduring of Costello's record sleeves, pastiche cubism that had at least one commentator fooled. As the artist "Sal Lorenzo", Bubbles also designed the 'New Amsterdam' EP.[22]

Costello's allusions

Costello's attention to the interest of the listener is nowhere more pronounced than in his readiness to reveal and celebrate the sources of the many allusions contained in his work, and these allusions provide a platform from which to observe his sense of the past.[23] The observation of allusion is a simple communicative process. Costello tells us a particular song derives from something else and listeners make the connection; in turn, listeners may come across references which might convince others, even Costello himself. Peter Burkholder points out that "the case for borrowing is stronger when it can be proved that the composer knew or had access to the existing piece" ("Borrowing", in Sadie 2001). For the reader, too, there is a question of being prepared for the allusion; as Earl Miner said, "The test for allusion is that it is a phenomenon that some reader or readers may fail to observe" (Preminger and Brogan 1993: 39). Christopher Ricks positions plagiarism "in the company of allusion" (2002: 219–40), as does Costello: "I had always tried to be ingenious when borrowing from Lennon and McCartney, but sometimes it's a thin line between influence and larceny" (*Bespoke Songs*, n98). However, Burkholder points out that "it is possible, even frequent, for composers to borrow material that listeners may not recognize and for listeners to hear similarities composers did not intend" ("Borrowing", in Sadie 2001). Costello may describe an allusion but the listener is unconvinced and refuses to recognize the link. Similarly, the listener may spot allusions that have nothing to do with Costello, who may not even have heard the source, leaving other listeners convinced or not. Artist and listener can interact: Costello may in theory pick up on a reference made by others and "validate" the reference retrospectively: a fascinating way of so doing is to build in references during fleeting concert performances of songs.[24] Finally, there is the question of the relationship between the specificity of an allusion and the generality of a style: some musical patterns are so commonly known or understood that they pass by, even if they remain a specific allusion for Costello or a particular listener. The processes of observing allusions thus depend to some extent on the attitude of the listener or critic. For *The New Princeton Encyclopaedia of Poetry and Poetics*, Helen Regueiro Elam was commissioned to write the entries for both "Influence" and "Intertextuality", the former concept belonging to literary history, the latter inflected by literary theory (Preminger and Brogan 1993: 605–8, 620–2). Influence suggests a search for stable meaning within the confines of a given form, where authorial intention is key. Intertextuality starts from a limitless range of potential connection, with less regard for disciplinary boundaries, valuing the critic's ability to form links between disparate works with no explicit reference to authorial intention.

The obvious points of allusion in Costello's works are words and music, but my review of those is preceded by an unexpected first group. Allusion in real life might seem unhealthy – "No, no, I'm not leaping from these high castle walls. It's my casual allusion to *Tosca*!" – but there do seem to have been actual allusions by deed in Costello's career or, put another way, Costello did things which, later in life, he interpreted as allusions. Elvis in the *nom de plume* Elvis Costello is an allusion, of course. When he appeared on the American television programme *Saturday Night Live* in 1977, Costello curtailed the Attractions' performance of 'Less Than Zero' in order to start 'Radio Radio': this he subsequently interpreted as an allusion to a similar TV-based switch by Jimi Hendrix (on Lulu's BBC show in 1969) (*This Year's Model* n02). In 1987, Costello appeared on a TV tribute to Roy Orbison, *Black and White Night*, and comments that "my role was that of utility player, covering parts on harmonica and using my elbows on the Vox Continental organ, as I'd seen John Lennon do on the film of the Shea Stadium concert" (*King Of America* n05). Finally, Costello's liner notes for *Kojak Variety* seem to be an allusion to those produced by Tony Barrow for early Beatles records (*Kojak Variety* n04). For a visual allusion, the cover of *Almost Blue* refers to that of Kenny Burrell, *Midnight Blue* (1963) (Carr, Case and Dellar 1986: 131).

Costello may or may not be an icon of pop music but one thing is certain: he's *hung out with* loads of them. Like a version of Woody Allen's Zelig, he appears in various contexts alongside an encyclopaedia of twentieth-century music: Bob Dylan, Bruce Springsteen, Van Morrison, Joni Mitchell, Elton John, Paul McCartney, the Rolling Stones, Burt Bacharach, Roger McGuinn, Jerry Garcia, Roy Orbison, Elvis Presley's backing band, Charles Mingus's backing band, Ray Brown, Earl Palmer, Tony Bennett, Chet Baker, Count Basie, Diana Krall, Bill Frisell, George Jones, Johnny Cash, June Carter, Emmylou Harris, Lucinda Williams, Gillian Welch, Billy Sherrill, Brian Eno, Lou Reed, Dave Grohl, Ringo Starr, George Martin, Larry Adler, Tom Waits, Jeff Buckley, Shane MacGowan, Jerry Dammers, Robert Wyatt, Tricky, the Beastie Boys, the Chieftains, Dusty Springfield, Chrissie Hynde, Daryl Hall, Solomon Burke, Allen Toussaint. It is easier to name the ones he hasn't got round to yet: among songwriters committed to the art, Jimmy Webb, Leonard Cohen, Randy Newman, Paul Simon; rock icons David Bowie and Neil Young; no John Cale, David Byrne, Steely Dan. What a musical life Costello has led!

My second group are allusions in words, and Table 1.1 presents a small selection from the chronological range of Costello's work. Allusions in words function in a variety of ways. The two examples from 'American

Without Tears'[25] refer to records as part of the story told, similar to the way records are heard in films: the reference to 'Who Shot Sam?' in 'Motel Matches' carries a cultural reference to country music as well as to the potential meaning of the words. 'Monkey To Man' (*The Delivery Man*) is based on Dave Bartholomew's 1954 original and, like an appendix to back up a fleeting footnote, an additional CD includes a performance of Bartholomew's 'The Monkey'. The reference to Otis Redding in 'Let Them All Talk' is a complex affair, referring to a song title that presents a cliché ("fa fa fa") in self-referential formal terms ("sad song"), and using its cliché to describe the use of a cliché! Some of the references are titles of songs, while others refer to lines in songs: identification relies on knowledge of the original. It is now in this sense impossible to observe that "we're all going on a summer holiday" without evoking Cliff Richard; by being the band they became, in 'From Me To You' the Beatles made an ordinary statement into a prominent reference. Single references and multiple references: Franklin Bruno points out that the first verse of 'Accidents Will Happen' "traps the singer in a web of earlier songs", including 'It's Now Or Never' (Elvis Presley's version of 'O Sole Mio'), 'You Keep Me Hanging On' (the Supremes' recording of the song by Holland, Dozier and Holland), 'I Just Don't Know What To Do With Myself' (the Bacharach and David song recorded by Dusty Springfield among others) and, in the chorus, 'I Don't Want To Hear It Anymore' (Dusty again, in 'Memphis', the song by Randy Newman) (Bruno 2005: 5).

With musical allusion we reach fertile ground, as both Costello and his listeners are devoted reference-spotters. The published literature includes examples of the writer's fancy without intentional "validation" by Costello, although one is sure to think that if there's one person who'd get an allusion, it is him. The wide range of Costello's listening is suggested by the lists he produced for the magazine *Vanity Fair* (Costello 2000, 2002a). Franklin Bruno spots a connection between 'Oliver's Army' and 'Don't Worry Baby' by the Beach Boys, at the level of musical phrasing: during the verses, four bars of tonic followed by two bars each of subdominant and dominant, as well as the connecting link between verse and chorus (Bruno 2005: 56–7). David Brackett has an imaginative study of 'It's Time' (*All This Useless Beauty*) that links elements of the song to past models: the words "this magic moment" to a song recorded by the Drifters in 1960, and the plagal cadence at 1'42 of Costello's record to several carefully examined aspects of records by the Beatles, Bob Dylan and Neil Young (Brackett 2005b: 357–67). This could be seen as an intertextual approach, by Elam's description, using Costello's song as a springboard for a kind of music-cultural history. However, the master of allusion as a playful aspect of listener pleasure, rather than a matter of authorial intention, is surely Greil Marcus. In a 1980 review of *Taking Liberties* (the US title of *Ten Bloody Marys & Ten How's Your Fathers*) Marcus heard Billie Holiday, Buddy Holly, Johnny Rotten, Carl Perkins, Bob Dylan, Frankie Lymon, Al Green, the Rolling Stones, Augustus Pablo, "the garage" [presumably garage bands], and Neil Young (Marcus 1993: 136). There's room for authorial playfulness in this technique as, later, in Marcus's view, a track from *Goodbye Cruel World*, 'The Great Unknown', "joins the great tradition of terrible rock'n'roll 'Great' songs, the only other example being Van Morrison's 'The Great Deception'", alongside other songs beginning 'The Great' by the Platters (Pretender), the Fleetwoods (Imposter), John Prine (Compromise), and "I swear, 'The Great Snowman', a record about Colonel Tom Parker that I heard in the fifties and have never been able to track down" (Marcus 1993: 260).[26]

Beyond the published literature, the Elvis Costello information website contains a listing of 133 songs with musical allusions identified by a range of both named and un-named observers.[27] The sources identified are wide-ranging, but can be grouped into collections. By far the most often named source is the Beatles, mentioned in 30 of the examples. Alongside the Beatles are many other musicians associated with the 1960s: Bob Dylan, the Rolling Stones, Beach Boys, Byrds, Yardbirds, Zombies, Hollies, Kinks, Doors, Small Faces, Them, Cream, Cilla Black and Dusty Springfield. Soul accounts for the next major set: Marvin Gaye, Aretha Franklin, Stevie Wonder, Otis Redding, the Four Tops, Supremes, Temptations, Meters, Booker T and the MGs. The 1970s, punk and after: David Bowie, John Cale, Stooges, Television, Clash, XTC, Pretenders, Billy Bragg. Pop music gives Abba and Burt Bacharach, and there are a few "pre-1960s" references to Woody Guthrie, Elvis Presley, the Everly Brothers, Kurt Weill, and some examples from musical theatre. Such discoveries depend upon the records listeners happen to have heard, but the list is nevertheless useful and suggestive, although it would be good to see cross-references indicated by precise timings. Some are spot-on: for example, the opening of 'Just A

Table 1.1 Allusions in words

Costello track and album	Allusion	Source (artist, track, date)
'Sneaky Feelings' (*My Aim Is True*)	"You'll force me to use a little tenderness"	Otis Redding, 'Try A Little Tenderness' (1967)
'The Beat' (*This Year's Model*)	"We're all going on a summer holiday"	Cliff Richard, 'Summer Holiday' (1962)
'Motel Matches' (*Get Happy!!*)	"Who shot Sam?"	George Jones, 'Who Shot Sam?' (1959)
'Possession' (*Get Happy!!*)	"If there's anything that you want"	The Beatles, 'From Me To You' (1964)
'High Fidelity' (*Get Happy!!*)	"Some things you never get used to"	The Supremes, 'Some Things You Never Get Used To' (1968)
'Let Them All Talk' (*Punch The Clock*)	"Fa-fa-fa-fa soul cliché"	Otis Redding, 'Fa fa fa fa (Sad Song)' (1966)
'Heathen Town' (extended *Punch The Clock*)	"And the devil will drag you under"	Frank Loesser, 'Sit Down, You're Rocking The Boat' (*Guys and Dolls*, 1950)
'American Without Tears' (*King Of America*)	"It's too late"	Carole King, 'It's Too Late' (1970)
'American Without Tears' (Twilight Version) (extended *Blood And Chocolate*)	"A fool such as I"	Elvis Presley, 'A Fool Such As I' (1959)
'Invasion Hit Parade' (*Mighty Like A Rose*)	"No pool, no pets, no cigarettes"	Roger Miller, 'King Of The Road' (1965)
'When I Was Cruel No. 2' (*When I Was Cruel*)	"See that girl, watch that scene, digging the Dancing Queen"	Abba, 'Dancing Queen' (1976)
'Alibi' (*When I Was Cruel*)	"Jesus wants me for a sunbeam"	Nellie Talbot, 'Jesus Wants Me For A Sunbeam' (hymn, c. 1900)
'Alibi' (*When I Was Cruel*)	"Papa's got a brand new…"	James Brown, 'Papa's Got A Brand New Bag' (1965)
'Monkey To Man' (*The Delivery Man*)	"Broadcast by Mr Bartholomew"	Dave Bartholomew, 'The Monkey' (1954)

Memory' (extended *Get Happy!!*) is uncannily similar to 0'17–19 of Phil Ochs's 'Flower Lady' (1968), the tune comically close to that of Burt Bacharach's 'Raindrops Keep Falling On My Head'.[28]

Listeners might wonder whether some allusions are actually discernible. For instance, Costello points out that the drum part to a demo of 'Black And White World' derives from 'Cold Cold Cold' by Little Feat (*Get Happy!!* n03),[29] but this might seem to us part of a language common to all rock drummers. Bruno has difficulty spotting the link Costello suggests between 'Accidents Will Happen' and Bacharach's 'Anyone Who Had A Heart' (Bruno 2005: 4). Allusions were sometimes shared between bands. 'Time Is Tight' by Booker T and the MG's is alluded to in 'Temptation' (*Get Happy!!*), as well as in 'In Quintessence', the opening track of *East Side Story* (1981) by Squeeze, which Costello produced. Costello allows that one of his allusions (to the Supremes, 'You Can't Hurry Love', again written by Holland, Dozier and Holland) was put to better use by the Jam in 1982: "'Love For Tender' made use of the same 'You Can't Hurry Love' riff that the Jam would take to the top of the charts with the vastly superior song, 'Town Called Malice'" (*Get Happy!!* n03).

Allusions create a strong sense of Costello's past, acting in his work as the privileged means of signalling allegiance and influence. They derive from various periods and genres of musical history. Pride of place is perhaps taken by American country and soul,[30] since they form the spine of the two cover-song collections, *Almost Blue* and *Kojak Variety*. A possible third stream is the music of New Orleans, culminating in *The River In Reverse*, the collaboration with the New Orleans songwriter and musician Allen Toussaint.[31] The most important factor here is suggested by the album title, *King Of America*, as Costello picks up from the "British invasion" of the 1960s, when young British men found an emotional connection with American roots music, often African-American, rhythm'n'blues, and rock'n'roll. The music acted as the key to unlock self-expression, perhaps the archetypal transformation being Van Morrison's, from Belfast blues to *Astral Weeks* in three or four years. Greil Marcus in 1974 characterized the Rolling Stones in the early 1960s (*12 × 5*, 1964) as "English robber-barons laying tracks across the U.S.A., they seized huge chunks of right-of-way" (Marcus 1996: 288); thirty years later Simon Frith was still able to observe that "for British rock musicians of all kinds, the musical identity that is most pertinent – and most problematic –

is *not being American*" (Frith 2004: 54). Even negatives emphasized the mesmeric hold: 'I'm So Bored With The USA', 'Crawling To The U.S.A.', 'American Squirm'.[32] Perhaps there was a sense of belatedness to Costello's generation, but the range of reference was familiar: 1950s rhythm'n'blues and 1960s soul, country via country-rock, Dylan and folk-rock all-pervasive. Referring to a period around 1970, Costello noticed that an "odd collision of American musical threads could be found in the contemporary recordings of both the Grateful Dead and The Band", adding that "it was old and new at the same time": timeless, or multiply timed (*Almost Blue* n04).

These foundations lead on to the immediate inheritance: American and British rock music of the 1960s and early 1970s. The Byrds receive the most sustained tribute, on 'You Bowed Down' (*All This Useless Beauty*); Costello describes allusions to 'I See You' on 'Lipstick Vogue' (*Girls Girls Girls* n89) and to '5D' on 'Dr Luther's Assistant'(*Get Happy!!* n03): the latter seems closer in its drawling melody and instrumental interludes (bridge 1'59–2'13, coda 3'10–25).[33] Roger McGuinn himself appears on *Spike* playing his signature guitar, the 12-string Rickenbacker. We shall see in the next chapter that the Band may have influenced the line-up of the Attractions, and 'Sweet Pear' (*Mighty Like A Rose*) seems to bear their trace. Bob Dylan was important as a general presence through the singer-songwriter genre. 'Possession' (*Get Happy!!*) "aptly departed from the grand marching style" of Bob Dylan's 'Is Your Love In Vain?' (see *Get Happy!!* n03), and his 'Subterranean Homesick Blues' lies behind 'Pump It Up' (*This Year's Model*).

Internet contributors point out Beatles allusions with zeal and, as with the Byrds, Costello found himself working with a real Beatle, Paul McCartney, also playing his signature guitar, the Hofner bass: the "added sixth" at the start (0'05) of 'My Brave Face' is a deliberate Beatles thumbprint.[34] Costello made a wise decision to perform 'All You Need Is Love' as a "northern folk song" at Live Aid in 1985, picking up on the song's television broadcast in 1967 to an international audience. Two other British bands to which Costello has made reference are the Merseybeats and Move. He covered a song recorded as a cover by the Merseybeats, 'I Stand Accused', and the original 'Everyday I Write The Book' (*Punch The Clock*) was intended to sound like them.[35] Costello picked up on some interesting things in the Move. 'All Grown Up' (*Mighty Like A Rose*) has a progression that sounds to me like the start of 'Blackberry Way' (1968).[36] Costello also hears the Move alongside the Byrds in 'Dr Luther's Assistant' (*Get Happy!!* n03) and thinks that "careful listeners may notice an inserted quote from The Move's 'Fire Brigade' at the end of the bridge" of 'Baby Pictures' (*Punch The Clock* n03): although it shares its rhythmic bounce and rapidity of chord change with the Move track, the exact quote is hard to spot.

In addition to the mainstream of 1960s and 1970s rock music, Costello sometimes refers to the pop music of the day: Abba, Burt Bacharach. The piano of 'Oliver's Army' alludes to Abba's 'Dancing Queen', so that Costello's defining pop hit owes something to the Swedish pop group and its two songwriters. 'How To Be Dumb' (*Mighty Like A Rose*) returns to those high-register octaves in the piano. Costello worked with Abba's Benny Andersson on *For The Stars*, and with Bacharach on *Painted From Memory*.

There are also allusions to aspects of the technique of four contemporaneous singer-songwriters. Speaking of 'The Boxer' (1970), Paul Simon commented that he "thought that 'lie la lie' was a failure of songwriting" (in Zollo 1997: 96). However, he gave significance to the ordinary "la la la" of everyday singing by sharpening the line to "lie la lie", and then worked the sound into the song. 'De Do Do Do, De Da Da Da' (1980) by the Police is a little essay in song on sense and communication. Costello uses this device in 'The Element Within Her' (*Punch The Clock*: 1'52–58, "She says 'No but you are la', la, la, la, la"), and 'Tart' (*When I Was Cruel*: "lie" eight times at 0'51–57). 'Let Him Dangle' (*Spike*), about the hanging of Derek Bentley in 1952, follows the judge's declaration with a repeated "doot" (0'22–25, etc.): too much pop silliness for the serious subject, or is the cursoriness and insouciance of British justice captured and mocked through a trite syllable?

One point of allusive vocal performance belongs to Van Morrison, where a song gives way to a particular sort of non-verbal scat singing and, for a moment, at 2'43 of 'The Sharpest Thorn' (*The River In Reverse*), it is as though Morrison is right there in the studio. The same happens at 3'53 of 'American Without Tears' (*King Of America*), while the backing vocals at 0'35 of 'Clown Strike' (*Brutal Youth*) get their wordless vocals from 'Jackie Wilson Said' (1972).[37]

At a certain point, allusion to Tom Waits's work after *Swordfishtrombones* (1983) is discernible. 'Stalin Malone' (*Spike*) seemed to pick up on spoken-word tracks on Waits's albums, something traceable back through to records of Beat poets. Marc Ribot became guitarist in Costello's band, having supplied angular lines to Tom Waits, while Mitchell Froom brought a certain sound quality, lacking bass and percussive, that I associate with the Waits records.[38] Specifically, 'Episode Of Blonde' (*When I Was Cruel*) can be compared with the track 'Swordfishtrombone' on the 1983 album.[39] Waits and Costello also share an interest in the harmony and instrumentation of Kurt Weill – see 'Miss Macbeth' (*Spike*) – perhaps via the producer Hal Willner.[40]

Finally, it is worth mentioning Sting, although Costello rarely makes positive reference to the singer-songwriter formerly of the Police, but there are parallels, such as a shared interest in jazz, Kurt Weill (also via Hal Willner), and John Dowland.

Sampling technology has enabled direct quotation from recorded sources, but Costello was well aware that his earlier practice of reference-making was effectively a performed version of sampling:

> Bearing in mind that this record was made many years before the trend towards "sampling", we made a pretty good job of lifting the main figure of Booker T and the MG's 'Time Is Tight' while the guitar part of 'King Horse' alluded to The Four Tops' 'Reach Out (I'll Be There)'. (*Get Happy!!* n03)

The main example of a prominent recorded sample is found on 'When I Was Cruel No.2' (*When I Was Cruel*), the sampled voice as well as the music (chord, orchestration) taken from 'Un Bacio E Troppo Poco', recorded by Mina.[41] The verbal allusion to Abba's 'Dancing Queen' in the same track resulted in a copyright credit on the sleeve of *When I Was Cruel*. Costello tried to sample the track 'Pop Life' (1985) by Prince, for 'The Bridge I Burned', but permission was denied (*All This Useless Beauty* n01).

In addition, the instrumentalists in Costello's bands may be making allusions of their own: Pete Thomas's reference to Little Feat, for instance. Steve Nieve loops a bit of the Bach melody, 'Jesu, Joy of Man's Desiring', four times at 2'44–58 of 'The Only Flame In Town' (*Goodbye Cruel World*), while the three fragments of 'America' from Leonard Bernstein's *West Side Story* at 1'52–2'05 of 'Button My Lip' (*The Delivery Man*) resulted in copyright credit on the sleeve.

Some oddities of my own to add to the internet list: Nieve's piano at the start of 'London's Brilliant Parade' (*Brutal Youth*) reminds me of the start of the British light classic, 'Westminster Waltz' by Robert Farnon, while 'Swine' (*The Juliet Letters*, 1'09–12) reminds me of the verse of Bacharach and David's 'What's New, Pussycat?' (0'27–31 of Tom Jones's 1965 recording); the start of 'Kinder Murder' (*Brutal Youth*) sounds similar to Angelo Badalamenti's *Twin Peaks* track, 'Fire Walk With Me'; and I keep hearing Marvin Gaye's *What's Going On* (1971: it could be 'Save The Children') at 0'14–24 of 'Oh Well' (*When I Was Cruel*).

I shall end this review of Costello's allusions by looking at the process of allusion in more detail with reference to three examples. The extended *Get Happy!!* contains a performance of 'High Fidelity' from the Pink Pop Festival in Holland 1979, a bizarre kind of *merging* of a song with another, 'Station To Station', the opening and title track of David Bowie's 1976 album. The reference starts from brooding, slow, obscure-sounding musical material: Nieve's semitone descent F–E corresponds to the C#–C of Roy Bittan's piano in Bowie (1'13); a guitar riff emerges in both; a gradual acceleration in the imitation corresponds to the tempo change in the original; and, in his vocal line, Costello seems to have integrated the outline of a melody from the Bowie original.[42] Finally, the euphoric arrival of the chorus of 'High Fidelity' corresponds possibly to the arrival of the fast section of 'Station To Station' (5'19, or the section referring to "cocaine" in the words, at 6'02). An impressive attempt to imitate the large-scale structure that Bowie constructed over ten minutes, at three and a quarter minutes this performance must have been entertaining for the musicians.

Costello has often referred listeners to 'Ghetto Child', a single by the Detroit Spinners from 1973,[43] as the immediate source of 'Alison' from *My Aim Is True* four years later. 'Ghetto Child' appeared a year after 'Could It Be I'm Falling In Love?', the Spinners' emblematic hit, produced by Thom Bell. Bell and Linda Creed wrote 'Ghetto Child', where seductive Philadelphia pop meets social commentary. On a 1992 BBC Radio One documentary about his career, Costello pins down the reference by singing the connection, the similarity of which resides in the respective choruses of the two songs.[44] The correspondence resides between the line "I know this world is killing you" in 'Alison' (0'54–1'04) and, in 'Ghetto Child' (0'57–1'04), the line "Life ain't so easy when you're a ghetto child". Costello sang the extract

Table I.2 'Ghetto Child' and 'Alison'

Detroit Spinners, 'Ghetto Child' (1973) (0'57–1'04)															
Life	ain't	so ea-	-sy	when	you're	a	ghe-	-	-	-tto	child				
I	2	3	4	I	2	3	4	I	2	3	4	I	2	3	4

Elvis Costello, 'Alison' (*My Aim Is True*, 1977) (0'54–1'04)															
A-	-	-	li--son				I	know	this	world	is	kil-	-ling	you	
I	2	3	4	I	2	3	4	I	2	3	4	I	2	3	4

of 'Ghetto Child' on the documentary, commenting that "It's that kind of staccato thing, that's what it was, musically that's what it was." By staccato, Costello means not so much notes of a short rhythmic duration, but the inner rhythmic asymmetry of the line. The Spinners' line is complicated by the loss of a beat in one of the bars: you could try hearing it (or conducting it) as: 4–3–4–4. But the words are, furthermore, decidedly asymmetrical in their relation to those beats, as Table 1.2 demonstrates. Other than its chorus, 'Alison' is a standard, country-inflected song, although the introduction picks up the rhythmic instabilities of the chorus, sensitively performed by the backing band, Clover. Costello was to return to the offbeat melodic line, for instance, on 'Distorted Angel' (*All This Useless Beauty*).

The story of Costello and Chet Baker is extraordinary. It is one thing for Dylan to start performing the Hendrix version of 'All Along the Watchtower' or Leonard Cohen to start performing the John Cale version of 'Hallelujah', but quite another what happened between Costello and Baker. Brown and Henderson's song 'The Thrill Is Gone' was presumably the type of song his father was familiar with: much recorded, the 1953 version by Chet Baker is thought to be the best, its slow pace lending gravity to the words. I imagine that Costello's version of the Rodgers and Hart song 'My Funny Valentine'[45] is also based on Chet Baker's 1954 version. Inspired by Baker's 'The Thrill Is Gone', Costello wrote 'Almost Blue' for *Imperial Bedroom* (1982). He had already recorded 'My Funny Valentine' in 1979, 'Gloomy Sunday' (from the Billie Holiday 1941 record),[46] and Cole Porter's 'Love For Sale' in 1981, at the time of *Trust*, then went into the cover-version period of *Almost Blue*.[47] Costello sets out the origin of the song 'Almost Blue', drawing attention to the proximity between model and imitation:

Costello and Chet Baker, who supplies a trumpet solo for Costello's recording of 'Shipbuilding' (1983). Costello's song 'Almost Blue' owes much to Baker.

Most concentrated of these songs is the ballad 'Almost Blue'. It was written in imitation of the Brown/Henderson song 'The Thrill Is Gone'. I had become obsessed with the Chet Baker recordings of that tune, firstly the instrumental and, later, the vocal take. It is probably the most faithful likeness to the model of any of my songs of this time. It has become my most covered composition. (*Imperial Bedroom* n02)

So what's the link? The pace is one thing, putting a spotlight on the words and their delivery. The chords follow a descending pattern which, if anything, crosses over from Costello's version of 'Gloomy Sunday'. The declamation of the first line of 'Almost Blue', the way that the words occupy the space of the musical line, is derived from 'The Thrill Is Gone': "almost blue" = "the thrill is gone". The way the song develops suggests that Costello is still writing in part a country rather than a jazz song: one tiny moment ("almost you" in the first verse, 0'32) sounds like country music, while "I see in hers too, now your eyes are" (0'46–52) is closer perhaps to the heightened emotion of Gram Parsons's 'Hot Burrito No.1' (covered on *Almost Blue*).

Then Chet Baker recorded 'Almost Blue'. Imagine that you grew up with, say, David Bowie songs in your dad's collection, you make up an imitation Bowie song, then you find out (after he dies) that *he*, Bowie, was performing *your* imitation song! In the meantime, Baker had played on a Costello record, the 1983 re-recording of 'Shipbuilding' for *Punch The Clock*; that was when Costello slipped Baker the tape of 'Almost Blue'. Telling the story, Costello adds detailed and allusive observation:

> Truthfully, my ideal was Miles Davis, though I was probably thinking of the Arabic lines of *Sketches of Spain* rather than his recent fusion records. (I had even attempted to imitate some of those figures in the background voices on both Robert [Wyatt]'s 'Shipbuilding' and 'Pills And Soap'. This last arrangement also took a cue from parts of Joni Mitchell's album 'Hissing Of Summer Lawns', although my vocal delivery disguises this quite well.) (*Punch The Clock* n95)[48]

He must mean the kind of multi-layered voices Joni Mitchell was using in tracks like 'Edith And The Kingpin' on *Hissing Of Summer Lawns* or the "Indian kids in Canada" section of 'Song For Sharon' on *Hejira*. There are two Chet Baker recordings of 'Almost Blue' (there could be more). Costello's preferred version is the one chosen for *Bespoke Songs*, from *Chet Baker In Tokyo* (1987, with Harold Danko, piano); the other version is found on the soundtrack to Bruce Weber's 1988 film documentary about Baker, *Let's Get Lost*. The film version has Frank Strazzeri on piano, and you half wonder if he's getting the bearings for his introduction from a standard jazz recording, like 'The Thrill Is Gone'. (The film version appears to be a live recording to an unkind audience: the album version seems to be a studio recording.) Richard Cook and Brian Morton comment on the Tokyo recording:

> Like Miles, Chet kept his eyes open for new pop standards and had enjoyed a brief association with Elvis Costello, playing an unforgettable delay-laden solo on Costello's own version of his anti-Falklands War anthem, 'Shipbuilding'. Chet returns the compliment with a sharp, well-thought-out version of Costello's 'Almost Blue', a song that offers a combination of romantic sentiment and hard-edged melody. (1996: 74)

Years later, Diana Krall covers 'Almost Blue' on *The Girl In The Other Room* (2004): classy piano introduction all hers, otherwise straight through.

Reviewing the evidence leaves us with criticism's question: what to make of these allusions? One point is that Costello is given more to the momentary allusion than the sustained pastiche; music is taking place in time, the duration of an allusion is something that can be measured and, in that sense, musical allusions differ from those in words of songs or even of poems on the page. The one sustained pastiche is 'You Bowed Down', Costello's song in the style of the Byrds (*All This Useless Beauty*).[49] Brief reference to the Detroit Spinners in 'Alison' might be compared with Elton John's sustained appropriations of the same genre produced by Thom Bell: 'Philadelphia Freedom' (1975) and 'Are You Ready For Love?' (1979). "Sustained pastiche" for Costello usually means "cover version", as found on *Almost Blue* and *Kojak Variety*. His musical allusions mainly function as knowing winks. '20% Amnesia' (*Brutal Youth*) has entered the world of Kurt Weill at 0'34–40,[50] but then a passing, distinct, reference to the Beatles' 'I Feel Fine' (at 0'48–49) leads back to the second verse. Sustained Byrds pastiche it may be, but 'You Bowed Down' still finds room (at 4'34) for a clear, if meaningless, reference to Television's 'Marquee Moon' (1977).

However, allusion certainly says something about Costello's ideal listeners: they are the sort of people who get the references. In addition, Costello's allusions are part of what he understands by creative labour, or even "popular music", in which originality as such is a relatively rare occurrence,[51] replaced by a range of terms: imitation, influence, reference, faithfulness to the tradition. I've suggested elsewhere that Costello belonged to a generation for whom authority in pop music constituted the intellectual terrain: they could be described as *academic* (Griffiths 2004a: 560–1). "I mean academics can be fans and fans can be academics", says Simon Frith.[52] Such a view was extant by the time of punk rock, when rock music became knowingly self-critical and knowingness the key element; one is able to sneer at precursors, make fun of them, because one understands them, even in secret or suppressed admiration. For instance, the Sex Pistols' *funny*[53] cover of 'Johnny B Goode' starts from a new and critical premise.[54] "Oh God, fuck off", Johnny Rotten at the start, then "I don't know the words", then "I hate songs like that: the pits". Funny and contemptuous at the same time, but it is a cover of 'Johnny B Goode' all the same. They knew its *shtik* well enough, its instant claim to rock'n'roll authority on the part of anyone who played it.[55] For these street intellectuals, pop music had become the repository of ideas, more so than books and music and films. A British generation born in the 1950s[56] all knew their pop *stuff*; if anything, Costello just knew more rather than better, or at least allowed himself to refer to it in a more discernible way.

* * *

This first chapter has approached the subject of Elvis Costello from several different perspectives: it has reviewed the "ontological" question of what "Elvis Costello" means and, after a brief detour into considering his "iconic" status, it has looked at his relationship to the past through allusions of various kinds. The questions raised by considering influence will return in our final chapter, which will look towards the future as opposed to the past. The following chapters expand upon the "ontological" aspect, by breaking down the elements of Costello's work into some of its constituent elements: music, words, and voice. A theme in this first chapter has been diversity of various kinds – contradiction, the co-existence of differing styles and references – but the next two chapters look for continuities among the contradictions.

2 Music

Analysing Costello's music

Elvis Costello had just learned to drive when he was put at the wheel of an old Buick with dodgy brakes and told to speed around a dangerous stretch of road between Nice and Monte Carlo with four female French models, while miming the words to his song 'The Other Side Of Summer'. "If I had plunged over the edge, this might not have been a bad place to conclude" (*Mighty Like A Rose* n02).[1] Costello's music is a conundrum that would not exist had he plunged, and *Mighty Like A Rose* (1991) might not have been a bad place to conclude; with the next album, *The Juliet Letters* (1993), things became more complicated.

Popular or classical?

The conundrum concerns nothing less than "classical" and "popular" music, understood in that dualistic way. Costello always had been a "popular musician", in Lucy Green's precise sense of the term: he learned to play the guitar by ear, played in groups from an early stage, and acquired repertory by imitating what he heard on records (Green 2002). By the time of *Mighty Like A Rose*, he was an eclectic and learned listener, keen to adopt different styles. However, at that point, having already learned to play the piano some ten years before, he learned to read musical notation, so that he became in addition a "classical musician"; he was extending his listening to the string quartet and other classical repertories.

So what? Commissioned to write orchestral music for a TV soundtrack (*GBH*), Costello tired of having to sing tunes which someone had to transcribe in order for them to be played by classical musicians and, although the common assumption in popular music was to leave the effort of so doing to producers, arrangers, orchestrators and transcribers, he went ahead and learned the dots (*Mighty Like A Rose* n02). Good for him.

However, it could be interpreted differently, in three stages of questions. First, the *pragmatic* situation, criticism:

- When reviewing a classical work, which criteria does the rock journalist summon?
- Does the classical critic attend only to the classical work, or keep going with the popular work?
- Which criterion does the classical critic summon: "contemporary classical" or the classical past?

Secondly, the *music-cultural* conundrum strikes to the heart of the popular–classical dichotomy. So:

- By going beyond the assumed practice of popular music, should Costello escape *popular* music studies and, for example, stop being an icon of *pop* music (assuming he ever was)?
- Can we get rid of the "popular" in popular music? (International Advisory Board 2005)
- By extension, when we say classical music, which classical do we mean?[2]

Finally, with these questions in mind, to go back to Costello, to check:

- Was *The Juliet Letters* a matter of *exploring musical diversity*, as we tend to say today, or was there more to it, something like "holding a genuine, if deluded, belief in musical *progress*, striving towards *better* music"?

Confronted with such critical decision-making, we are presented by Wayne C. Booth with five options,[3] which I paraphrase:

1. mutual toleration: live and let live, rejoice in multiplicity.
2. monism, sometimes combined with "courteous toleration": one mode is uniquely true and legitimate, and is either one already in hand or one to be hoped for in the future. This is sometimes called dogmatism, or even fanaticism or fascism.
3. eclecticism, which attempts to "winnow the true from the false", in each mode, often in the hope of producing a new synthesis free of falsehood (and perhaps becoming a new monism): this is sometimes called pluralism, or "qualified relativism" or "operationalism".
4. scepticism, which claims that no position is true because every mode is refutable by its rivals. This extends to "full" or "utter" relativism: "What is true is only whatever is true for you, and whatever is true

for you is true." There are potentially as many truths as human beings, and there can be no genuine contradiction.

5. modal pluralism, "a meta-mode that offers an unqualified embrace of many modes". The key point is that human beings cannot escape a plurality of philosophical systems or critical perspectives. The truth of each valid mode could be translated into any other valid mode, but this may be a vain task or "suited only for the mind of God".

One expects people in popular and world music to cling to relativism (Booth 3 and 4) like a trusty sword. In order to celebrate a blues recording or appreciate an Irish folk song, they seek to evade any "monist" claim (Booth 2) of "classical music" to be elevated by a number of factors: the possibility of greater duration, organic connection between disparate elements, varied and challenging compositional techniques, distinguished track record. But not everyone in pop music thinks like a relativist; for example, John Cale captures the sense of pop music as an inferior practice, *un*courteous toleration: "I've no business being in rock and roll. I've said it over and over again that I'm a classical composer, dishevelling my musical personality by dabbling in rock and roll" (Cale and Bockris 1999: 218). Costello looks back with dismay on the reception of *The Juliet Letters* as someone desiring mutual toleration (Booth 1) but received by monist perspectives (Booth 2). A defensive paragraph attempted a summary:

> It is not as if we had protested that we were creating a brand, new language of modern music. Nor were we attempting to ingratiate ourselves with a mass audience with some watered-down classical hybrid. All we were doing was writing some songs together. (*The Juliet Letters* n02)

The last line is a pragmatic but trivial point about form, true of his first band, Flip City. The first-person plural is interesting, since *The Juliet Letters* is a genuine collaboration. Otherwise, the options are stark, between the "brand new language" (Booth 2) and a pluralist hybrid (Booth 3, albeit a "new synthesis *full* of falsehood"), including a dig at the "mass" audience.

At the time Costello curated the Meltdown festival in London in 1995, a dispute arose in the British press centred retrospectively on *The Juliet Letters*. For Andrew Clements, classical music critic of the *Guardian*, the problem was not so much that Costello was engaging in "cultural synthesis" as such, which Clements was ready to praise in a book by John Rockwell. However, "British music remains, for good or bad (I think unquestionably for bad) a world of two, scarcely overlapping cultures, in which each views the other with suspicion" (Clements 1995: 9). Clements admired *King Of America* and *Blood And Chocolate*, two "wonderful albums" in 1986, but thought Costello was now turning to poor models of classical music, *The Juliet Letters* presenting "clichés of a string quartet, couched in a musical language that has trawled through the string-quartet repertory of this century for reusable gestures". Critically selective of models in popular music – "[Costello] wouldn't recycle the gestures of early rock'n'roll" – for the string quartet "he's perfectly happy to adopt a musical language that has long outlived its useful shelf life. The result is pastiche and parody rather than something vital and relevant." This is "the blindest of musical alleys".

> I wish he, or more likely a younger, more culturally ambiguous figure could combine elements from both traditions, build upon a language of British post-modernism, and create something fresh. This would be a totally new music, not putting the wine of Costello's lyrics into the mildewed bottle of twentieth-century modernism. (*ibid.*)

Responding, John Woolrich, a professional composer, first took on Clements's authority in popular music, claiming of his line about recycling early rock'n'roll: "that's exactly what he [Costello] *does*".[4] Woolrich offered several examples of classical composers – Haydn, Mozart, Stravinsky, Bainbridge, Turnage, Adès – who engaged in stylistic crossovers and borrowing. Clements's "dream of a 'totally new music' is silly and thoughtless." He suffered from the "English disease of negativism", his argument from the "myth of originality" and the "metaphor of progress" (Woolrich 1995: 28).

In reviewing this dispute, first note that both contributors were able to make informed assertions about Costello's so-called popular work. Woolrich sounds more like Booth 1: live and let live, although his *compositions* might suggest a different answer. Clements desires a genuine eclecticism that will lead to something "totally new" (Booth 3), criticizing Costello from what sounds like a monist defence of classical technique; note also Clements's canny and evaluative separation of words and music.

Elsewhere, adopting a critical stance towards rock music, Allan Moore in 1993 asserted Booth 4: "The extreme relativism that this implies is both unavoidable and to be embraced, for it asserts that not only music's meaning, but its values too, are the preserves of listeners" (Moore 1993: 185).[5] In 1995, David Brackett sounded like Booth 1: "to Costello, art music is merely more source material, not an elevated musical practice that, once ascended to, may never be left." Brackett evokes the theory of postmodernism: Booth 3, postmodern style, and Booth 4, the postmodern condition (Brackett 1995: 168).

Costello always allows Booth 4, the sceptical perspective, since every listener is free to switch off or walk out,[6] but this overlooks something Costello's songs train you to expect: battles for control of power closer to the monists of Booth 2. Brackett's book is tolerant of diversity in popular music and brings postmodernism on board, but he was in 2005 the most insistent of the *Popular Music* debate's twenty-three contributors on having to preserve the dualism for the sake of popular music:

> Here [at a North American university] popular music is de-
> fined negatively as the music (along with non-Western music)
> that is not taught in all the other courses offered by the
> faculty of music, or, for that matter, in instrumental/vocal
> lessons or in performing ensembles. Compared to jazz and
> classical music (institutionally distinct categories in this case),
> popular music is the new kid on the block. (International
> Advisory Board 2005: 138)

Brackett refers to *institutional* power plays, the contest of faculties, and, when Costello started out, British musical culture bore a striking resemblance to a neatly organized class system. For example, Costello would have aimed to be heard on BBC Radio One (pop music for youth), his father would have appeared on Radio Two (popular music for adults), while for both of them Radio Three (classical music) would have been beyond reach, the pair of them like father-and-son builders turning up in a white van to fix a big house in the posh, leafy part of town.[7] The danger of the presentation to follow here is that Costello's work is seen as a gradual ascent to an Everest of technical complexity, albeit a mountain peak that turns out to be a problem. But there really is something of that in the story: the songwriter of 'Less

Than Zero' turns from pop songs as the only game in town towards the pop song as one possible expressive medium among many others, as the composer of *Il Sogno*.

Time

> "Well, you're limited timewise. You can only *ramble on* so long, and then it isn't interesting anymore. Or else people would be writing symphony length songs. They don't seem to work in that context." (Robbie Robertson, in Zollo 1997: 395)

"Musically, Costello has transcended the three-minute popular song," says James Perone, offering the example of 'Radio Sweetheart' (Perone 1998: 11). Transcend the popular song as it may, 'Radio Sweetheart' (1977) is a good thirty seconds short of three minutes. Costello was raised on vinyl, his imaginative head filled by the 45-rpm single or 33 1/3-rpm long-playing record, both of which needed flipping over halfway through: the idea that the song on record lasted between two and four minutes was a basic starting-point. For musical minds raised on singles and albums with two sides the arrival of CD was a key development, inviting greater continuous length, for better or worse. Although CD dates to around 1982, Costello remembers *Mighty Like A Rose*, as late as 1991, as "probably the last record that I imagined as a two-sided vinyl disc" (*Mighty Like A Rose* n03). Costello was productive both before and after CD's arrival, and the timings in Table 2.1 suggest that only a gradual increase is found: in the world of the song, however, thirty seconds can be a very long time indeed.[8] From the notably short average of *Get Happy!!*, the totals show a steady increase but the average track peaks at 4'18 for *Painted From Memory*, the style of which, perhaps, led to a certain slowness. If there are leaps to be found, there is a nudge forward between *Trust* and the trio of *Imperial Bedroom*, *Punch The Clock* and *Goodbye Cruel World*,[9] and then between *Goodbye Cruel World* and *King Of America*. On the other hand, never underestimate Costello's ability to pull off concision and compression: nearly twenty years after 'Welcome To The Working Week' and 'Mystery Dance' (*My Aim Is True*), 'Shallow Grave' (*All This Useless Beauty*) also stays under the *two*-minute barrier. "Many of the songs for this album were under or around the two-minute mark", as opposed to a "conventional length composition" (*Get Happy!!* n03).

Table 2.1 Average length of tracks on Costello's albums

Album	Date	Tracks	Total time	Average
My Aim Is True	1977	13	36'49	2'48
This Year's Model	1978	13	39'21	3'00
Armed Forces	1979	13	40'12	3'60
Get Happy!!	1980	20	48'21	2'24
Trust	1981	14	41'53	3'00
Almost Blue	1981	12	32'42	2'42
Imperial Bedroom	1982	15	50'57	3'24
Punch The Clock	1983	13	45'32	3'30
Goodbye Cruel World	1984	13	44'24	3'24
King Of America	1986	15	58'04	3'48
Blood And Chocolate	1986	11	47'55	4'18
Spike	1989	15	64'30	4'18
Mighty Like A Rose	1991	14	54'28	3'54
The Juliet Letters	1993	20	62'52	3'06
Brutal Youth	1994	15	57'22	3'48
Kojak Variety	1995	15	54'21	3'36
All This Useless Beauty	1996	12	48'20	4'00
Painted From Memory	1998	12	52'26	4'18
When I Was Cruel	2002	16	65'57	4'06
North	2003	11	40'38	3'42
The Delivery Man	2004	14	56'41	4'00
The River In Reverse	2006	13	53'07	4'00

In turn, the basic formal design of the tracks rarely alters: listening to Costello, one soon discovers that words like introduction, verse, chorus, bridge, coda are adequate, the words "improvised instrumental solo" refreshingly rare, although the listener needs to be attentive to micro-differences within those divisions.[10] In terms of track length, Costello rarely allows a track to *change* (style, subject-matter, speed) within the track: examples are found in 'Veronica' (*Spike*), 'I Almost Had A Weakness' (*The Juliet Letters*), and 'You Bowed Down' (*All This Useless Beauty*). *The Juliet Letters* opened doors of exploration – the Wagnerian 'Dear Sweet Filthy World', and 'I Thought I'd Write To Juliet' – while 'I Want You' (*Blood And Chocolate*) has a distinct introductory section. What happens in a Costello song, to the point of being generally the case, is that a speed is set for the specific song, and the music then follows that song's meaning through the standard formal divisions. In this, he follows American song-writing models like Brill Building, country, soul and gospel. When Costello started out, his acceptance of temporal limits was not only a denial of the formal extensions of progressive rock but also of what Tony Banks has called the "imaginative pop" of bands like Genesis, Queen and 10CC (Buckley 2005: 90). If there was talk of *Armed Forces* as the work of a British Springsteen, *Born To Run* of 1975 contained formal contrasts within tracks in generating operatic epics such as 'Thunder Road' and 'Jungleland'. Costello's formal consistency is seen in Table 2.2, which analyses two tracks eighteen years apart: even though 'You Bowed Down' contains an exceptional tempo change, the broad contours are much the same.[11]

Costello's harmonic language

Costello controls chords as well as voice, melody and words and, from the start, he used a wide range of guitar-based chords, adding piano-based chords at a later point. The listener assumes the basic reference points of tonal music: keys, cadences, inversions (partly a matter for the bass player), modulations.[12] Some tracks, with drones and blues-based progressions, consist of limited harmonic movement. It is appropriate for 'Tokyo Storm Warning' (*Blood And Chocolate*) or 'Bedlam' (*The Delivery Man*) to hammer away at the same chords, the music's passivity the platform for the words to make their mark. One of the most remarkable examples is 'When I Was Cruel No.2' (*When I Was Cruel*). A sampled voice, sounding like the word "bon", is repeated 71 times over the seven minutes of the track, and acts musically as a sustained (or "pedal") inner note C, for a song in F minor largely based on chords I (F,Ab,C) and V (C,E,G), C being a note common to both chords. However, occasionally the sample/pedal clashes expressively with the chord: see the closing phrase at 1'30–50. A piano figure derived from the first of Erik Satie's *Trois Gnossiennes* (1890) appears at 3'14.[13] Towards the end (c. 4'30) of the static 'Button My Lip' (*The Delivery Man*) Steve Nieve plays atonal clusters, before its F sharp minor gives way to the A major of 'Country Darkness'.

One of the most effective thumbprints in Costello's songs is the descending diatonic bass scale, starting the same but ending in various ways.[14] This descending line, starting at the tonic and moving step by step all the way down to the tonic, is heard (in various keys) at the opening of 'Accidents Will Happen' (*Armed Forces*), in 'All This Useless Beauty' (*All This Useless*

Table 2.2 'Radio Radio' and 'You Bowed Down'

Time	Word indicator	Formal section
'Radio Radio' (This Year's Model, 1978): 3'03		
0'00		Intro × 4
0'13	I was tuning	Verse
0'26	I was seriously	Link
0'38	Radio is the sound	Chorus a
0'46	They say you better listen	Chorus b
0'57	Better do as you were told	Chorus c
1'02		Intro × 2
1'08	I want to bite the hand	Bridge, dominant preparation at 1'18
1'22	Some of my friends	Verse 2
1'34	Either shut up	Link 2
1'47	Radio is the sound	Chorus a/b/c
2'11	Wonderful radio	Intro × 12 as coda
2'51		Cadences
3'03		End (dead)
'You Bowed Down' (All This Useless Beauty, 1996): 4'51		
		Intro × 2
0'16	1: I expect	Verse 1 × 2
	2: I'd promise	
0'46	So we broke that vow	Link 1
1'01	You bowed down	Chorus × 2
1'13		Intro × 1
1'20	1: When you first	Verse 2 × 2
	2: Now they say that	
1'51	And so you parade	Link 2
2'06	You bowed down	Chorus × 2
2'17	You value	Bridge × 2 (3/4 time)
2'36	If you just bowed down	4/4 time, dominant preparation at 2'40
2'44	1: And now every time	Verse 3 × 2
	2: I remember a time	
3'14	So you're in demand	Link 3
3'29	You bowed down	Chorus × 4, harmonic variation at fourth repeat
3'52		Intro × 8
4'51		End (fade)

Beauty), and the tail of the chorus of 'Oliver's Army' (*Armed Forces*). With the band in expressive disarray, 'Suit Of Lights' (*King Of America*) surprises by landing on V of vi (E,G#,B) rather than I (C,E,G) (e.g., between 0'18 and 0'28), but eventually gets to I (C) at the chorus end; at the bridge (1'50), Bruce Thomas wanders lonely as a cloud from the note G an octave lower, twice; but the band announces the descending scale at 3'28, with each bass note fully harmonized, Nieve adding what sound like Handelian fills at 3'49, by adding passing notes in his left-hand bass part. Slowed down, the descent of 'Possession' (*Get Happy!!*) sounds like 'Suit Of Lights', but also alludes to Bob Dylan's 'Is Your Love In Vain?' (*Get Happy!!* n03). The link from verse to chorus[15] of 'White Knuckles' (0'20) is unusual in that the scale descent from I (E) starts by supporting chord vi (C#,E,G#) in first inversion and, after a deviation to B minor (0'27), E as tonic (E,G#,B) is reached only at 0'40. The chorus of 'You'll Never Be A Man' (*Trust*) starts off the descent from A (0'38) to cadence on A (0'43–48), but then resumes the scale descents, first on D major (notes D, C#, B, A: 0'48), and then transposed to F major (F, E, D, C: 0'56 and 1'01). The theme is that of scale-steps leading downwards: '13 Steps Lead Down' (*Brutal Youth*) starts off the descent from E for its catchy chorus (the notes E, D#, C#, B: 0'22), twice repeated, but cuts off (at 0'29) to a section on chord vi (C#,E,G#, the "relative minor" of E). The four-note descent resumes (at 0'50) but this time, at its third repetition (0'57), the scale descends all the way to F# before settling again on C# minor (an "interrupted cadence" at 1'04), finally going all the way down the steps to the much-delayed tonic (E) at 2'14.

Bass descents can vary. One is the chromatic version, I–V7 of IV–IV–flat iv,[16] as found in the chorus sections of 'Riot Act' (*Get Happy!!*: the notes D–C–B–B♭), 'High Fidelity' (*Get Happy!!*: the notes A–G–F#, F eventually appearing at 1'00), and 'The Other Side Of Summer' (*Mighty Like A Rose*: G–F–E–E♭). Variants of these descents appear in the chorus of 'Opportunity' (*Get Happy!!*), 'New Lace Sleeves' (*Trust*) and the bridge of 'King Horse' (*Get Happy!!*: 1'46). A particular version of the chromatic filling-in between I and V is found at 1'34–43 of 'Poor Fractured Atlas' (*All This Useless Beauty*), in which each chromatic note supports a chord (see Table 2.3).[17]

Some other thumbprints to listen for: one, possibly derived from guitar-based writing, is ending a line on the minor chord ii to lead back to the

Table 2.3 'Poor Fractured Atlas' (*All This Useless Beauty*, 1996): chromatic bass line, 1'34–43

Chord	D	A	C	G	B♭	A
Bass line	D (I)	C#	C	B	B♭	A (V)

tonic, rather than chord V, for instance, D–A–G–*Em* in 'This Is Hell' (*Brutal Youth*: 0'59–1'05). Note also the deliberate simplicities, such as the "comforting I-iii" progression: '(The Angels Wanna Wear My) Red Shoes' (*My Aim Is True*: 0'14–20), 'Deep Dark Truthful Mirror' (*Spike*: 0'02–06), 'You Tripped At Every Step' (*Brutal Youth*: 0'12–15), 'Jacksons, Monk And Rowe' (*The Juliet Letters*: 0'15–17); dependable I–V–IV–I progressions in 'Possession' (*Get Happy!!*), 'Suit Of Lights' (*King Of America*), 'Turning The Town Red' (expanded *Goodbye Cruel World*); or I–IV–V–IV in 'Rocking Horse Road' (*Brutal Youth*).

Circular progressions and mixtures

Perone describes 'Radio Sweetheart' as an interesting case of a song which avoids having a marked verse section (Perone 1998: 11): "engaging and surprising", says Alan Robinson.[18] It is also a harmonic progression which expands and returns in a circular fashion. I refer to this as a mixture progression, as though E major has in this case "borrowed" G major from its tonic minor, E minor (which forms the basis of the introduction).[19] Thus the big dominant (B7) can resolve both to E as the perfect cadence but also to G, the relative major of E minor. The same principle is used for 'Big Sister's Clothes' (*Trust*), as shown in Table 2.4. Most of the chords for both songs sit easily on the guitar.

Costello might have inherited mixture progressions from the Beatles, McCartney in particular, whose 'Here, There And Everywhere' (1966) is a textbook case: its G major refers both to E minor as *relative minor* and G minor as *tonic minor*, as well as *its relative major*, B♭ major, the shift, at "I want her everywhere" taking the music from the notational world of one sharp to that of two flats.[20]

Mixtures are found at various points in songs, for example, at the start of some tracks where "chord I to major IV" becomes "chord I to minor iv":

Table 2.4 'Radio Sweetheart' and 'Big Sister's Clothes'

Time	Chord progression
'Radio Sweetheart' (1977, expanded *My Aim Is True*)	
0'00 (fade in)	Em; Em–Am–Em
0'36	G–Em–C–D; G–Em–A–B7
0'49	E–C#m–F#m–B × 2
1'01	F#m–G#m–F#m–F#
1'07	E–B7
1'15	G–Em–C–D; G–Em–A–B7
1'32	E–C#m–F#m–B × 2
1'45	F#m–G#m–F#m–F#
1'51	E
1'58	E (pentatonic call-and-response)
2'28	End (fade)
'Big Sister's Clothes' (*Trust*, 1981)	
0'00	E–C#m × 2
0'07	E–C#m–A–B × 2
0'20	G–Em–C–D; G–Em–C–B7
0'34	Em–G–C–B7; Em–G–C–B7–C–B7–C
0'54	G–Cm–G–Cm
1'00	Em–C–Em–C–B7
1'09	E–C#m–A–B × 2
1'22	G–Em–C–D; G–Em–C–B7
1'36	Em–G–C–B7; Em–G
1'46	C–B7 × 4
2'00	Em

see 'Jack Of All Parades' (*King Of America*, the opening riff and 0'14-18) or 'The Other Side Of Summer' (*Mighty Like A Rose*: 0'11–15). Little mixtures can be dropped in, to provide small moments of colour, as at 0'40 in both 'Human Hands' (*Imperial Bedroom*) or 'TKO (Boxing Day)' (*Punch The Clock*). The bridge section of 'New Amsterdam' (*Get Happy!!*) plays, briefly but expressively, with major–minor relation at "Back in London" (1'11–18): Em–A–E–Am–D7. 'Accidents Will Happen' (*Armed Forces*) refers to mixture chords during the chorus and fade. 'High Fidelity' (*Get Happy!!*) shows a minor-key verse resolving to a major-key chorus, the musical trick of the Picardy third.[21] 'Clubland' (*Trust*) is the same, and includes a terrific reharmonization of the verse material for the third verse (at 1'53–2'08), so that the standard progression, I–VI–ii–V, repeated (bass line: B–G–C#–F#)[22] is transformed into the parallel chords: B–A–G–F#–D–E. 'Let Them All Talk' (*Punch The Clock*) uses minor and major to delineate formal sections: minor-chord introduction (0'00), major-chord verse (0'14). An example of "the 'Wonderful World' flat six" (in theory, an A♭ major chord in C major, in practice, where Louis Armstrong sings "And I *think to myself*") is found at 0'55 of 'Kid About It' (*Imperial Bedroom*); there are flat sixes also at 0'35–38 of 'Imagination Is A Powerful Deceiver' (extended *My Aim Is True*), 1'02 of 'Dear Sweet Filthy World' (*The Juliet Letters*), and 2'04 of 'Fallen' (*North*). Costello saved some good examples for *The Delivery Man*: the bridge of 'Heart-Shaped Bruise' reinterprets the C# minor at 1'24 as the C major of 1'38, both resolving to the perfect cadence A (chord V) to D (chord I). 'She's Pulling Out The Pin' is an extended example, whose first minute progresses from G to B♭ via three distinct sections: the first (0'00–31) circles from G through B♭ back to G, the second (0'32–42) lands surprisingly on B♭7, the dominant of E♭ (at 0'41), the third (0'43–59) resolves to B♭. The music provides a witty correspondence to the story.

Songs that modulate

"Pure pop for now people" was one of the Stiff label's catchphrases[23] and 'Oliver's Army' includes a classic pop trick, the modulation "up a tone", in this case from A to B. In order for this to happen, after the second chorus the opening riff has ended on the dominant of *A major* (1'33), a chord of E major, whose note B becomes the B of G# minor (1'34), which is chord vi in *B major*, so commencing the bridge section in B.[24] Although modulating at the same time, the song preserves the sense of "heading to the minor", a familiar effect for the bridge of a major-key song. At the bridge, the song is safely in B; however, extended dominant preparation (1'43–52, the final F#7 at 1'49), with "the boys from the Mersey and the Thames and the Tyne", ensures uplift for the tonic's return and the final verse.

There are relatively few modulating songs in Costello's output (it can be a bad idea),[25] but some are interesting. Relatively simple tricks like those in 'Oliver's Army' can be found at 1'20 of the country pastiche 'Different Finger' (*Trust*), an example which would qualify for what Walter Everett calls a "truck-driver modulation" (Everett 2000: 311–12): the gear/key is D, depress the clutch/dominant (B7) in order to set up the higher gear/key, E. Both versions of 'American Without Tears' have simple modulations up the tone: the *King Of America* version opens with the instrumental introduction pitched *another* tone "too low", so that the song opens with immediate uplift, perhaps creating the sense of a story already under way. We shall examine two examples from *Punch The Clock* presently: 'The Element Within Her', which starts in F and ends in G, but gets there by a winding route, and 'The Greatest Thing', which has an overall harmonic structure Ab–E–B–G (two major-third drops a minor third apart). Finally, 'Lovable' on *King Of America* has three shifts upwards (A–B–C–D), one too many perhaps, but not all the same: the first and third (1'35 and 2'22) are truck-drivers (clutch on F# to go to B, and on A to go to D), while the middle one (1'58, to C) enters excitingly in mid-chorus, mid-phrase (at 1'58).[26] A dramatic later example is at 2'07 of 'I Still Have That Other Girl' (*Painted From Memory*), starting in F but referring to tonic minor "mixture" chords, before a big shift up a semitone to G flat. The drama song 'I Thought I'd Write To Juliet' (*The Juliet Letters*) wanders far from the initial tonic of F minor to end eventually in G minor (3'03–4'06), but taking in B major (1'30 and 2'38), G major (1'48) and E major (2'22) along the way. 'She's Pulling Out The Pin' (*The Delivery Man*) ends in Bb, a minor third from where it started.

A few examples go the other way: *down* a tone. Due to its juxtaposition of different recordings, the zany and 'Battered Old Bird' (*Blood And Chocolate*) manages to end a tone *lower* than where it started, cutting from the recording in D to the one in C, twice. 'Human Hands' (*Imperial Bedroom*) is in G major but ends on F major by the trick of sitting on the *minor* dominant (D minor) from 0'05 and making it an F major (at 2'38–39). 'Our Little Angel' (*King Of America*) is a simpler case of a song in A minor ending on its G major contrast section. 'Jack Of All Parades' (*King Of America*) ends on an interrupted cadence: the song includes mixture chords from its A major home, but the piano eventually ends on F major in the first inversion, the cue for 'Suit Of Lights' to start in C. On the cassette version of *Girls Girls Girls*, 'Jack Of All Parades' ended a side, with the cadence left to dangle in the silence.

The piano, and the Attractions as musicians

> "So when I write the song on guitar and transfer it to piano, I lose touch with what I did. And also because I was working with gifted pianists like Richard Tee, Barry Beckett, they might change the chord subtly. Change the bass of a chord. So the song might evolve harmonically because of some other musician's input after I took it off the guitar and gave it to them." (Paul Simon, in Zollo 1997: 103)

> "On guitar, to make some chords, your fingers have to go into acrobatics. On piano, you just move one note over. It's laid out in a way that's a little easier to deal with. And changing a note on the bottom is easy, whereas on guitar it would be tricky if not even possible." (Robbie Robertson, in Zollo 1997: 388)

Costello indicates two moments in his musical development: learning to compose at the piano, and learning to read music. The first is described in *Imperial Bedroom* n02:

> The major change of the previous eighteen months had been a gradual shift to the piano as my main composing instrument. This not only invited a more arranged approach to the songs, but also reflected the music to which I was listening.[27]

Learning to read musical notation is often referred to in the notes: *The Juliet Letters* n92, or *Brutal Youth* n02: "In the previous year I had learned to read and write musical notation." These comments enable us to date Costello's composing at the piano to about 1982, and his studies in musical notation to about 1992–3.

Costello commented on the role of the piano in conversation with Timothy White in 1983:

> "I think it would be unfair to the other two Attractions, Bruce and Pete Thomas, to say that Steve has a greater say overall. Obviously, he has the most scope with his instrument because he's the main melodic interest on most tracks, and from the

nature of his instrument he has more range than the bass or
the drums. But I think overall it's a fairly even input."

He then refers to Nieve's orchestrations on *Imperial Bedroom*, observing
that:

"It's marvellous that he has the technical, musical ability to
write things down, that he can communicate complicated
ideas to players that can only work with written music. I don't
have that ability. I don't write or read music at all. I have to
describe things to people if I'm working with a writer or
arranger. I have to communicate by humming the lines, which
can get very tedious." (in White 1983)

We can only guess why in 1977 Costello adopted a line-up with piano
rather than an extra guitar, but I suggest that the pianist he ended up with,
Steve Nieve (*né* Nason), is the key to thinking about Costello's musical
development, at least up to *Spike*, the Steve Dedalus to Costelleo Bloom.
Their personal relationship endured difficult periods: Thomson describes
early 1987 as the nadir, with reconciliation in late 1992 (Thomson 2004:
246–7, 302). The hatchet was yet to be buried at the time of the BBC radio
series in early 1992, so that the pianist never speaks, the one consistent pity
in a faultless biographical documentary (see pp. 69–71 for an extract).[28]
After 1992, their partnership happily resumed to reach fresh creative peaks.

Why is the piano significant? Playing the piano like Wilhelm Kempff is one
thing, but what Costello seems to mean is playing the piano with enough
control for it to take over from the guitar as chief "chord-generator" for
songs. After all, he was able to call on tremendously proficient *players*,
whatever the instrument. The distinction between guitar-based songwriting
and piano-based songwriting is worthy of study in its own right (Moore
1993: 54–5), and it would be possible to match separate histories on the
difference: the guitar-based rock'n'roll of Chuck Berry and Buddy Holly
contrasted with Fats Domino and Jerry Lee Lewis at the piano; the guitar-
based singer-songwriting of James Taylor and Paul Simon contrasted with
Randy Newman and Elton John at the piano; Ani di Franco's guitar contrasted
with Ben Folds's piano; Lou Reed's guitar contrasted with John Cale's
piano.[29] For Costello as listener, the likely inspiration was the Band, in which

Steve Nieve with Costello and the Attractions; during concert performances recorded in 1996, Costello and Nieve appeared as a duet.

both Garth Hudson and Richard Manuel were keyboard players, contributing at various times to Bob Dylan's supporting sound; recall also the E-Street Band behind Bruce Springsteen: Roy Bittan, piano, Danny Federici, organ, a split in keyboard-based resources the Band also employed. However, this is also a context where "pub rock" may have had a direct effect, since the scene included several talented pianists.[30] Bob Andrews provided a solid piano foundation for both Brinsley Schwarz and Graham Parker's Rumour; Paul Carrack for Ace and, briefly, Squeeze, the earlier version of which included Julian "Jools" Holland; Chaz Jankel for the Blockheads. However, Steve Nieve didn't come from that immediate background and was, at least by training, the one element of Costello that links to the other great keyboard source of the time, progressive rock and, less so, heavy metal. Pianists in those genres, such as Tony Banks, Rick Wakeman, Keith Emerson, Mike Ratledge and Jon Lord, were all, as the phrase invariably had it, "classically trained".[31] Nieve in the Attractions could be characterized as a prog-rock pianist in a pub-rock band.

Costello expresses the musical shift arising from the piano as "a more arranged approach" to songwriting; piano-based composing can mean a difference in control of voice-leading and the bass part, and in Costello's case doing so drew attention to the shifting roles played by Steve Nieve and Bruce Thomas on bass. A key question is how much of the instrumental parts Costello controls, a basic aspect of how we perceive the music as belonging to Costello as author and how much any band-based music is collaborative. A further distinction can be made between Nieve the pianist and organist, the latter lacking the percussive quality of the piano: eventually, that "Attractions organ sound" can seem like an internal reference brought out, for instance, at the bridge (2'32) of 'Monkey To Man' (*The Delivery Man*). A different set of issues arises with the drummer. Pete Thomas had played in Chilli Willi and the Red Hot Peppers, whose three tracks included on *Naughty Rhythms*[32] indicate their eclectic reach, notably the Western swing of 'Breathe A Little', relying on Thomas's considerable ability to adapt and keep up.

It is worth emphasizing the musical abilities of the Attractions whenever the word "punk" is used in this context: they were all skilful *players*, and must have regarded with, at most, courteous toleration any "de-skilled" connotation of punk, in relation either to not being able to play as provocation, the London punk approach (Siouxie Sioux, Sid Vicious), or to the more art-derived cultivation of untutored invention, the Manchester approach (the Fall).[33] It so happens that British punk bands avoided keyboards, with the exception of the Stranglers; singer-songwriter Joe Jackson was also a classical pianist and seen at the time as belonging to the same "new wave" as Costello.

Like many of the pub-rock bands, the Attractions were a superb ensemble, heard at their early best on *This Year's Model*, where 'Radio Radio', 'No Action' and 'Chelsea' all have tremendous attack, which may mean that they were all as individuals wanting to be slightly, spunkily ahead of the beat. The musical material was most appropriate: 'Radio Radio' has the rhythmic energy of the opening of Beethoven's 'Waldstein' piano sonata, the motor power of eight fast eighth notes, or quavers, with the first given a rest; 'No Action' contains irregular cuts where everyone needs to know the rhythmic formula; '(I Don't Want To Go To) Chelsea' contains a memorable melodic gesture in the guitar as the band skanks as the musical equivalent of imitation Jamaicans in blackface. *Mad About The Wrong Boy*, the album issued by the Attractions *sans* Costello in 1980, is worth digging up if only to establish, swiftly and comprehensively, that while the cat was away, the mice were playing anything but their master's canon, substituting instead: prog-style "imaginative pop" with sharp contrasts within the song; throw-away comedy, bad jokes rather than pointed irony; and words "stuck in for the purpose", achieving at most a vague sense of gloom and doom.

Thomson suggests that Nieve was close to leaving the Attractions around the time of *Get Happy!!* (1980), but considers his role to be crucial on *Trust* (1981) (Thomson 2004: 150, 164). Nieve's contribution is decisive on *Imperial Bedroom* (1982), which is also Bruce Thomas's finest hour on record as an Attraction. This presented Costello with a problem: his musical identity had become bound up with Nieve's role as pianist. I am also of the view that *Imperial Bedroom* is the first entirely successful *album* from start to end, and that Nieve had a lot to do with it.[34] Not only did he seem to have the Emerson–Wakeman rack of keyboards to hand – the 'Like A Rolling Stone' organ of 'Man Out Of Time', the harpsichord of 'You Little Fool', an accordion for 'The Long Honeymoon',[35] lots of little piano voices and touches, such as the gorgeous, repeated A flats at 2'25 of 'The Long Honeymoon' – but he also supplied orchestrations from somewhere in that classical training: romantic horns for 'The Long Honeymoon', the light music of '… And In Every Home', the stoned fade of 'Town Cryer'.

The piano, precisely, then runs into trouble on *Punch The Clock*. In my hearing, *Punch The Clock* is a failing less of production than of arrangement, classical piano set alongside brass interjections. *Goodbye Cruel World* adds to the confusion, in production as well as arrangement. At this point, Costello recognizes that his dilemma really *is* the Attractions, which at heart means Nieve as carrier of a particular version of piano-playing: bass and drums are not part of the musical issue, for all that there may have been difficulties in daily life.[36] Nieve's part in *King Of America* is tiny but tremendously telling: he enters late in the day on 'Jack Of All Parades', leading the song towards the "interrupted cadence" that sets up 'Suit Of Lights', messy but poignant, the very sound of people falling apart. The key thing about *King Of America* was that its various keyboard sounds (accordion, "doctored piano", organ) were options rather than necessities. The Attractions moodily re-gathered for *Blood And Chocolate*, where the organ is called for and the piano appears on two tracks only: the demented and 'Battered Old Bird' and 'Crimes Of Paris' (the latter low in the mix). Never again did Nieve have the heroic prominence of *Imperial Bedroom* (Mercer-Taylor 1995: 40).

With *King Of America* and without the Attractions, Costello encountered not only the styles of American music but also the musical values of American musicians, which he sums up in this brilliant aphorism:

> The essential difference between English and American musicians could be very crudely defined in these terms: American musicians will always ask "How do we end?" English musicians only ask "How do we begin?" (*King Of America* n95)

Much can be read into that sentence: the art-school lineage in English rock music, perhaps, which Costello viewed with scepticism, once describing such music as having an "icy clean line that came straight out of art school" (*Armed Forces* n02). In 1985 Costello thought that "American music is more interesting at the moment", which Mick St. Michael reads as referring to American rock and roots bands such as X or Los Lobos (St. Michael 1986: 117), when American bands like REM, the Long Ryders and Dream Syndicate arrived to perform in England. In his great history of the period, David Cavanagh describes the ensuing contrast with post-punk British indie music, the American bands "demonstrably streets ahead as musicians and performers", and "liberated by punk rock in more subtle ways than their British contemporaries". Peter Buck of REM came to the bold conclusion that the claim of punk rock, "we can do anything", "meant we could do these weird folky things and not have to be a hit band" (in Cavanagh 2001: 187). On the other hand, says Cavanagh, "the indie scene in Britain was no less trend-obsessed and style-conscious than the chart pop it wanted to destroy." The stars of that point in Cavanagh's epic are the Jesus and Mary Chain, who "played music as though it were an outlet of expression that would be available to them only once or twice in their lives". Their short sets, consisting largely of feedback, correlate in the most extreme form to Costello's point about English (or Scottish) musicians starting with little sense of ending. Cavanagh parodies the insular British response: "Hour long sets! My dear, these foreigners have so much to learn" (*ibid.*: 187–8). Art-school musicians and music-based musicians could be different creatures, the Attractions more the latter.

Costello praises the Attractions' later ensemble performance on 'Poor Fractured Atlas' (*All This Useless Beauty*), and their performance of 'The Other End Of The Telescope' (*All This Useless Beauty*) can be heard as an extended essay on the subject. The music is by Aimee Mann, with words adapted by Costello, but her version sounds more like *a record* (of the song), whereas the Attractions' is *a recording of their performance of their arrangement* (of the song). The Costello and Attractions performance makes more of the role of voice-leading, discernibly so, where the original Til Tuesday performance[37] uses more root chords, as well as being produced as a more "mushy" sound. Table 2.5 shows the song's basic outline. In F major, the very first notes of the guitar, B♭ and C (with the C held in the organ), set a harmonic agenda that works all the way through to Steve Nieve's coda, the harmony making use of E♭ as an alternative settling-point to the dominant, C (as at 0'20 or 2'24 in the bridge). Bruce Thomas is crucial as a melodic bass player, precisely "on the note", but also inclined to fill spaces with connecting melodies. For instance, listen for the four-note melodies between B♭ and F, descending: Thomas simply fills the space at 0'23, then as chordal steps at 0'31. The descent from F to C is implied at the very

Table 2.5 'The Other End Of The Telescope' (*All This Useless Beauty*, 1996)

Time	Section	Word indicator
0'00	Verse Ia	Shall we agree
0'22	Verse Ib	And in time we won't even recall
0'31	Verse Ic	Smoke as smoke disappears in the air
0'40	Chorus Ia	I know
0'48	Chorus Ib	You'll see me off [chord sequence echoes opening of verse Ia]
0'52	Chorus Ic	At the other end
1'06	Verse 2a	The promise of
1'24	Verse 2b	Then down the hall
1'33	Verse 2c	One day you are up
1'41	Chorus 2a	I know
1'50	Chorus 2b	You'll see me off
1'54	Chorus 2c	At the other end
2'06	Bridge a	Lie down baby [chord sequence echoes opening of chorus Ia]
2'15	Bridge b	Your head is so sore
2'29	Verse 3a	You're half naked
2'45	Verse 3b	And it's so hard
2'54	Verse 3c	The answer was
3'03	Chorus 3a	I know
3'11	Chorus 3b	'cos late in the evening [chords repeated × 3]
3'27	Chorus 3c	At the other end
3'36	Coda	[instruments alone]
4'05	End (fade)	

opening though not clearly stated, heard in the chorus at 0'48 (and 1'50, and repeated three times in the passage at 3'11), then properly in the verse at 1'06. Meanwhile, the descent from F to C forms the basis of the melody at 0'40, which then ascends for the approach to the hook line at 0'51, as well as for the core melodic material of the bridge at 2'06, and this is harmonized at 2'15, the bass now descending from D; the bridge also reinterprets a passage from the chorus (at 2'06). The "background" material then decorates outward to the smallest details: Nieve's decoration at the chorus (0'54), a tiny second in the second verse (1'11–12), a little open fifth and descending arpeggio on synthesizer at 3'16–19, and the wonderful instrumental coda (3'36–4'05). This floats on chord IV, B♭, but listen to Bruce Thomas ascend (3'43) through D, E, G, back to B♭ (3'52). Nieve also fragments the scale into two-, three- and four-note descents, gaining the tonic F at 3'43, ascending to C at 3'45, tonic again at 3'52; his final touch is to leave the bass at the dominant, C (4'00). Pete Thomas follows Nieve with delicate and fast cymbal work, introducing a repeated rhythmic pattern from 3'51 to 4'00. The voice adds a decorative slide in pitch, or glissando (that descending scale, C to F) at 3'33 and supplies beautiful falsettos at 2'00 (C) and 2'29 (D), the latter one of Costello's great vocal notes on record.

Enriched harmony: the line to *North*

Having demonstrated technical mastery of the pop forms, Costello went further and began to stretch the songs towards richer harmonic content. Why he did so is something we can only guess at: his upbringing surrounded by the harmony of big-band arrangements, watching Nieve's musical skills like a detective, the need musically to express or to take the melodic and harmonic material further, and a sense that a different harmonic language would suit different, more "adult-oriented" themes in song. Recognizing a connection with the tradition of the *lied*, 'Favourite Hour' (*Brutal Youth*) evokes the "murmuring brooks" of Wilhelm Müller's *Die schöne Müllerin*, set to music by Schubert in 1828.[38] This section will examine points in Costello's output in terms of musical *progress*, an idea discredited by pluralist perspectives but an important direction and ambition to recognize in Costello's case.[39]

'Party Girl' (*Armed Forces*) is a rich song, covering great musical distance in its first 1'29. Based in A, it includes distinct sections in G at 0'46 and C at 0'59, before three-and-a-half oscillations between D and E from 1'05 to 1'17 (Bruce Thomas wandering freely), and a big dominant E (Steve Nieve in piano concerto mode at 1'35–37). Notable is the pair of inner ascending chromatic lines, 5–5#–6–7 natural, the first (E–E#–F#–G) at 0'33–38, transposed (A–A#–B–C) at 0'38–44.[40] Second time round, the song deviates from the script at 2'25 (corresponding to 1'02 first time round), and heads towards a classic oscillating end (2'33: C to A, seven times in all), with Steve Nieve again in concerto mode, and fading at 3'18.[41]

The bridge of 'Human Touch' (*Get Happy!!*: 1'20–30) seems "out of control", its chords compressed shifts on the guitar: C#m–G#–F#–A–

G#–C–C#m–D–C#m. A notable development occurs in 'Shot With His Own Gun' (*Trust*): 0'48 of this track can stand as the point where a whole musical world opens up for Costello, tied to the shift from guitar-based to piano-based writing. It is an odd song, dealing with sordid affairs set to rather aimless words: "shot with his own gun" rhymes with "dad is keeping mum". Costello performs with Nieve alone at the piano. The song is in Am/C and reaches a typically uncertain chord: D, F, A♭, C, the "half-diminished seventh". The F minor chord (F, A♭, C) opens up A flat (0'48) as its relative major for a progression which ends on a plagal cadence in F major (0'57).[42] The shifts in key hinge on the use of notes common to different chords: G♭ (respelt as F#) is the common note in the change from G♭ (G♭, B♭, D♭ at 0'52) to D (F#, A, D at 0'54), and D is the common note in the change from D (F#, A, D) to B♭ (D, B♭, F at 0'56). To sum this up as a formula: D♭/B♭/**G♭** (=) **F#**/A/**D** (=) **D**/B♭/F.

Imperial Bedroom was an ambitious album, adding to these directions in two tracks, 'The Long Honeymoon' and 'Boy With A Problem'. Harmonic progression in 'The Long Honeymoon' is used to extend the music of the chorus. At 1'36 the music has settled on G minor (a fifth above the key centre C): Nieve's piano decorations (1'30–38) present little speeded-up compressions (E♭, D, C to D, C, B♭) of the notes Costello is singing at the time. Playing with the ambiguity of diminished chords (able to lead to both B♭ and D♭), at 1'40 a descending progression starts from D flat, progressing D♭m (1'42)–B (1'44)–Bm (1'46)–F#–Bm (1'48), then a little slide (A–G#m–Gm: 1'50) to cinematic guitar (1'54). C minor is returned to at 2'19. On the face of it, it would seem that B minor (a key with two sharps) is a long way from the home key of C minor (a key with three flats),[43] but inner voices are linking one progression to the other. Note that the Attractions pick up on these details: for instance, Bruce Thomas plays inversions at 1'48 and, as usual, Nieve adumbrates motif material appropriate for the melodic context: at 1'30–38, Nieve's piano part is like a speeded-up correspondence to the voice, or its rhythmic diminution. Finally, Costello ensures that the slide at 1'50 is tied to the song, masking its additional function as engineering a return to home ground.

'Boy With A Problem' goes further, since harmonic boldness is there from the start and is tied closer to the theme of the song. The song compresses much musical movement into its 2'08 duration, as shown in Table 2.6. It can be broken down into six sections. Five of the sections end on dominants, the first and last suggesting an E♭ major to follow, while sections 3, 4 and 5 lead towards C major. Section two lands on A♭ major six times, momentarily settling on that chord (0'46–48) before section 3 supplies a simple shift from A♭ to G as dominant of C (1'00–03). The first section uses a simple major–minor mixture and could in theory return to C after its final chord. The third section consists of a classic Costello descending chromatic bass line (A♭–G–G♭) but lurching to an unexpected F♭ at 0'54, answered by an unusual A (B♭♭!) at 0'58. Sections four and five remain relatively close to the home key, while the final section follows the pattern of the first, leaving the song dangling in mid-air (the boy's problems, in Chris Difford's words, unresolved).

With *Imperial Bedroom*, Costello had the expressive resources available to create a certain kind of "adult" harmony reminiscent perhaps of the albums recorded by Frank Sinatra on Capitol in the 1950s: the road to *North* is in place. The sense of musical progress continues to inform the following two albums – *Punch The Clock* and *Goodbye Cruel World* – before giving way to diverse musical styles strategically employed on *King Of America* and *Blood And Chocolate*, *Spike* and *Mighty Like A Rose*. Three tracks from *Punch The Clock* are noteworthy, and the following analyses focus on chord progressions shaping the form of each track.

'The Greatest Thing' uses a "Bo Diddley" rhythm, clever formal cuts and tonal transpositions, so that the opening riff is heard at four different levels of musical pitch (marked a, b, c and d in Table 2.7). Between these resting-points lies a variety of engineering work: riff (b) is arrived at through a small modulatory sequence, and is effectively the tonic major equivalent of E minor; riff (c) is a fifth above riff (b) and is a case of the music being "on"

Table 2.6 'Boy With A Problem' (*Imperial Bedroom*, 1982): 2'08

Section	Time	Word indicator
1	0'00	I feel like a boy
2	0'27	It's the last thing
3	0'49	Days in silence
4	1'03	I crept out last
5	1'26	I've got a problem
6	1'41	I feel like a boy

Table 2.7 'The Greatest Thing' (*Punch The Clock*, 1983): 3'00

Time Section	Chord progression
0'00 Drum introduction	
0'07 Riff (a) and Verse 1	G–Em
0'31 Chorus 1	C–Am; Em–G; F–D; C–G ("plagal cadence" × 1)
0'41 Verse 2	G–Em
1'00 Chorus 2	C–Am; Em–G
1'05 Harmonic transition	F–Am–D–Bm
1'09 Riff (b)	E–C#m
1'28 Chorus 3	D–Bm; F#m–A; G–E; D–A ("plagal cadence" × 1)
1'38 Riff (c)	B–G#m
1'57 Chorus 4	E–C#m; G#m–B; A–F#m; E–B ("plagal cadence" × 2)
2'07 Chorus 4 repeat	E–C#m; G#m–B; A–F#m; E–B ("plagal cadence" × 3)
2'17 Drum transition	
2'22 Riff (d)	G–Em
3'00 End (fade)	

the dominant rather than "in" the dominant;[44] riff (d) is a dramatic plunge to the "flat 6" of the dominant of E, i.e., from B to G, but ensures that the song ends where it began.

'The Element Within Her' also uses transpositions to clever effect, in under three minutes. The opening melody ("La la la") is heard at all of four levels, the first clustering on A (major or minor), the second on E, the third leading to a perfect cadence in C, the final on B at the fade. As the listener will find by cutting from the end back to the beginning, the song as a whole has gone "up a tone", but not in the manner of a truck-driver. Meanwhile the verse, an ascending sequence, is heard at two different levels: x and y. This is shown in Table 2.8.

Finally, 'TKO (Boxing Day)' contains an interesting example of what might be called a "framing" effect, where the opening A♭ minor, a semitone "too low" for the main key of the verse, returns to conclude the track (see Table 2.9).

On *Goodbye Cruel World*, 'Home Truth' has a meandering, mixture-based progression for its chorus. Starting from D, the verse ends on its dominant A (0'32), and then it is like a ball passed along a line of players: A hands over to A minor (0'33), through C to F (0'38) before creeping up to B♭

Table 2.8 'The Element Within Her' (*Punch The Clock*, 1983): 2'50

Time	Section	Chord progression
0'00	Opening melody ("La la la") a	F–Am–E (V of **A**)
0'14	Chorus I	E ending on A
0'28	Verse I (*x*)	D–G; Em–A; F–B♭
0'39	("La la la") b	C–Em–B (V of **E**)
0'46	Chorus I repeat	E ending on A
1'00	Verse 2 (*x*)	D–G; Em–A; F–B♭
1'12	("La la la") b	C–Em–B (V of **E**)
1'19	Bridge	F–C–G–C; G–C
1'30	("La la la") c	F–C–Dm7–G–C (perfect cadence in **C**)
1'41	Verse 3 (*y*)	G–C; Am–D; B♭–E♭
1'52	("La la la") a	F–Am–E (V of **A**) × 2
2'07	("La la la") c	F–C–Dm7–G–C (perfect cadence in **C**)
2'16	Cut to ("La la la") d	G–Bm–F# (V of **B**)
2'50	End (fade)	

Table 2.9 'TKO (Boxing Day)' (*Punch The Clock*, 1983): 3'27

Time Formal section and chord progression

0'00 **A♭m** riff
0'07 Up a semitone for Verse I: **Am**–F–C–Dm–F–A major
0'22 Link: Dm–G as dominant of **C major**
0'34 Chorus I: C–F–G; C–Fm–**C** (note harmonic mixture: C–F–C; C–**Fm**–C)
0'50 Verse 2 (Am to A)
1'05 Link 2 (dominant of C)
1'18 Chorus 2 (C)
1'26 Bridge: Fm–A♭ to variation of Chorus I (E♭/Cm at 1'31 and 1'38) to **A♭m** (1'43)
1'46 Up to **Am** again for Verse 3
2'01 Link 3 (dominant of C)
2'13 Chorus 3 (C)
2'29 Extension repeated but this time...
2'46 ... settles on **A♭m** for riff
3'27 End (fade)

(0'45). Down to G minor (0'49), back up to B♭, then through C back "home" to D (0'53). Again, notice Nieve's piano decorations, playing with the melodic cluster (A, B, C), then (B♭, C, D). There is a dramatic bridge section at 1'51, dropping from D to C# minor, and engineering its way through E and F#m to land on D at 2'02, picking up from the end of the chorus to lead back to the verse. 'The Comedians', with its jaunty 5/4 rhythm, looks ahead to 'This Town' from *Spike*. However, 'Joe Porterhouse' shows busy but purposeless harmonic work.[45]

Mighty Like A Rose certainly returned to musical matters, with at least two highlights. 'Invasion Hit Parade' has three distinct areas, saving the best till last. The song is a cavalcade of images and references.[46] The verse sits on a D dorian mode, referring to G and C, but framed by D itself. The chorus (at 1'19) sounds like a beat group jamming on D/Am, but at 1'28 introduces a strong ascending progression (Am–F#7–Bm–B7–Em) and a short chromatic descent (1'35) before ending on F to G7 (1'43). It is that F in the last pair that kicks off the coda progression (once at 2'49–3'07, then at 4'04, a sixth repeat to the fade at 5'29): F–G–F#–A#m–A–C#m–/–.

The final track on *Mighty Like A Rose*, 'Couldn't Call It Unexpected No. 4' also appears on *GBH* (the last track 'Closing Titles'). Costello is happy simply to repeat the sequence without contrast, three times in this case (a tiny extension at 1'41 to 1'53). Apart from the circus sounds (for the benefit of Mr Kite), it is the happy sense of circularity that charms listener and player, wandering and return, while Costello maps over this a strongly linear melodic line, utilizing his vocal range to good effect (see Table 2.10).

Costello is right in thinking of 'Favourite Hour' from *Brutal Youth*[47] as one of his best musical pieces to date:[48] indeed, in my view, a "best of" compilation without it makes little sense. The harmonic excursions – mixtures

Table 2.10 'Couldn't Call It Unexpected No. 4' (*Mighty Like A Rose*, 1991): 0'12–50

Time	Chord progression
0'12	D–Bm–F#m–G–A × 2
0'25	C#m–G#m–E(maj7)–G#m
0'31	A–C#m–A–C#m
0'38	G#m–A–E–A–C#m
0'46–50	A7–D

and common-note connections – are tied perfectly to the melodic line. In Table 2.11, note especially the italicized sections of the chord sequence. The melody makes the most of expressive intervals of the seventh, at 0'23, 0'26, 0'32, 0'37, 0'39–40 (the line through to 0'44 especially fine), 0'45–46 (an augmented sixth!), to lead up to the peak at 0'54 (A–F#–G). The span of the melody exploits Costello's vocal range and imposes its emotive line upon the words.[49]

'Upon A Veil Of Midnight Blue' (extended *The Juliet Letters*) and 'I Want To Vanish' (*All This Useless Beauty*) form further links between 'Favourite Hour' and *North*. In 'I Want To Vanish', notice the Romantic slush of 1'00–17, E♭7 to A♭ leading to C over G (at 1'11), cadencing in C (1'15) before a pregnant augmented chord (1'18) leads back to F major home (1'21). *North* (2003) was a destination for these tendencies. Costello presented an album that may have evoked a Sinatra album already in the shops, and may indeed have expressed the heart's swings in real life between Cait O'Riordan and Diana Krall, but above all he played to his most sustained command of harmonic richness. Appendix 2.1 (pp. 94–5) presents notes to guide the listener through the album's musical content: keep the words to hand.[50]

As a collaboration, *Painted From Memory* belongs to the works of both Costello and Burt Bacharach. For Bacharach the album was a small step but for Costello it confirmed the giant leap his control of musical material had taken: remember that Bacharach (born in 1928) was over a quarter-century older than Costello (born in 1954). 'Satellite' (*Spike*) had been Costello's

Table 2.11 'Favourite Hour' (*Brutal Youth*, 1994): 0'00–1'09

Time	Chord progression
0'00	D–F#m–Bm–D7
0'15	G–Bm–Em7
0'23	A–D–A–
0'32	C#dim7–D–
0'41	Bm–*Em*–
0'45	*E♭7–D–Bm*
0'52	*Gm*
0'55	*B♭m*
0'57	*F*
1'00	Am–Dm–G
1'09	D

Costello collaborated with Burt Bacharach on *Painted From Memory* 1998, but he had attempted to imitate Bacharach's music in 'Satellite' on *Spike* 1989.

earlier attempt at pastiche Bacharach and by coincidence was heard by Bacharach during its recording. Costello comments (*Spike* n01) that it was "only when we were composing and arranging together eight years later that I realised how very far 'Satellite' was from his actual writing and arranging style". In 'Satellite', Costello adapts surface elements of Bacharach's sound: curious orchestration that foregrounds tuned percussion and timpani, a particular extended resolution (E, D#, C#, D# over B: heard at 3'22), and harmonic progressions that may be closer to the Bacharach of 'Baby It's You' (originally for the Shirelles), which was covered by Costello with Nick Lowe in 1984. Set next to 'Satellite', *Painted From Memory* shows a tremendous advance, at least in terms of the musical style, especially its supple phrase-structure. The chorus of 'Toledo' (0'58) illustrates this; it is an eleven-bar phrase, with four beats per bar, divided as bars (2 + 3: 0'58, 1'02) + (3 + 3: 1'09, 1'16), and repeated (1'23–48). The phrasing of the harmony follows the melody, which is in turn allowed to extend or contract as appropriate to its emotional demand and the stress of the words. The dramatic bridge (3'08–52) of 'God Give Me Strength' expands and contracts its phrasing, building to the moment of pent-up expression at 3'48–50. Table 2.12 presents bar divisions,[51] which reflect melody, harmony and rhythm combined, but their asymmetry and unpredictability is the thing to listen for.[52] These are tricks of some of the great Bacharach songs.[53] Harmonically, there are some of the developments which we've seen in Costello's line to *North*: an irenic major coda to a minor song in 'In The Darkest Place' (worth noting too the invading F sharps at 1'49); a mid-phrase shift up a semitone in 'I Still Have That Other Girl' (at 2'07: truck-drivers denied entry); some "common-note" reinterpretations in 'Such Unlikely Lovers'. Costello uses his vocal "spread" as a compositional resource, including falsetto in 'Tears At The Birthday Party' and 'Such Unlikely Lovers', and there are some well-timed vocal contributions from female voices. Orchestration is superb throughout. I would even go so far as to suggest that there are some unifying devices, especially little snippets of melody that return. Listen for the rising melody followed by the leap: "Do your friends come around" in 'In The Darkest Place', the opening of 'Such Unlikely Lovers', the first line of 'What's Her Name Today?', and, now descending, in 'Painted From Memory' – "And so this had to be painted from memory". It would be a pity were *Painted From Memory* to disappear from view.

Table 2.12 'God Give Me Strength' (*Painted From Memory*, 1998): 3'08–52

Phrasing	Word indicator
2	God, if she'd
3	Grant me her indulgence and decline
2 + 3	I might as well wipe her from my memory
2 + 3	Fracture the spell as she becomes my enemy
4	And maybe I was washed out like a lip print on his shirt
3	See, I'm only human, I want him to
3	Hurt
3	I want him, I want him to
2 (etc.)	Hurt

Musical notation and the path to "classical" music

> Blending classical and pop: for gosh sake kids don't try it. (Morton and Death 1998: 33, 'Wagner versus the Shangri-Las')

> Since the 60s it's been the norm for pop performers to build records one layer at a time. This made allowances for lack of formal training while also ensuring a level of density in direct proportion to the recording budget. When you know you're going to hand out the sheet music, tap the stand and count in a bunch of musicians a different vocabulary follows. (Hepworth 2003: 72)

> "But certainly in popular music and rock and roll, that's not the problem [that knowledge can get in the way of spontaneity]. The problem is people don't know enough." (Paul Simon, in Zollo 1997: 113)

Costello hasn't spelled out the benefits of musical notation, and they're never easy to pin down or explain, especially to musicians and listeners who get by perfectly well without them. But knowledge is power, and notation can change *everything*: the notes introduce an almost-visual precision to musical understanding, and musical ideas arise from musical material. "Tones are beings who understand each other, as we understand tone," wrote J. W. Ritter in 1810. "Every chord may already be a mutual note-understanding, and come to us as an already created unity" (in Rosen 1995: 70). In addition, the whole of score-based repertory comes to life. For Costello, the string quartet appeared to be the initial impetus, echoing something Randy Newman once said:

> "I may be wrong, but I think a good song is to be respected as much as any other piece of music. I might have some sort of bias about people not being musicians. Not being able to put stuff down or not being able to write ... a string quartet, or something." (in Zollo 1997: 271)

GBH (1991), Costello's first collaboration in television music with Richard Harvey, was an important gateway, but *The Juliet Letters* (1993) was the first stand-alone product of this new-found knowledge, in which the Brodsky Quartet responded to Costello's enthusiasm. Costello has said of *The Juliet Letters* that "the music you most confidently attribute to one party invariably turns out to be the work of the person you least suspect" (*The Juliet Letters* n92), and it was two of the quartet's members who produced the two catchiest numbers, 'Taking My Life In Your Hands' and 'Jacksons, Monk And Rowe'.[54] The first of these is good to listen to, even though the music teacher given to theoretical rectitude might circle several points: ghastly consecutive fifths at bars 25–6 of the score (0'16–17), lumpy root positions from bars 19 to 22 (0'55–1'04), over-zealous expressive intensity at the end of verse 1 (bars 13–17, at 0'37–49), and the very end hopelessly overcooked (bars 59–61, at 3'04–16). On the other hand, untutored innocence produces the clash of the high E tonic against the two dominants (of E and of C# minor) at bar 27 (1'21–22). Problems lurk here, especially for the aim of sustaining tonal material over a long period: in 'I Almost Had A Weakness' (beginning at 0'21), the repeating chord sequence is the background for comic words, but the chords are too much of a good thing. Costello's music is best in *The Juliet Letters* when it sounds like Wagner via Debussy (Holloway 1979): 'Why?' (D♭ and A♭ juxtaposed with G, as at 0'49–52), 'Dear Sweet Filthy World' (the dissolve at bars 37–38 (2'03–10) following the B minor section (1'34–2'02)), 'The Birds Will Still Be Singing' (the passage from bars 36 to 47 (2'23–3'13), and the instrumental coda (3'31–4'21)). *The Juliet Letters* would benefit from a talented male singer, with a background in either the classical repertory or musical theatre, extracting a suite of about eight songs for a recital. If it turned out to work only as "a Costello record", this would point to a problem which our final work presents, on a dramatic stage.

> "The songs are the most important thing. I want the songs to mean something to people. I don't mean by that that I want them to be significant. It's just that too much rock has cut itself off from people. It's become like ballet or something. Ballet is only for people who can afford to go and see it. It's not for anybody else. You don't get ballet going on in your local pub."[55]

It is unfair to dig up something said in an interview thirty years earlier, but Costello may have had a point, and if it no longer holds – that is, ballet is no longer strictly for toffs – then that's something to celebrate. *Il Sogno* is Costello's ballet music for Shakespeare's *A Midsummer Night's Dream* (*Sogno di una notte di mezza estate*). Commissioned in 2000 by the company Aterballetto, the music was composed rapidly for first performance in Bologna in October that year. The music was then revised for a studio recording in 2002 by the London Symphony Orchestra conducted by Michael Tilson Thomas, which was issued in 2004. An edited version, entitled "suite", was issued a year later to accompany the concert recording, *My Flame Burns Blue*.[56] The first recorded version has 24 tracks in just under an hour, the suite 18 tracks in just over three-quarters of an hour. Appendix 2.2 (pp. 96–8) presents listening notes for a selection of movements.

I shall try to sum up my problem with *Il Sogno*, problems that don't apply to *North*. As in opera, musical theatre or film, listening to a ballet score raises the question of how much to allow for context; during a full stage performance one's musical attention may be diverted by watching dancers perform. In addition, however, *Il Sogno* has been performed in the concert hall, and now exists as an orchestral recording. The liner note reveals that such questions were already germane:

> We would read through the cues and Michael [Tilson Thomas, conductor] would say, "What is happening in this passage? There's no activity there." I'd say, "That's where the dancers do something very active against a background of still music,"

> and he had to remind me, "The dancers won't be there!" In
> the end, I tried to create a piece of music to which people
> might respond without any visual cues. (*Il Sogno* n04)

The problem can be traced back to the evocation of eighteenth-century wind-band music on the track 'Harpies Bizarre' (*Mighty Like A Rose*): the issue is not that Fiachra Trench orchestrated the piece in this quirky way, more that Costello is presenting imitation classical music as a real thing. The music is visual, the interlude a *film music* to accompany the *theme* of that point in the song. *Il Sogno* suggests that Costello approaches "classical" music as he approaches all of the "popular" genres: he is aware of musical history, has acquired technique, and regards the medium as the means to an expressive end. He was more interested in the activity of composing classical music rather than any idealized concept of classical music epitomizing musical material on its own terms, a complicated claim anyway, since it raises the issue of how musical material is defined at any given time, its nature, as well as its social and historical situation. For classical music as music produced from about 1750 to 1820, Charles Rosen provides a trenchant summary:

> I do not want to turn Haydn, Mozart and Beethoven into
> Hegelians, but the simplest way to summarize classical form
> is as the symmetrical resolution of opposing forces. If this
> seems so broad as to be a definition of artistic form in general,
> that is because the classical style has largely become the
> standard by which we judge the rest of music – hence its
> name. In no other music do the parts and the whole mirror
> each other with such clarity. (Rosen 1976: 83)

A more productive comparison for *Il Sogno* may be found in the soundtrack albums, *GBH* and *Jake's Progress*. Like *Painted From Memory*, as collaborations, these two records are difficult to present purely as Costello compositions, since composer Richard Harvey is co-credited on all their tracks. Nevertheless, with the opening track of *Jake's Progress*, for example, one somehow downplays the expectation of musical interest that *Il Sogno* raises, effortlessly admiring its nature as functional music – varied, interesting, and competent – and maybe that is how one should approach *Il Sogno*. The very first track of *Jake's Progress* is similar to some of the movements of *Il Sogno* summarized in Appendix 2.2: firmly tonal, competently orchestrated, allowing of reference to what sound like Romantic models, and inclusive of contrasts within the movement (see Table 2.13).

The sociology of Costello's classical music is complicated, and raises questions about the social situation of the orchestra. Costello's classical music evokes a time when its "target audience", the music's most informed recipients, really did experience the music as something to *read* as well as to *hear*: one studied scores. Because that social context no longer exists, and the score remains unpublished, the exercise invites the recording to be heard as background music, and even as mere background music. The struggle

Table 2.13 *Jake's Progress* (1995), track one ('Jake's Progress Opening Sequence')

Time	Description
0'00–18	Introductory opening from repeated D♭: viola solo, piano. Delicate harmony and scoring
0'18–38	Reminiscent of Costello and Harvey's music for *GBH*, this includes a "thumbprint" shift (at 0'18–23) from D♭ major to F minor and back.
0'38–1'00	E♭ minor to A♭, as dominant of D♭, then to B♭ minor. Shift engineered (0'50–1'00) from B♭ minor to D
1'01–40	Contrasting faster section sets off with repeated "pulse" A, electronic keyboard and drum kit, then melody (*x*) on French horn at 1'18 to 1'30, divided at 1'25. Melody uses a "modal" shift from D major to A minor. Repeated in flute at 1'30 before abrupt shift to next section.
1'40–2'00	Modulating section starting with a "cutting" melodic figure in strings at 1'40. D minor, 1'40, A minor, 1'44, F minor, 1'48, G minor, 1'52, with baroque-style harmonic sequence and counterpoint
2'00–2'20	Elgarian, lyrical section, D minor
2'20–2'36	Melody (*x*) returns in D major on trombone combined with string figure from 1'40.
2'36–2'50	Short transition on F: melody with descending inner line C–B natural–A, leading to G
2'50–3'56	Slow section starting in F picks up from material at 2'36. But melody *x* returns (still horn in D) at 3'11, then is played in various instruments and keys (flute in C at 3'37), finally to horn, ending on C.
3'56–4'12	Uses melody from 2'36, F leading to G, then fragment G–A–B♭, twice, to unexpected close.

Costello collaborated with the Brodsky Quartet on *The Juliet Letters* (1993) and performs Randy Newman's 'Real Emotional Girl' on their *Moodswings* (2005).

to get the thing commissioned, completed, rehearsed, performed, recorded, is delivered to listeners who are unprepared, however sympathetic. In a stinging but accurate criticism, Alex Ross, the music critic of *New Yorker* magazine, also suggested that, as a musical celebrity, Costello is performed and recorded ahead of jobbing young composers, who might begrudge his ability to jump the queue.[57] After all, where were Costello's apprentice piano pieces? Where the discarded string quartet? As a final means of evaluating *Il Sogno*, two pieces could be brought on for comparison, both of which make reference to external elements: Aaron Copland's ballet *Appalachian Spring* of 1948 is a masterly composition in an extended tonal idiom; John Cale's music to the film *Process* of 2005 (a challenge to the listener to stay beyond track three) presents perfect, consistent piano meanderings in a post-tonal mode by someone from the world of "pop music".

We conclude our survey by returning to the "ontological" issues the book started with, and the question "What is the work of Elvis Costello?" When we listen to Costello *sing* and *play* his own material, there is a certain mode of musical understanding set in motion, principally the idea that Costello is his own best performer. With the mode of "classical music" that *Il Sogno* evokes, a different mode operates, in which Costello's authentic presence is beside the point. When Costello dies, the former mode will go with him, but Schubert's piano sonatas are alive and well every time they are played: if anything, they're in better shape than when Schubert lived. At the risk of an ugly sentence, one might say that with music played by *people other than one's self* who are not *trying to be who you are*, the mode of "classical music" is in play. Here also, one's relation to the past is less a matter of crafty allusion and more the outrageous claim to have produced something that can hold its own alongside established "classical" works in this mode. So here's the thing. In one concert hall, the London Symphony Orchestra is performing *Il Sogno*, in another concert hall *not* Elvis Costello and the Attractions (together again at last!), but the Brodsky Quartet playing Haydn and Bartók. Costello's allusive music runs at last into the question the singer-songwriter avoids: why choose an imitation when you can have the real thing?

Summary: popular and classical revisited

I imagine that, like Joni Mitchell, Costello would loathe critical debates about categories. Who cares? Get over them! Be that as it may, studying Costello's music puts popular music in an uncomfortable position, suggesting that the adjective may already say more about the institutional setting in which it is invoked. His classical work also challenges us to think what we mean by that adjective, and might be even more uncomfortable. Here are five options:

- a fixed canon of musical works that have lasted a long time;
- a more circumscribed set of such works that display features such as organic unity, convincing durational reach achieved through tonality, and specific techniques. It is music played from score by instrumentalists and singers trained in particular techniques; it is studied by reading as well as listening;
- the subset of "contemporary classical" works;
- another subset of "visual music" of the kind produced for films;
- a means of employment for orchestral musicians.

To date, in my opinion, by way of critical judgement, Costello's classical work succeeds only as the fourth. This is not to say that his head is not full of the first two possibilities, even the one about producing something that takes its place in the canon. One insists that the fifth is *de facto* a good thing. But I think *Il Sogno* works only in the sense of being visual music.

To sum up, Costello's songs and instrumental works are exercises in tonal music, the music a foundation for words and vocal melodies, or for stories and visual images. Costello's musical mind seeks challenge and new expressive resources. His musical quality has progressed and expanded with time and education, through studying the piano and learning to read music. His music is *well worth studying*.

Making music, making records

> All popular artists get caught between making records and making music. If you're lucky, sometimes it's the same thing. (Springsteen 2003: 139)

> [My task] was to capture them in their dilapidated glory before some more professional producer fucked them up. (*King Of America* n95)

The second comment is Costello on producing the Specials and the Pogues. After the first singles and album on Stiff, enormous amounts of Costello's effort has gone into making records with, from his perspective, frustrating attempts to form or find a corporate structure that would do commercial justice to the product. Costello has never taken the advice of a Bacharach song: 'Make It Easy On Yourself'. I want now to home in on *Punch The Clock* and the discussion between Costello and producer Clive Langer recorded for Radio One's series on Costello, first broadcast in 1992: the production of *Punch The Clock* is useful for my purpose for having polarized opinion. Amazingly in retrospect, it was "album of the year" in the *New Musical Express* for 1983; and Mick St. Michael was favourable in 1986, seeing the album as an improvement on *Imperial Bedroom*:

> With the exception of the Nashville sessions where Costello half-heartedly subjected himself to the rigid artist/producer relationship that typified country music since it began, Elvis had never encountered a producer whose ideas differed so radically from his own. And whereas Nick Lowe's task in years past had been to coax the best possible sound from Jake Riviera's *enfant terrible* in the confines of the recording studio with the least trouble, the interaction between Langer, Winstanley and Costello was clearly somewhat more creative. That's not to decry "Basher" Lowe's straightforward production methods – the aural sensations of *Imperial Bedroom* attest to the initial consequences of his absence – but while *Punch The Clock* found the new producers filling the breach, they were now clearly calling some of the shots. (St. Michael 1986: 104)

Interviewed by Barney Hoskyns for *RAM* in 1983, Costello also appeared to be positive about *Punch The Clock* and, like St. Michael, was suggesting an advance on previous records:

> "Clive and Alan have the patience to construct something the size of [Madness'] 'Our House', which Nick Lowe lacked. Nick is like Stax, where they're more like Motown or Van McCoy."

> "On *Punch The Clock* we had the discipline of a production team, who do actually take ideas and put them in a bit more logical order than I did when I was ordering the music of *Imperial Bedroom*. I mean, what Geoff Emerick did on that

> record was nothing short of a miracle, to make sense of some
> of the stuff that I wanted to do."

There was praise, too, for Langer and Winstanley's drum sound:

> "It's a more natural drum sound, isn't it? Without giving
> anything away, though, they do use techniques to doctor the
> drum sound, it's not all natural. That's one of the great
> ironies, that they often use lots of trickery to get a simple,
> natural sound."

That said, Costello sensed that some tracks on *Punch The Clock* had "misplaced arrangements, which don't get to the heart of a song", allowing that he will be able to "correct" them in live versions. He can already see that there are weak songs on the album: 'King Of Thieves' is too crammed, and 'Love Went Mad' was discussed as being better replaced by 'The Flirting Kind' in the CD order. Langer is also credited for keeping Steve Nieve in tow: "ruthless in getting him to play the same thing twice". Costello describes the greater compression of *Imperial Bedroom*:

> "The voice is incredibly loud on that record, it's almost like
> this voice alone in the room with you. There was a conscious
> effort to turn all the instruments down and put the voice up.
> It's like if you listen to old Walker Brothers or Dusty Spring-
> field records, the backing is compressed and only surges up
> when the voice stops, and we were attempting to do the same
> thing in a modern recording studio."

Even at that early stage, Costello can see that "the loss in humanity on records coincides with the revolution of the solid state valve" (Hoskyns 1983).

By the time of the 1992 BBC documentary, Costello seems to have changed his view, and emerges (partly through the programme's editing) as opposed on principle to the production style of *Punch The Clock*. I have transcribed the relevant section in full, including the views of Bruce Thomas (BT) and Pete Thomas (PT), since the discussion seems to offer telling insights into the processes and tensions involved in making a record. Sections in italics are scripted inserts from the original documentary.

Production discussion, BBC Radio One series[58]

'Pills And Soap' was later remixed for inclusion on Punch the Clock, *an album produced by Clive Langer and Alan Winstanley, whose crisp commercial vision had contributed to a spectacular run of hits by Madness and Dexy's Midnight Runners. It seemed that Elvis, in danger of becoming an esoteric cult act, was finally acknowledging the demands of the current singles market.*

EC: Clive's brief was definitely to be harder on my songwriting from [a] structural point of view, 'cos I'd been completely indulgent on *Imperial Bedroom*, going any way I wanted both in the structure and the style and the execution of the songs, and his job was to look for hooks; and suggesting, like, you know, well, he got me to write a couple more, 'cos I had too many morbid ballads to begin with. So he said we need some more rhythmic songs.

BT: He was trying to get a hit. We were trying to get a hit! That wasn't that far behind *This Year's Model* and *Armed Forces* stuff. We thought we might still be in with a chance of pulling something back, you know, and this was the thing, you know, they were the big pop producers at the time, and we were saying, well all right, they know how to make pop records and make hits, let's get them to produce it and maybe we'll get a couple more hit singles and we'll be back in business again.

PT: That was the first time anyone had really got us playing tricky arrangements that had to be right. He was more interested in getting the arrangement right rather than the feel of it because most of it would go on later. It wasn't like we were trying to get the whole thing in one go, which you did with Nick [Lowe]. You basically get the drums right, maybe the bass, and then they'd go on to work on the rest of it, sort of thing. I mean there probably were exceptions but it was more a question of building things up, which was different. But it's good in a way because at least you know you're gonna get somewhere in the end. You know the end result is gonna be good, and it got us playing some different rhythms and things, you know, like, 'Everyday I Write The Book' was this sort of funky, this real, like, English whitey attempt at some sort of funk beat. But it was a bit, you know, so ... We would have just done it like the Merseybeats, that song, you know, that

Clive Langer and Alan Winstanley produced Costello's *Punch The Clock* and *Goodbye Cruel World* (1983–4), bringing a distinctive approach to the process of making records.

was how Elvis wrote it. I can remember it was, like (*sings melody while clapping four beats, two soft, two loud, creating a sense of "square" rhythm*).

In commercial terms, the collaboration with Langer and Winstanley worked perfectly; the contemporary dance groove of 'Everyday I Write The Book' gave Elvis Costello and the Attractions their very first American top forty hit and Punch The Clock *became their best-selling album since* Get Happy!! *three years earlier. But Elvis never seemed comfortable with the new production team's deliberation and attention to detail. Such a contrast to the crazy spontaneity of Nick Lowe.*

CL: The idea was to make Elvis popular again and to make some pop records after he'd done, you know, the wild ones, and I think we did it well. I think it's just a different kind of discipline, you know, I've got different ears to Nick Lowe. I was brought up a few years after him, later. I was probably more into pop music than American country kind of stuff, and that's what came out, probably. Alan's a very disciplined engineer, very strict, which they probably weren't used to. When we were going over a backing track we'd be happy just to listen to the drums to make sure that every little thing the drum was doing was in time and perfect, and we wouldn't indulge in the pleasure of, maybe, and the excitement of hearing the whole band playing. In the control room we'd just have the drum "soloed" to make sure they were all right because that's all we were bothered about. I should imagine Nick might have it blaring out and the whole band's jumping and everyone's having a great time but a few days later they might find there's a tom-tom mike that's fallen off, and even if we had everyone playing together we'd then strip it, and once we were happy with the drums we'd then do the bass, work on the bass for quite a few hours, every slide would be in the right place, which is probably, it's easy to understand why someone doesn't like that process, it's not the yee-ha rock'n'roll way of doing it.

EC: I have been pretty hard on the two records that I made with Clive Langer and Alan Winstanley. I think really only because it's the only time I've really given myself over to a production sound rather than working in kind of collaboration with the producer. I always sound like I'm deriding Clive and Alan's production style, but they were real pop producers so inevitably the records date to the time they were made in and, with all due respect, I think that sound hasn't dated very well.

CL: I still think it sounds good. But I understand what he means, you know, I've talked to him a lot about it, and his criticisms, I do, I understand them. I just don't agree with him.

To bolster the points made with regard to 'Everyday I Write The Book', especially Pete Thomas's drummed illustration, Table 2.14 gives brief notes on the three versions of the song available on record. The difference between the final studio version and the two previous ones is striking, as though it were a cover version made to imitate a distinctive genre. As well as musical differences such as speed and form (the extended coda), it *sounds* very different: the arrangement is altered, while the mix of those instruments and backing voices is more deliberate and precise. As Langer suggests, to return from this track back to a Nick Lowe production, such as *Armed Forces*, illustrates the point in an immediate and perceptible way.

Costello makes a magnificent point in summary: that by taking bearings from the pop music of the day, the record inevitably dates to that time. The 1980s (in Costello's words: "the decade that music and good taste forgot") is a temporal period that also became a sound signifier. Costello's liner notes for the music of this time describe a "clipped and sterile studio sound", observing that the "tinny, unyielding tone [of the Yamaha DX7 synthesizer]... does more than anything else to 'datestamp' this recording" (*Punch The Clock* n03), to "date-stamp the album to an exact week in 1984" (*Goodbye Cruel World* n04).[59] However, Costello's comment also suggests that there are musical sounds that do *not* "date to the time they were made", and I imagine he means something like the "timeless" sound of American, folk-derived rock music like the Band. Be that as it may, what's wrong with *Punch The Clock* might be less its production as such, and more the arrangement of instrumental accompaniment, insofar as these can be separated. The problem might reside in bringing together Nieve's "classical" piano, which had gradually assumed a central position in the band, through *Trust* and *Imperial Bedroom*, and the soul-derived brass section of Dexy's Midnight Runners. Its nadir can be heard at the coda of 'The Invisible Man', where Nieve has to fill in space between the simple pentatonic hits of the brass section: listen between 2'30 and 3'02 to hear piano and brass speaking different musical languages. Meanwhile, on the opening track 'Let Them All Talk', after the brass fanfares, what on earth is Nieve playing during the verse behind Costello's words (listen to the piano between 0'14 and 0'44)? It is hard to think of

Table 2.14 Three versions of 'Everyday I Write The Book'

Live recording, 1982[a]	Studio recording, 1983[b]	Studio recording, 1983[c]
2'20	2'19	3'52
Crotchet = c. 120	A notch faster than live version: crotchet = c. 132	Crotchet = c. 90
E flat major; 4/4 beat Led from guitar, and including Attractions organ and keyboards	E major; 4/4 beat Greater prominence for piano part, imitating voice	E major; 4/4 beat Arrangement includes marimba, string synth, backing vocals, and piano counter-melody at chorus. Precise "placing" of each part in sound texture; observe chorus (0'43–57): voice, backing vocals, carefully controlled drum and bass, piano counter-melody doubled by electric guitar.
	Drum style driven from bass, using the range of drums, and regular fills	Style of drumming driven from hi-hat, with support from rest of kit
Chorus ends I–flat four–I (0'31–34)	Chorus ends I–IV–I	No "plagal" end for first chorus, but seamless flow back to verse
Two verses and chorus. Brief bridge (1'27), then verse three (1'34). 1'58: three times repeat of hook line at end. Ends with Beatles "added sixth" chord (2'17).	Same formal outline as live version, if in a brighter recording. Brief bridge (1'23), then verse three (1'31). 1'54: three times repeat of hook line; no "added sixth" at end.	Bass part precisely delineated Form broadly similar (bridge 1'59–2'07), but second bridge at 2'51 leads to extended coda, 2'56–3'52 and fade.
Definite end	Definite end: 2'12–19	Fade

[a] *Punch The Clock* first reissue (1995).
[b] *Punch the Clock* second reissue (2003).
[c] *Punch the Clock* version (1983).

a good rock model for "piano plus brass", other than Langer and Winstanley's productions for Madness: Allen Toussaint's arrangements for the Band's *Rock Of Ages* live album (1972), for instance (and by extension, *The Last Waltz*, 1978), although he fostered a more *legato* style of brass-playing than the punchy, Stax stabs of the Dexy's team, and the early Dexy's sound was more about guitar and organ with brass rather than the piano. So the accident waiting to happen arose perhaps because Nieve had attained an unassailable position as pianist in the Costello sound world and his, the piano's, centrality was forcibly juxtaposed alongside the brass element of *Punch The Clock*.

To sum up, by the time of *King Of America*, Costello had adopted a different approach, praising the way that "the players all made wonderful use of this extra space" (*King Of America* n95). His encounter with a certain version of commercially led production was over, and this became only one among many possible approaches to making records.

Voice

Basing a recorded song on the idea of the voice must be fun, since the song in performance, and its recording if made, becomes partly about the voice in the moment of performance.[60] For 'There's A Story In Your Voice' (*The Delivery Man*), Costello concocts a lively chord sequence, with "plagal cadences" galore, that changes key to the dominant (from G to D) as the endpoint for both verse and chorus (0'15–22, 0'57–1'04). The words are country clichés: walking in shoes, wine and woe, hurt and fortune, Gideon bibles in motel rooms; "voice" rhymes with "choice". The band shuffle along, with evocative guitar twang (0'35) and dutiful tambourine (0'38), dropping out at one point (2'58–3'03). What a good pop *song* writer, old Costello, you think. However, at 1'04, it changes: enter Lucinda Williams. The song now gives way to the record, which becomes very much concerned with the story a voice carries. Here is a voice that amazes and, in order to describe it (assuming one wants to do that), words head towards adjective and metaphor: of Lucinda Williams, Bill Buford says "a sound so sandpapery that Emmylou Harris described it as capable of peeling the chrome off a trailer hitch" (Hornby and Schafer 2001: 192). I'm reminded of a weird line of Tom Waits: "You're full of rag water and bitters and blue ruin."[61] For example, at the second line (1'19–34), the voice presents a range of notes, some precise in intonation, some close but not quite; the words are enunciated in a particular, "slangy" way, which presumably corresponds to the spoken dialect of a region. The last chorus is clunky on the page ("cheap sunglasses", 2'35), but still works as a hollering duet. It is a great record, but disappointment lurks in recreating the song in subsequent live performance, and how limp Costello's solo performance seems on the *Live In Memphis* DVD (2005). Watching it is like enjoying a well-prepared picnic in the rain: never mind, it is still a nice song.

Lucinda Williams is a classic case where words struggle to capture "the grain of the voice", in Roland Barthes's much-used phrase.[62] Allan F. Moore's useful discussion attempted to pin down "grain" into observable features (Moore 1993: 43), while Walter Everett has presented a detailed list with many examples, which I summarize and extract below as a route into making precise observations on Costello's voice (Everett 2000: 278–9: examples all from this source):

1. range (working upwards: from Johnny Cash through Elton John to Art Garfunkel; from Tracy Chapman through Joni Mitchell to Mariah Carey)
2. degrees of diaphragm support: from none (Lou Reed) to strong (Freddie Mercury)
3. locus of greatest resonance: chest (Bill Medley), head (Diana Ross), nose (James Taylor)
4. timbral quality: light and supple (David Bowie), simple and expressive (Aretha Franklin), multiphonics (James Brown), timbral modulation (Eddie Vedder)
5. intonation: on-pitch (Roberta Flack), off-pitch (Bob Dylan), "on top of" the note (Mary Wells)[63]
6. vibrato: between absent (Paul Simon) and constant (Joan Baez)
7. absence of pitch: rap, spoken interludes in songs
8. falsetto, described by Everett as "the constriction of the arytenoid muscles that cause vocal membranes" (Roy Orbison)
9. timbrally matched choral blending (Everly Brothers)
10. tremolo (Aaron Neville)
11. "all sorts of approaches to" articulation (Janis Joplin "unmatched for her variety of high-voltage techniques"), including: phrasing, portamento, note-bending and glissandi, dynamic shadings and other matters of stylistic ornamentation
12. a singer's level of ease or tension (David Byrne)

Several, but not all, of these headings are applicable in Costello's case. Costello himself refers to the "almost impossibly low register" (Everett 1) of 'Home Is Anywhere You Hang Your Head' (*Blood And Chocolate* n95), but its low A (at "you hang your head") is bettered by the G of "She's been suitably stunning" on 'Beyond Belief' (*Imperial Bedroom*), or the E at the end (2'12–13) of 'Oh Well' (*When I Was Cruel*). Low is easy to pin down, high more difficult, since the male singer has the falsetto as well as the high sung note as the top of his range. The highest note Costello has recorded may be the high B at 3'00 of 'Let Him Dangle' (*Spike*), which sounds like the top of his *sung* range without going into a scream or falsetto. That measures his range as about two octaves and a quarter. In addition, there are the various pitch-derived noises a voice can make, as illustrated at the start and end of 'Man Out Of Time' (*Imperial Bedroom*). It seems as though Costello opened up to his falsetto (Everett 8) around the time of *Spike*, where it can be heard on 'Chewing Gum', and at several points of side two of *Mighty Like A Rose*: 'Sweet Pear' is a great example of the voice's entire range being used as an expressive device. By the time of *All This Useless Beauty*, falsetto is an integral part of his expressive vocal resource: 2'18 of 'Little Atoms', and the end of 'Distorted Angel'. As with other elements of Costello's technique, *When I Was Cruel* integrates falsetto as an available resource: see 'Tear Off Your Own Head', 'Dust 2 ...', a single line of '... Dust', 'Radio Silence', 'Tart', and 'Dissolve'. 'Tears Before Bedtime' on *Imperial Bedroom* is a good example of Costello's overdubbed backing vocals covering his vocal range: "one of a number of tracks that employ an over-dubbed vocal group or disguised voice in order to distort the perspective or the identity of the narrator" (*Imperial Bedroom* n02). Costello is able to perform notes with great rapidity, as shown by the end of 'Our Little Angel' (*King Of America*), and 3'34 of 'The Other End Of The Telescope' (*All This Useless Beauty*). At duration's other end, he can hold a single note for a long time, controlling its vibrato, as heard on many of the songs on *North*. Costello's voice is often discernibly loud in volume (Everett 11). On the BBC radio series, Paul McCartney performed a comic imitation of his bespittled din. Towards the end of 'Nelson Mandela' by the Special AKA (1984, 3'40), Costello can clearly be heard, leading the troops. An odd but interesting moment is found at 2'25–34 of 'The Letter Home' (*The Juliet Letters*), with bad intonation employed for effect. *Speaking* words to the beat-poetry of 'Stalin Malone' (extended *Spike*), Costello sounds ill at ease, unsure of his spoken accent (Everett 7). [64]

Moving on from observable features of Costello's voice *per se*, 'God Give Me Strength' (*Painted From Memory*) is an example of a song which utilizes Costello's vocal range, from his low B at the opening to his high A in the bridge. Many of Costello's *melodies*, which could be thought of as the musical meeting-point of harmony and voice, exploit his range to the full. As with many singers, the low range is often the focus for restrained commentary: containing impressive harmonic tricks, the early Flip City track 'Imagination Is A Powerful Deceiver',[65] sounds odd because the melody doesn't lift up in pitch. There are plenty of examples of big and high vocals, but the very end of 'Taking Your Life In Your Hands' (*The Juliet Letters*, 3'08–11) is Costello's 'Nessun Dorma', achieving that highest B again.

The four minutes and seven seconds of 'You Tripped At Every Step' (*Brutal Youth*) is a not-untypical example of how much variety Costello can extract from his voice, including his own backing vocals. In D major, the verse has the low register used for conversational words, before the chorus heads up to a higher and stronger F sharp for its cadence. Shifting to B flat major, the bridge includes a brief, if rather ugly, high passage for expression (1'46–47: A, A flat, G). The backing vocals are art concealing art, details that contribute to the whole. Listen for an angelic, Chi-lites vocalise at 0'04–09, a close-harmony vocal at 0'36–38, a vocal for rhythmic punch at 0'43–48, and an amazing falsetto with expressive vibrato at 0'50–53 (on the repeat at 1'30–35).[66] At 3'00–15, the second (and third!) vocal becomes a dramatic character "singing back" to the main vocal. At 3'25–28, and 3'36–38, the backing vocal is onomatopoeia, "trip" as warning signal. At 3'32–36, the second voice answers the main phrase, creating a series of short melodic ascents. The Chi-lites vocalise closes the track to the fade.

Another example for observing Costello's skill is the single version of 'Blue Chair' from 1987.[67] There seem to be two voices present: one with *a bit of a cold*, choked and breathless (listen to "mistake" in the second verse: 0'58–59), and another that's bang-on, whiplash, a snake disappearing into the grass (the line immediately following "mistake", "cries for you", at 1'02–04). You might imagine Costello recording the "bit of a cold" bits on a grey day, sniffling and hung over, the other bits on a bright morning after a jog in the park and a good breakfast. But, of course, what he's doing is *controlling* the "bit of a cold" voice. This seems remarkable to me, that gymnastic ability, and the beholding of such moments can seem sublime, other-worldly, super-natural. Choosing Frank Sinatra's 'I've Got You Under My Skin' for his *Desert Island Discs*, Costello described just one note in such terms: "I also think that, from a musical point of view, the note that Sinatra hits on 'don't', in 'don't you know, little fool', the second time he comes in, is supernatural."[68] The idea of magic or the super-natural applies more to the natural voice than to the learned instrument, and raises the question of where voices come from. In Costello's case, there is one obvious answer.

> I am the third in four generations of musicians in my family.
> I don't imagine I am going to stop now. (*Extreme Honey* n97)

> "I had different voices every day."[69]

Aired on BBC Radio Two, *The Joe Loss Show* for 18 October 1968 was special because it brought to an end a four-year run of the programme.[70] It opens with 'In The Mood', which had usurped 'Let's Dance At The Make-Believe Ballroom' as the band's signature tune in 1937. As this is a farewell broadcast, the band's big hits are included, and 'March Of The Mods' follows, a hit for the orchestra in 1964: although the title may sound like a reference to the Who or Small Faces, it was in fact an easily identifiable, "tiddley-pom" tune. Larry Gretton and Ross MacManus take turns at 'The Red Balloon', a top ten hit for the Dave Clark Five a month before, with MacManus (I think) taking the verse in French. A few listeners' requests: a bunch of them right there in the audience! MacManus then gives a terrific performance of 'Can't Take My Eyes Off You', which had been released as a single by the orchestra a year earlier (backed by 'If I Were A Rich Man') and was a hit for Andy Williams earlier in 1968. Time for a guest, and Val Doonican is presented as a big catch for the show: two songs follow, after which the band does a number based on the Bo Diddley groove. There's some comedy with Gretton and MacManus: is MacManus the one with the Scouse accent? The Breakaways, the female backing group, do a version of 'Take Me In Your Arms And Love Me', a hit for Gladys Knight and the Pips in 1967. Time for a break, and part two starts with an arrangement of the theme tune for the BBC comedy *Steptoe And Son*. MacManus is back to sing 'Help Yourself', a recent number one hit for Tom Jones. Time for the second guest, Mary Hopkin, "that sweetie from Wales" says Joe Loss. It's 'Turn! Turn! Turn!' first, Pete Seeger's song. She gets to read out a few more listeners' requests, and then is asked if she knows the song, 'Those Were

The Days'. Of course she does: it's still there at number one in the charts! Cut now to the orchestra's other big hit, the 'Wheels Cha Cha', their cover of the String-A-Longs' original, hard to describe but instantly recognized, often used on TV as backing music for a muscle man and other variety acts. Ross MacManus and Andi Silver team up to sing 'Jesamine', a hit for the Casuals that summer. The band goes out with 'Congratulations', Britain's Eurovision song contest entry (and number one hit) for Cliff Richard, which had come second in the competition that year. Big thanks all round: presenter, producer, Joe Loss himself.

It was a variety show, a remnant of forgotten practices: a resident group bashing out cover versions of songs still in the charts ("sound-alike arrangements", as they were called); an orchestra able to imitate the instruments heard on recordings; someone who could write arrangements in a relatively short time; songs and instrumental numbers in carefully arranged co-existence; professional singers who can turn their voices to anything, and are also called on to perform comedy skits; a presenter who also does comedy; listener requests (for people in hospital, birthdays, anniversaries); professional standards and etiquette – Loss, not the presenter, introduces the guests, big thanks at the end. There was no consistency of musical style: there were songs originating with Gladys Knight, Pete Seeger, the Casuals, Val Doonican, which might be filed in different parts of the record shop, but their co-existence here was possibly a good thing. There was also no special emphasis on authenticity: Mary Hopkin has the hit with 'Those Were The Days' and it's "her song", but it's a cover all the same, not that anybody notices or cares.[71]

This was the world inhabited at that time by Elvis Costello's father, Ross MacManus.[72] Originally a jazz trumpeter, MacManus summed up his *own* career shift as moving from the musical world of "Dizzy Gillespie, Miles Davis, Gerry Mulligan" to an altogether lighter world alarmingly suggested by the first song shown to him by Joe Loss: 'You Make My World Go Tick-a-Tick-a-Tock'. An interviewer described MacManus as a "general utility man" for the Loss show, able to sing anything and turn his hand to Spanish (Latin-American) tunes, Italian love songs, French, English and Irish accents (for comedy) as the need arose. He was with the Loss band from at least 1955, but his peak seemed to arrive in the mid-1960s. Loss had the idea of imitating the ska sound that was popular in Britain: 'My Boy Lollipop' was a hit for Millie in 1964, and 'Ob-La-Di, Ob-La-Da' was the Beatles' imitation in 1968. Thus, in 1964 MacManus wrote and recorded 'Patsy Girl' with a group called for the purpose 'Ross MacManus and the Joe Loss Blue Beats'; it was sung with a Jamaican accent, and became a top twenty hit in Germany in 1966. The record is worth tracking down for its flip side, too. 'I'm The Greatest', which, like 'Patsy Girl', was written as well as performed by MacManus, is based around Cassius Clay, MacManus speaking rapidly at the start and including references to butterfly and bee, and singalong interjections, "I'm the greatest", "I'm the prettiest".[73] Asked to name his favourite track, MacManus chose 'Serenade In Blue' from *Joe Loss Plays Glenn Miller*, a record which sold slowly but steadily on EMI's Music for Pleasure label in 1969, describing his own work as "fine singing, hanging on my eyebrows".[74]

Does Costello join Whitney Houston, Jeff Buckley and Rufus Wainwright as singers who inherited the genes? Costello's father had a terrific voice, as versatile as the music-social context demanded; a big range (in an interview he imitates Paul Robeson in a rich baritone); a big sound, often called for when the tracks ended with dramatic notes for the voice; clear diction at all times. Expressive, too, but in a different way from Costello: if anything, his vibrato and intonation were better, the intonation precise and vibrato carefully controlled within the progress of the note. Costello's voice, by comparison, has more authentic presence, reflecting upon the premise of singing one's own material.

A final point to extract from the Loss show concerns the non-vocal contribution. Costello has spoken admiringly of Leslie Vinyl, who did the arrangements for the orchestra, often writing them straight from the record: the story is told of his transcribing guitar feedback for orchestra. A great Costello comment: "There's a funny little window between the world of Alma Cogan and the world of Jimi Hendrix, and that's the world I grew up in, so I owe him a real debt."[75] Costello's respect for artisan musical values originates in this background: with "popular music" as a form of employment, both popular and critical taste can be regarded with distance, if not disdain.

Another point to make about Costello's voice is that he is not a trained "classical" singer. The only recorded example where he has attempted what might be construed as a classical song is his performance of John Dowland's 'Can She Excuse My Wrongs With Virtue's Cloak?' (expanded *The Juliet Letters*). Labelling this a classical song raises again the awkward question of what "classical" means. Since it was published in Dowland's *First Book of Ayres* in 1597, in period-based terms the song belongs to the late Renaissance, with the classical music of Haydn and Mozart a long way in the future. There have been fierce debates about how such early music should be performed, and great distance between the styles adopted by, say, David Munrow and Anthony Rooley (who directed the recording of Dowland's work for the excellent Florilegium series in the 1970s). Even so, by being a score to be rendered, interpreted and edited, Dowland's song belongs to the same approach to performance that continues in the traditions of song as text-setting, including the *Lied* and *mélodie*. One reads the Dowland score, even while listening to a performance, differently from the way one might read the published score of a Costello song, a transcription after the event. One listens *for* rectitude, in the same way that the singer in these traditions performs first for rectitude, however much interpretative license is essayed in any given case. Of the several recordings I've heard, the one by Rogers Covey-Crump with lutenist Jakob Lindberg (Bis, 1990) seemed best, though I'd be hard-pressed to explain why. However, having heard some of those recordings and then turning to Costello's performance, recorded at the Meltdown Festival in 1995, is a peculiar experience.[76] The instrumental accompaniment was odd, including a piano and a violin trailing off before the second verse (2'31–33); the song was urged in its later stages towards a marked conclusion. But this pales next to the primary response: it's Elvis Costello! The singer's specific identity is immediately recognizable: Daniel Taylor (Atma, 1998) is striking in the way the countertenor voice invariably is, but not *personally* so, and I happily recognized Jan DeGaetani's voice (Bridge, 1999) from her recordings of modernist repertory,[77] but even that was not the same kind of recognition that greets Costello. How did he get on with Dowland? Note that this is not a *difficult* song: its range and rhythmic detail are easy for someone who can pull off some of *The Juliet Letters* or *Painted From Memory*. Two technical faults appear, if faults they are. Costello has an odd *twang* in his pronunciation. Listen to "are those clear fires that vanish into smoke?", as "are" becomes "arrr" in a way that sounds either American or even British West Country. It might be the product of listening to American country music, but it could also be a performing style handed down from his father. Secondly, pitch and tone: the examiner at a student recital might comment, with notes ringed on the score as evidence, "his intonation is wobbly from the start", his voice occasionally "fades out" as though tired (which it probably was), and the note is occasionally approached from under, at 0'56 and 1'09, for instance. "Never look up to a note, always look down," his father had advised (*Almost Blue* n04).[78]

Before we leave the classical voice, the final track on *For The Stars* (2001) reverses the Lucinda Williams moment on *The Delivery Man*. 'For The Stars' is a pop song with gorgeous melodic intervals for a classical singer, Anne Sofie von Otter, and this time it is Costello's entry (at 0'39), going on about trumpet lessons, that carries the effect of recognition and the natural voice: see their two-voiced melody from 0'54 to 1'16 to find Costello twice straining and "graining" her effortless melodic line. Attending to Costello's performance of John Dowland raises the question: is he any good? Watching Costello and Nieve perform 'Veronica' on TV, a song that closes with a high and loud enunciation of the title's name, someone in the room responded: "That's just awful." And it was a *right din*. Where vocal grain is concerned, and more so than in classical performance, it is possible to take against someone, and Simon Frith brings Costello together with the number one candidate for this response: "Most recent Dylan presents me with my Elvis Costello problem: I find the musical ideas and intentions fascinating and honourable but the voice so unmusical as to make it hard to listen for long."[79] Greil Marcus is another writer who struggles with Costello's voice, while making analogies with other singers including Bob Dylan. These comments are taken from his collection *In the Fascist Bathroom* (1993):

> The singing is impossible to follow: you tune out. (p. 137, of *Taking Liberties*)

> Costello pulls in his voice. He pulls back from his own songs, until what you hear in his voice is simply another instrument in a merely coherent arrangement of something that has become beside any point he might have started out to make. (p. 259, of *Goodbye Cruel World*)

> EC is a typical first-rate rock'n'roll singer with a third-rate voice: almost no physical range, little coloration. Sam Cooke might have been able to bring life to the three-piece-suit-with-watch-and-chain arrangements on *Goodbye Cruel World*; given Costello's limits, diffuse phrasing on top of diffuse

instrumentation produces only a nullity. As with Bob Dylan, Costello's true – and vast – range as a singer is primarily conversational: pauses, emphases, gestures, asides, bursts of rage or compassion, an argument in which values are weighted, weighed and found wanting. (p. 260)

The new versions of his own songs spoke to their recorded versions, wrestled with them. (p. 261, of *Goodbye Cruel World*)

Costello has no *bel canto* gifts to draw on; his timbre will always be moral. Throughout *King Of America*, he lets his voice quiver at the end of a line, suspends it in the air, makes you aware that he is trying to get something across. There are little cracks and tears in Costello's voice when he brings it up to meet a chorus; the struggle to communicate becomes its own subject matter. (p. 312)

It's the voice that cuts, that hurts: a voice of absolute power-lessness. (p. 313, of 'Our Little Angel', *King Of America*)

The singer cries out against some great wrong, but while he makes the song impossible not to understand emotionally, the exact nature of the great wrong evades him, forcing him into poetry, away from the plain speech the Irish ballad was made for. (p. 313, of *King Of America*)

Marcus captures the expressive range and contradictory effects of Costello's singing although, as we have seen by careful consideration of Everett's headings, it is simply not true that Costello has "almost no physical range". In comparative terms, Costello is Marmite on slightly burned toast for breakfast set next to the *pains aux chocolat* of Jeff Buckley or Rufus Wainwright. That said, Costello is extremely adept as a pop voice, his vocal contribution to *Painted From Memory* the decisive evidence. The voices for Bacharach and David were a particular and delicate mix of "authentic inauthenticity" or "inauthentic authenticity" closer, it could be argued, to Donald Fagen of Steely Dan or Neil Tennant of the Pet Shop Boys than the jazz traditions of Ella Fitzgerald, Sarah Vaughan, Billie Holiday. Though manufactured, the songs of Bacharach and David could lurch suddenly into canyon-like depths. Dionne Warwick's light soprano was often the instigator of performance traditions, but there was also a school of dependable British singers like Cilla Black, Sandie Shaw, Tom Jones, and Dusty Springfield.[80] Interviewed by David Hepworth, Costello compares pop singers of the generation that preceded and followed him. A grumpy patch reveals interesting points and principles: scepticism about technology, the importance of playing as well as singing, a sense of the past, and a sense of the weight of the past on the present (Hepworth 2003: 69):

> "They can't sing. I blame headphones. It's made everyone deaf to pitch."

> "They're not meaning to modulate, they just drift, they have no sense of pitch because none of them play instruments."

> "That's ninety per cent of singers today – no taste. Just sing the bloody melody, what's the matter with you?"

> "Nobody's going to sing that kind of phrasing better than Stevie Wonder, so why bother?"

We might at times borrow Wordsworth's great phrase, "the spontaneous overflow of powerful feelings",[81] to describe Costello's voice, especially *over*flow. Excess, of loudness or expression, was always lurking and Costello grew convinced of its necessity, around 1991:

> I might have thought to sing the tune as I believed it were beautiful. It is hard to deny that I was in a contrary frame of mind at this time, subjecting even the tenderest melodies to an extremely violent and guttural attack. (of 'How To Be Dumb', *Mighty Like A Rose* n02)

> I had developed the odd notion that all potentially beautiful melodies should be placed under severe strain, and therefore treated it to a very harsh vocal delivery. (of 'All Grown Up', *Bespoke Songs* n98)

The last verse of 'Riot Act' (*Get Happy!!*) is an example of trying to *will content into* the song through the voice. The idea was that the words, "colour" and "remarks off the cuff" referred to the "Columbus incident" of 1979 (*Get Happy!!* n03).[82] It is like the vocal equivalent of italics although, as with writing, rewrite can sometimes produce a better outcome than emphasis. Another example is the word "blood" (see 2'47–57, prepared by silence and "molto rallentando") at the end of 'This Offer Is Unrepeatable' (*The Juliet Letters*): if word and note require *that* much effort, one thinks, something must be amiss. Finding 'Little Palaces' (*King Of America*) "a bit too earnest", David Gouldstone focuses first on the words and their subject:

> The sections I'm not so happy with are those dealing with child-battering. There's no reason why Costello shouldn't write a song on the subject, but in my opinion he's confused the issue by mixing it up with the problem of sub-standard housing. (1989: 142)[83]

However, his ears point towards a further problem: "Neither do I like the way he sings 'knock' – he sounds as if he's striving for effect instead of letting the song speak for itself." A fundamental problem of expression arises, as the voice appears to relish and even to celebrate the emotion it intends to criticize. Like the cinema's lingering close-up, vocal expression inflates the detail, especially at the word "knock" in the phrase "you knock your kids about a bit", four times in all (1'44, 1'49, 2'44, 2'50). Costello effectively *says* in his performance: "I'm setting out to express my contempt for any such action, like a good protest singer", but he *sings* it as: "Here's what it's like to give the kids a good thumping." Both are present simultaneously, both dependent on what we hear as listeners. "There is music in words and meaning in music. This is probably why so many show singers over emote. They do not seem to trust the music because they are actors at heart and trust in words" (Fitzpatrick 2005: 79).

Where 'Tramp The Dirt Down' (*Spike*) was *ad feminam*, 'How To Be Dumb' (*Mighty Like A Rose*) is *ad hominem*, directed at bass player Bruce Thomas for his autobiographical novel *The Big Wheel*, published in 1990. The book contained barely veiled vignettes of identifiable individuals, perhaps casting people in a bad light, but there's very little sex,[84] surely the grand theme of the tell-tale memoir; weirdnesses are presented in often surreal settings. A good third of the book was taken up with memories of a childhood in the north-east of England and holidays in Southwold on the east coast; such memories are the spur for considering the nature of time, a familiar theme after a lifetime as a bass-player in rock bands, employed primarily to keep time in tandem with the drummer, and enduring seemingly endless periods of touring. Where Thomas hides behind sobriquets, Costello's song is directed at a general "you" (though there's 'New Bruise' as a dance craze in the second verse, among a sequence of bad wordplay). Musically, the song is a standard form, with a catchy chorus ("How to be dumb") and perfunctory bridge section ("Trapped in the house"). The words are unrelentingly nasty: Thomas is described variously and progressively as "the funniest fucker in the world", a liar, dumb, a mistake, a perpetual sucker, envious, pretentious, lacking in courage, a hypocrite and dilettante, ugly and stupid. The vocal delivery can only add a physical sense of injury to insult. To return to Wordsworth,

> For all good poetry is the spontaneous overflow of powerful feelings: but though this be true, Poems to which any value can be attached, were never produced on any variety of subjects but by a man, who being possessed of more than usual organic sensibility, had also thought long and deeply. (1984: 598)

Some vocal performances

> "The performance of songs is a wonderful opportunity. It is a great privilege. It is a great way to test your courage. And to test the song. And to test the audience." (Leonard Cohen, in Zollo 1997: 339)

> "So people cheer, you know? Because it's suddenly about me and them. Right in the middle of this story about two people suddenly it's me and the audience – just for a moment. Great thing about songs." (Jackson Browne, in Zollo 1997: 416)

A singer who covers an already existing performance must decide upon his or her similarity to or difference from the previous version. Elsewhere, I've called the faithful, tribute-band type of cover a "rendition" and the more creative, taking-over type an "appropriation" (or "transformation") (Griffiths 2002: 52). It could be argued that Costello doesn't do renditions: he may not want to, or his voice creates the impression that he is unable so to do. In the expressive moment of singing, Costello "puts his heart" into the song, and by doing so makes it his.[85] Commissioned for the soundtrack of the film *Notting Hill* (1999), his performance of 'She' should be close to a rendition, but even here his voice takes over Charles Aznavour's original.[86] Instrumentation and pace are preserved, but Costello translates many of Aznavour's most distinctive vocal characteristics: for Aznavour's light tenor, Costello's full baritone; for Aznavour's decorations (the "mordent" in particular: moving rapidly away from and back to the note), Costello's legato; for Aznavour's respectful detachment from the melody, Costello's ineluctable commitment. Preserving the original key of D flat major may be the decisive comparison, since it means that Aznavour's voice "sits on" the melody and gives the song a light sense of longing; by having to strain more from the start, Costello is able and willing to impart a heavier sense of "seething". Costello's voice added an extra dimension to the English restraint of the romantic film.

The same sense of commitment to the moment of performance inheres in Costello's concert performances of his own songs. Of course, being at a live performance and listening to the recording of a live performance are quite different things, with the added musical interest of the stripped-down arrangements found on the five-CD set recorded with Steve Nieve in 1996 – *Naked Songs*, a Rickie Lee Jones title – or the orchestral arrangements found on *My Flame Burns Blue*, recorded in 2004. If Costello is always and already an appropriator, I further speculate that there's a distinction between covers of songs or singers where he performs with the clear and generous aim of matching their performance (imitation being the sincerest form of flattery) and another category of voices that he *wants to be*. In that select latter group I include, in ascending order of pitch: George Jones, Gram Parsons, John Lennon, Carl Wilson, Robert Wyatt, and Chrissie Hynde. Costello is fascinated by the idea of taking on another *persona*, once describing "method singing" (*Blood And Chocolate* n95) by analogy with a style of acting:

> The fan or admirer in many of us may imagine a different creative history for our favourite singers, actors and artists. What if Elvis Presley had lived to record 'Brilliant Disguise' by Bruce Springsteen or Picasso had painted the Forth Bridge or Winona Ryder had taken the part of the daughter in *The*

Godfather III? Or perhaps these things are better the way they are. (*All This Useless Beauty* n01)

Elvis Presley didn't live to record 'Brilliant Disguise', but Elvis Costello did. It is one of the tracks he recorded in 1992 for a tape sent to George Jones. The Springsteen original is from *Tunnel Of Love* (1987).[87] Costello recorded these songs "in the manner in which I had read was quite common in Nashville, namely by mimicking the singer's style to sell a song". By this he means imitating George Jones, not the different and diverse singer-songwriters:

> So taking just one day in the studio in the company of Pete Thomas and Paul "Bassman" Riley, we cut songs by Hoagy Carmichael, Tom Waits, Bruce Springsteen, T-Bone Burnett, Bob Dylan, and George Gershwin in my mad and, at times, comical approximation of the Jones style. (*Kojak Variety* n04)

So here's a curious idea: Costello pretending to be George Jones performing a Bruce Springsteen song he can imagine being performed by Elvis Presley. In the event, Costello performs 'Brilliant Disguise' close to Springsteen's original recording, but strips away its production: the phrase that kicks off the bridge (1'58–2'04) brings a country touch absent in the original. Nick Tosches gets close in words to pinpointing George Jones's remarkable technique and emotional effect:

> Gliding to high tenor, plunging to deep bass, the magisterial portamento and melisma of his onward-coursing baritone send off white-hot sparks and glissades of blue, investing his poison-love songs with a tragic *commedia-è-finita* gravity, inflaming his celebrations of honky-tonk abandon with the heat of careening, heartfelt delight, and turning songs such as 'Warm Red Wine' into harrowing wails from the abyss. (Tosches 2000: 357)

Another song for George Jones saw Costello sing Bob Dylan, and an amusing confusion is found in Costello's cover of 'You're Gonna Make Me Lonesome When You Go' from *Blood On The Tracks* (1974). The vinyl album didn't have the words printed, and Costello either couldn't find his copy of Dylan's published lyrics or just worked them out from the record. As a result, he misheard the line, "mine [that is, my relationships] have been like Verlaine's and Rimbaud's" in the original as "mine have been the lanes and rambles", which makes sense in picking up from the "flowers on the hillside blooming crazy" in the song's bridge. Costello is generous in confessing his error, since the recording sounds more like a fluff than a proper mishearing. With George Jones in mind, he countrifies Dylan's folky song with vocal precision: in particular, starting with "lonesome" in the refrain, he stretches Dylan's line to a top G for a Jones-style whoop.

Performing 'Love Hurts' with Emmylou Harris must have been a strange thing: how often had Costello pretended to be Gram Parsons while singing along with the record at home? Costello was a big fan of Parsons: in writing about the band booked for *King Of America* it seems a point of principle that we know that he knew the band from their link to Parsons more than to Presley. It is appropriate that two of the best recordings on *Almost Blue* were covers of Parsons: 'I'm Your Toy' the cover of 'Hot Burrito #1' from the Flying Burrito Brothers; 'How Much I Lied' from the first Reprise album, *GP*. Both are placed strategically on *Almost Blue*, as the slow song on side one and as the final track. 'How Much I Lied' in particular illustrated the expressive possibilities of the cover version. Unlike some of the other tracks on *Almost Blue*, 'Good Year For The Roses' included, it sounds like a genuine piano-led Attractions performance, as Nieve's arpeggios and decorative figuration substitute for the jaunty tune that opens the Parsons version. In both, the vocal line dips down at "know" and "blind" in the first two verses,[88] but Costello stretches to the G during the chorus (at 1'29). By letting the tune speak for itself, restrained and choked-up at the same time, Costello acts the song and convinces of its veracity. One big difference is that the Parsons original brought in backing vocals for the chorus, with the multiple voices giving a sense of community, the singer's male friends rallying round perhaps: Costello is all alone. Costello's 1981 cover of Leon Payne's 'Psycho' makes it into Dave Marsh's 1001 greatest singles (Marsh 1989: 416–17), and was originally the B-side for 'Sweet Dreams'. Maybe Costello has a greater attachment to individual *singers* in country than soul, where it is more a case of happening to like particular songs: 'Getting Mighty Crowded', 'I Can't Stand Up For Falling Down' (*Get Happy!!*), 'Don't Look Back' (extended *Get Happy!!*).[89] Franklin Bruno draws attention to a Ray Charles cover, 'Sticks And Stones' (1960), recorded in 1994 (extended *Kojak Variety*) (Bruno 2005: 117–18).

Having worked with Paul McCartney around the time of *Spike* in a collaborative position once occupied by John Lennon, there must have been something different for Costello, one imagines, in subsequently performing and recording a Lennon song. Furthermore, 'You've Got To Hide Your Love Away' is one of Lennon's most identifiable and personal Beatles songs. Costello's performance was recorded for an Irish TV drama and comprised the supplementary tracks for the CD single of 'You Tripped At Every Step' (*Brutal Youth*). Costello's minimal version is energetic and expressive: a tambourine bashes out beats, and a yelping backing vocal underlines the "Hey" of the chorus. There's a pointed rewrite: "hearing them, seeing them" turns into "hearing them, seeing her" during the second verse (1'10 in the Costello record): something to do with the TV programme perhaps, or a Costello detail. Pace is almost identical: Lennon comes in at 2'11 (*Help*, 1965), Costello at 2'38, the extra twenty seconds from repeated verse-derived chords at the coda. Costello must have performed that song in his bedroom for many years, so that pinning down his performance in recording was like finding an old family photograph. Of the Costello–McCartney collaborations (Thomson 2004: 253), the most "Lennonish" position is the odd but interesting 'You Want Her Too' on *Flowers In The Dirt* (1989). Costello is a sort of *alter ego* to the song's narrator.[90] A bizarre swing-band orchestration finishes the track in the manner of Tom Waits's *Frank's Wild Years*.

With Robert Wyatt and Carl Wilson, I think that Costello heard something outside himself in their high pitch and ethereal quality. Costello comments on both singers through recordings: 'Shipbuilding' had to respond to Wyatt's original, where 'Sweet Pear' is a fantastic conception, like a link between Carl Wilson of the Beach Boys and Rick Danko or Richard Manuel of the Band. Costello links 'The Other Side Of Summer' (*Mighty Like A Rose*) to two tracks from the Beach Boys' *Holland* (1973), 'The Trader' and 'Funky Pretty'. 'The Trader' supplies the piano sound, perhaps, but is an unusual track that divides (at 2'25) into a pastoral second section. 'Funky Pretty' has vocals improvised over a funky rhythm. As well as these later Beach Boys references, one can hear earlier pop hits like 'Barbara Ann' or 'Sloop John B' in the backing vocals and strong bass lines.

Costello's desire to be Chrissie Hynde informs several songs in imitation of her writing style, and Hynde appears as a singer on 'Satellite'(*Spike*), providing the "kind of vocal harmony on 'Satellite' that I had imagined for years" (*Spike* n01). Her signature vocal moment is at 2'34–42 of 'Back On The Chain Gang' (1982): a rich vibrato for solo and backing vocal, the key changing (from D to E via a bridge in D minor), and words "making us part" in a song about emotional struggle. The start of 'Kid' (1979) has the same vocal intensity, while 'Brass In Pocket' (1980) combines intimacy and sass. 'You'll Never Be A Man' (*Trust*) "borrowed some musical ideas from The Pretenders' 'Brass In Pocket' and several other songs by Chrissie Hynde" (*Trust* n03), while 'Turning The Town Red' "sounds like another of my many attempts to write a Chrissie Hynde song" (*Goodbye Cruel World* n04), listing three others: 'Men Called Uncle' (*Get Happy!!*), 'Kid About It' (*Imperial Bedroom*), and 'Mouth Almighty' (*Punch The Clock*). The coda to fade of 'Turning The Town Red' (2'36–3'16) sounds to me like Chrissie Hynde, the close of 'Kid' from 2'13 (noting the terrific added vocal at 2'36). The opening melody of 'Kid About It' quotes directly from that of the Pretenders' 'I Go To Sleep' (1981): Costello's demo is snoozier, slower and nearly an octave lower, in A compared to the G of the record. For 'Men Called Uncle' (0'35–42), maybe it is 'Don't Get Me Wrong' (1986, 0'38 following) where the voice "sings to" an instrumental part. Better than the final version, the slower-paced demo of 'Mouth Almighty' (extended *Punch The Clock*) suggests that Costello was imitating Hynde's vibrato in the verse section.

Costello's cover of Randy Newman's 'Real Emotional Girl' is in my view an ill-judged vocal performance. Like Robert Wyatt after recording 'Shipbuilding', Costello is supposed to have wept after singing for this record: "He simply burst into tears," says Thomson (2004: 384). Newman's original, found on *Trouble In Paradise* (1983), lasts 2'28 at crotchet = *c.* 66. Costello's cover, found on the Brodsky Quartet's record *Moodswings* (2005), lasts 3'52. Slowing the pace is the basic error-generator, emotion-generator. The original is both medium- and slow-paced: the score of the Newman song indicates correctly, for the middle section, "slower, poco rubato", following up with "a tempo". The original recording achieves the trick of being both emotionally committed and detached, both harmonically full and empty; the quartet's arrangement sentimentalizes Newman's stately, Beethovenian restraint. The middle section, in its striking and stark emptiness, perhaps with Mahler in the background, looks back to Newman's 'I Think It's Going To Rain Today', on his first album, in 1968.[91] But listen to Dusty Springfield's beautiful cover ('I Think It's *Gonna* Rain Today'), on *Dusty Definitely*, 1968 (Peter Knight arrangement, Springfield having heard a demo disc) to show it can be done. In the Brodsky version, substituting warm strings for piano's cold percussion is a bad move: when Newman tells you that she's "real emotional", "real" is both necessary because nothing in the sound gives it away as well as being pointedly real, genuine, authentic ("real" sung to the C as the tonic peak of the opening melody).

Finally, Nick Lowe wrote '(What's So Funny 'Bout) Peace, Love And Understanding?' and first sang it for a 1974 single for Brinsley Schwarz. Elvis Costello and the Attractions' version was first issued as the B-side of another Nick Lowe single, 'American Squirm' in 1978.[92] Dave Marsh thought that "for this one single Elvis Costello and the Attractions were as good as any rock band in the world. Singing clichés, they redeemed them – and discovered themselves." Marsh heard Nick Lowe as "the voice of a man who'd been through the Balkanization of the counterculture", while Costello "eradicated Lowe's cynicism and replaced it with joyous acceptance and thinly veiled remorse" (Marsh 1989: 385–6). Marcus also heard the original as a "joke on sixties pieties", "full of irony". However, he thought Costello sang it only "with apparent conviction", a stance the listener knows to be "a joke", but "a dialectical joke, maybe": it is left to the final guitar chords, not the voice, to boil off the irony and "validate" the song's sentiment (Marcus 1993: 357, 37). Both critics offer salutary examples of the cultural weight a voice can carry, though listeners to the original might no longer sense the irony, apart from Lowe's spoken interlude at 2'14–24. After all, everyone plays the original arrangement: key, pace, instrumental melody. The recorded version of a concert from Steve Earle's 2003 tour, charged with emotion by Earle's opposition to the Iraq war and his protest song 'John Walker's Blues',[93] closed with the song as coming-together and defiance. In their two-voiced 1974 performance of the Bacharach and David song 'Baby It's You', originally recorded by the all-female Shirelles in 1961, Costello and Lowe seem to evoke the performance tradition of the Everly Brothers records, in which the great question is: who is each singer singing *to*?[94]

Covers of Costello songs by female singers might suggest interesting perspectives on their gender-related subject position. Costello disliked one of the earliest of these, Linda Ronstadt's cover of 'Alison' (*Living In The USA*, 1978), but it was a bold song for her to choose, not least because it raised the issue of her female voice's relationship to the "Alison" of the song. Mapped directly from Costello's version, it could have been a lesbian appropriation, but the cover substitutes "he" for Costello's "you", making Ronstadt the female friend who's betrayed by Alison. Slick LA accompaniment reinforces the air of domesticity, as though life was mirroring daytime soap on TV. 'Just A Memory' was a demo included on the New Amsterdam EP (*Get Happy!!*), but was recorded, transformed into 'Losing You' for Dusty Springfield's 1982 album, *White Heat*. This was a low point in Springfield's career, and it fell to the Pet Shop Boys to provide her voice with a comfortable sofa for 'What Have I Done To Deserve This?' in 1987. A remarkable third verse is added at 1'08 of the cover with a striking second line: "I count the pages of the letter I write/One, two, three, four, five, six, seven, eight, nine." The chorus so nearly comes off, at 1'28 through the bridge (1'49) of the cover to the "interrupted cadence" end at 2'47; the corresponding points in the original are at 1'01 through the bridge at 1'24 to the end at 2'14. However, neither of these versions has the sheer boldness of Judy Collins's unchanged covers of songs by Bob Dylan.[95]

To sum up, Costello's voice is the front line of his engagement with musical history and all of the themes that he explores in words and music. Since his voice tends towards "spontaneous overflow", a song founded on restraint, or a resistance to sentiment, is likely to get transformed in his presentation. The voice often shapes Costello's own melodies, so that musical content is intimately bound up in vocal projection, and anything the words have to say will be affected by vocal delivery: stories in the voice. Although I suspect most people would regard Costello as songwriter first, singer second, both aspects are inextricable. As many of his cover versions suggest, Costello is notable in interpreting his own and already existing songs.

Appendix 2.1 *North* (2003): listening guide, combining timings, chord progressions, formal sections, and other commentary

'You Left Me In The Dark' (F)
An introduction in two paragraphs, 0–0'26, 0'27–42, presents a sophisticated harmonic world, the second sounding like some of the music from *Il Sogno*. Voice at 0'43, music firmly in F. 1'25: link section with reference to G♭ and advanced chords ("You left me standing alone"). 1'47–57: "You left me in the dark' hook, ending Dm–E♭(9) (1'52), Bacharach there perhaps. Second verse adds string accompaniment. Final violin F over E♭ "left in the dark".

'Someone Took The Words Away' (F)
Picks up on advanced chords of first song: Dm–Cm. F major, 0'38: Am–A–D; 0'49: Gm–C; 0'54: F–B–E–B–E (1'05). Bridge section that follows will provide basis for sax solo later. Return to second verse. The advanced chords of the bridge as basis for Lee Konitz alto sax solo, ending on G dominant, three times through: 2'48–3'20, 3'21–53, 3'54–4'31. Slow, sustained, lovely. (Basic chords: Dm–Cm–Em–Dm–Cmaj7–D half-dim–C–Am7–Dm7–C/G–G.)

'When Did I Stop Dreaming?' (F)
Introduction: B♭9–F × 2, E7–Am7, D7–Gm7, C (5#). 0'29: verse with chromatic non-harmonic notes: B♭–E♭7–F (0'40: "when did I stop dreaming?"); 0'50: Gm–C7–A7–Dm (the A7 at 0'55 lovely); B♭–D♭–F–C (1'18). Two verses, bridge at 2'16 (A♭/E♭/G/B♭ (Joni Mitchell's *Court And Spark*?) to Fm7, eventually to C dominant (2'51). 3'00: third verse. Short coda based on bridge, twice through: 3'54–4'33, 4'34–5'19. C dominant to end.

'You Turned To Me' (C)
Simple 3/4 melody in C: second line heads to Am (0'31); third line to B flat to C; descending melody to cadence (0'50). 0'55: Cm–B♭–B♭m–A♭. 1'14: A major 7. 1'19: Randy Newman film music, E flat. 1'28–32: G dominant to C at 1'34. Second verse to perfect cadence C at 2'24, the first to end a song in the cycle to date. Simple on the surface, but complex elements underneath.

'Fallen' (D flat)
A simple lyrical song. Introduction and first verse D♭, pedal notes (0'38) with chromatic inner voices: B♭♭–A♭ (0'48–49); second verse. 1'22: verse of recitative, 1'53: strings enter for B♭m section; flat six, B♭♭, 2'04–07. 2'08: back to D♭ for curtailed final verse and perfect cadence at 2'28–32. Short piano coda to balance introduction to 3'04.

'When It Sings' (D)
Chromatic descending bass: D–D/C#–D/C; 0'08: Bm–Bm/A#–D/A; 0'16: G–Em, piano alone then with voice, extended at 0'56: C–Em–B♭–A–D at 1'04.

Contrast section, 1'12: Bm–G; 1'20: C#–F#m–Dm (F bass)–F7 (F bass)–Gm; 1'34: B♭/F–A/E♭ (vocal peak), so that return of D at 1'48 sounds disjointed. Verse 2 to 2'27; second contrast to 3'01: second peak 2'50–3'00. Final verse as before to 3'50. Long final tonic: 3'36–52.

'Still' (C)
Opening pedal notes, piano alone then voice: C–D–B♭–G. 0'18: C–F–Dm–B♭–G ("cowboy" cadence). Strings at 0'24. 0'36 to chorus/contrast and F, then Gm7–C; 0'42: Am–Dm–Gm–E♭–C (cowboys at 0'46–47); Am–Dm, then 1'00: A–D–E; 1'06: Am–Dm–Gm–E♭–C (1'10–11), cadence at 1'12. Opening material in F to 1'35. Contrast section still in F to slower cowboy cadence, 1'47–49. 1'56 cut back to C for coda to end at 2'21, a performed fade. This is the first song at something other than a slow pace.

'Let Me Tell You About Her' (F)
Standard chromatic line, F–A♭m–Gm–C. 0'19: F–E♭–B♭–B♭m. Cadence to 0'29. 0'30: chorus section B♭ up to Dm (0'41/0'59), and peak cadence: 1'01–07. 1'08: third section ("some things are too personal"): A–Dm × 2; 1'23: B♭–F–Gm–C. Back to start at 1'39, run through again to end of chorus at 2'39. Lew Soloff flugelhorn solo, 2'40, improvised solo over "third section" chords; second time to 3'11, third time to 3'41 to end at 4'20 on C dominant (4'07–20), a return to the "imperfect cadences" found in the first three songs.

'Can You Be True?' (C)
Big orchestral flourish on C pedal to 0'20. In C, two sung phrases then, 0'40, over to heartland section of song: Am with 0'42: B7–Em–E7 shifts to big Am at 0'54. 1'14: contrast section: C7. Lovely Am 'Moon River' moment at 1'34–40, to melodic peak over Am at 1'47. C at 2'04, verse again at 2'13, but mostly about the heartland section (2'32–), big Am at 2'46 and 3'15. Plagal F–C: 3'17–21. Perfect cadence to long final tonic 3'31–42.

'When Green Eyes Turn Blue' (G)
Piano introduction extracted from later bridge section (2'46–50). Song starts Am7–D–Gmaj7; 0'29: C–F#–Bm; 0'44: B7–Em; 1'00: D pedal–G to 1'15. Second verse with band to 2'19. Bridge, 2'20: Am–chromatic D–G; 2'36: F#; 2'44: Bm; 2'46: Gm; 2'48: E♭; 2'50: D. Third verse: 2'58 to 3'58, to final G, 4'03–12.

'I'm In The Mood Again' (B flat)
Two verses of major-key wandering, to Dm at 0'20 and 0'52, ending on F dominant. 1'05, Gm, bridge creeps chromatically upwards: Gm–A♭m; 1'14: D♭7–G♭maj7; 1'23: B♭m–Bm; 1'32: E7–A; 1'38: F dominant. Verse 3, 1'42 to 2'09 (Dm at 2'02); interrupted at 2'10 for chromatic cadence. Final B♭ tonic 2'19–32.

Appendix 2.2 *Il Sogno* (2004): listening guide, combining timings, chord progressions, formal sections and other commentary

Section	Time	Notes
		Tracks 9 and 10: 'Oberon And Titania' and 'The Conspiracy Of Oberon And Puck', 5'20 in all

Section	Time	Notes
A	0–0'25	(E–D#–B–D–C#–A#) × 5. Single note B.
B	0'26–1'06	C major tune, tonic pedal note, pastoral oboe and percussion. Tune to sax at repeat. Short link.
	1'06–24	Same tune but reharmonized as Bm–C#m, with added note in harmony. Sax followed by strings.
C	1'25–4'13	Rhythmic groove in orchestra: C–B♭ in bass, E–D in melody times three, E–F# fourth time. Four-bar phrase repeated six times (C–B♭ repeated 24 times in total), the last two of which include saxophone improvisation. Melody from 0'26 enters for four more phrases, followed by two phrases of Bm contrast (from 1'06), back to C for three phrases on which the drums extemporize a solo. Then five more phrases: the melody for four phrases, and a final phrase as coda. The basic groove has repeated: 24, 16, 8, 12, 16, 4 (80 in all).
D	0–1'06 (track 10)	The music then cuts to a C/G pedal. Now "fourness" resides in a repeated C/G pedal around which harp and strings add material. Different chords at 0'40 lead to F and end at 1'06.

Comment: Response to this piece may depend on how one hears the repeated groove: their quantitative aspect is only a part of the picture, much as for Ravel's *Bolero* (1927), perhaps the model especially for the melodic material at 2'24–31. To me it lasts too long with material that is too thin. My ears recoil especially at 1'06–24, which sounds like music for a BBC television drama set in Yorkshire.

Section	Time	Notes
		Track 13: 'The Identity Parade', 4'40

Section	Time	Notes
A	0–0'35	Sleep music: E♭–C–E♭ motive. 0'15: three times repeat of idea ending with string tremolo.
B	0'35–1'06	Ostinato figure × 11. Counter-melody in strings (third ostinato) and tuned percussion (fifth ostinato). Harmonic change at the ninth ostinato.
	1'06–20	Twice-repeated figure: strings with bassoon
C	1'21–57	Staccato string passages with two pairs of Stravinskyan cuts at 1'25 and 1'31, 1'39 and 1'47. Brass at 1'57 lead into next section.

D   1'57–3'05 Ostinato-based passage. The groove has a 3+3+2 pulse,
                  the bass motion is G–A♭, against which key melodic notes
                  F–E/E♭–F#. The sequence of repeats is: 2+x+11+x,
                  where x is a "chorus" section at 2'06–16 and 2'57–3'06
                  (chords B♭–G/B bass–C–Em). The second of these cuts into
                  next section.
E   3'06–26   Mendelssohnian interlude for strings and wind in E minor.
        3'26–34   C7 chord, twice.
F   3'34–4'00 Back to the groove × 7.
        4'00–26   Cadential figure built on groove (2, 2, 2), three times
                  punctuated by silence, diminuendo.
        4'26–34   Brief recapitulation of staccato strings from B
        4'34–40   Brief recapitulation of sleep music, ends on D

Comment: This track displays variety but, again, much depends on how interesting one finds the ostinato-based sections. The untuned percussion, Peter Erskine's drum kit, seems to me a problem in grounding the rhythm. I admire the material at B, reminiscent of the film composer Nino Rota. The ears prick up at the Mendelssohnian section, E, either with postmodern amusement or to think, what on earth is this? The recapitulations are neatly compressed.

Track 17: 'Oberon Humbled', 3'40

A   0–1'10   B flat major. 0'32–1'10: appoggiaturas in melody. Small
                  pause at 0'55.
B   1'10–48   D flat major, three times repeated sequence (D♭–E♭m–
                  D♭m), second and third with overlaid high strings and per-
                  cussion. "Oom-pah" accompaniment.
C   1'49–2'28 Development of material from B: D flat and ends on V.
D   2'29–3'40 2'29–3'02: twice repeated sequence: E♭m–D♭–C♭/A, B♭m.
                  3'02–19: linking phrase
                  3'20–40: coda G♭–G♭m–D♭m, ending on "interrupted
                  cadence" of G/C/D/F.

Comment: Sections A and B are simple tonal music but, as the music "dissolves", C and parts of D have interesting harmonic development. Nevertheless, the tendency is to repeat and juxtapose rather than develop material to a different tonal region. Gerald Abraham was discussing Grieg, but what he wrote applies to aspects of *Il Sogno*:

> Yet Grieg is far from being a perfect miniaturist. The great
> miniaturist must be a magnificent craftsman, making every bar
> tell, never using a note too many, making the most of the
> medium in which he works. And Grieg is not. His workman-
> ship is usually neat, but he drops so easily into conventional

figures, particularly in his song-accompaniments ... The most serious of all Grieg's weaknesses is his inability to conceive more than two bars of music at a time. Even when he gushes, he cannot sustain the melodic flow. (Abraham 1964: 158)

Track 21: 'Bottom Awakes', 1'41 (this track is not found on the 'Suite' version)

A	0–0'17	Delicately scored, A flat major, ending on C minor
B	0'18–58	Disney-like string material. B♭ major–D minor–C minor (to C/E♭/G♭)
C	0'58–1'24	Return of A material (A♭), once in strings, then once back in glockenspiel. C minor link to coda.
D	1'25–41	Coda, picks up on cadential material earlier in the work: comic G7s to end on C major

Comment: This one is chosen especially for the scoring at the start of the track, A and C reminding me again of film music by Nino Rota. The following section sounds like music for a Disney film by Randy Newman, although the violin solo at 0'45–57 is too sugary for my ears.

Track 24: 'The Wedding'

Comment: 'The Wedding' is worth listening to because the work seems to end several times. To be sure, the purpose of the piece is to recapitulate material from the work as a whole, like an overture late in the day. But listen for the endings: a conclusion first at 1'54 and 2'02, from the world of Bernstein's *Candide* (1956); then, to my ears a truly terrifying and laboured conclusion (all C major) from 2'22 to 2'53. "The sogno motif" (E♭–G♭–F) returns, at 3'25, seemingly always at pitch. Another big ending at 4'01, F clashing with G♭, before the final end on F at 4'12.

3 Words

The language is unforced, but not distinguished. It is highly suitable, therefore, for being sung. (Hobsbaum 1996: 134)

Musicians like things that don't mean too much. (Larkin 2001: 50)

"My point is that the balance – where you put the balance – is crucial in defining what kind of song it's going to be. And, you know, for certain people who are very word-oriented, you can put much more emphasis on words and lyrics and they will follow you. And other people – *most* people I think – are not word-oriented and kind of just hear an overall soundscape." (Paul Simon, in Zollo 1997: 95)

What are Costello's songs *about*? Anything and everything. "Nothing seemed beyond the realm of the pop song," Costello said of *Spike*,[1] and went on to list its variety:

That album was a collection of songs about drunken comedians, junk-bond saleswomen, satellite pornographers, a 1950s murder case, a pair of terrified soldiers, a woman who scares children, a woman who scares adults, the alcoholically deluded, and various other potentially violent malcontents. (*Mighty Like A Rose* n02)

Nothing if not eclectic but, in these two further comments by Costello, limitations and types are mentioned:

"Despite what some of the *weightier* songwriters of today will tell you, there are some ideas pop music won't carry effectively. They'll always sound pompous or over-reaching." (in Flanagan 1990: 237)

Table 3.1 The subjects of song

Costello's subjects	Poetic genres	Musical genres
I want someone/I lost someone	Lyric, drama, tragedy, narrative, epic	Song, song-cycle, ballad, opera
I believe in something	Hymn, satire, epic	Hymn, national anthem, political song
Someone died	Elegy	Funeral march, lament
Dukla Prague Away Kit	Comedy, satire, fancy	Comic song, fantasy

> "There are probably only five subjects in all human song: I
> want someone, I lost someone, I believe in something, some-
> one died and a *Dukla Prague Away Kit*." (in Fitzpatrick
> 2005: 79)

"Only five" returns to the idea of genre, so that Costello's five categories
map onto transhistorical types in poetry or song.[2] Costello's "I lost someone" can be seen either as the sad extension of "I want someone" or the
bleak premonition of "someone died": in Table 3.1 it is included with the
former. Sheila Davis has five such "modes": history (the way I believe it was),
realism (the way I see it is), romance (the way I feel about it), fabulation (the
way I think it could happen (though it's improbable)), and fantasy (the way
I imagined it (though it's impossible)) (Davis 1985: 83). Costello's comment
differs in that history, realism and romance are concurrently present in his
first four categories, while his final category represents both fabulation and
fantasy.[3] Costello also described the dichotomy of words and music in
'Oliver's Army' (*Armed Forces*) in transhistorical terms:

> "There was an intention to put a comparatively strong lyrical
> idea – strong in the sense of not ineffectual, or not insubstan-
> tial – against this really poppy backing. It's not a new trick."
> (in Bruno 2005: 92)

"Not a new trick": here is the Roman writer Horace, writing in his *Ars
Poetica* about 65 years before Christ:

> The aim of the poet is to inform or delight, or to combine
> together, in what he says, both pleasure and applicability to

life. He who combines the useful and the pleasing wins out by both instructing and delighting the reader. (Bate 1970: 56)

The poet Robert Frost wrote:

It should be of the pleasure of a poem itself to tell how it can. The figure a poem makes. It begins in delight and ends in wisdom. The figure is the same as for love. No one can really hold that the ecstasy should be static and stand still in one place. It begins in delight, it inclines to the impulse, it assumes direction with the first line laid down, it runs a course of lucky events, and ends in a clarification of life – not necessarily a great clarification, such as sects and cults are founded on, but in a momentary stay against confusion. ("The Figure a Poem Makes" (1939), in Herbert and Hollis 2000: 45)

Delight and wisdom, and "a momentary stay against confusion": but eliciting meaning from the words of songs presumes, among other things, that the words make sense.

"'Strict Time', which is one of those druggy, word-play songs, has the line, 'She was smoking the everlasting cigarette of chastity'. That's about the moment when you want to kiss the girl but she won't put the cigarette down. A lot of people would have written a whole song on just that one thing, but I was trying to cram too much in. There are four or five lines that precede it that are just gibberish." (Costello, in Flanagan 1990: 244)

David Gouldstone hears 'Strict Time' (*Trust*) as giving "the impression of being unfinished, a doodle rather than a fully worked out idea", adding that "nevertheless, it has some good lines, and the perky piano riff makes it worth listening to" (1989: 80); "weekend courting in the suburbs", summarizes Brian Hinton (1999: 209). Hinton sees this issue as separating him from Gouldstone, as well as Costello from various other songwriters:

> David Gouldstone's book *A Man out of Time* has gamely tried
> to dissect Costello's work song by song, as I did in earlier
> books on Joni Mitchell and Van Morrison – far more linear
> wordsmiths, both. With Costello from *Get Happy!!* onwards,
> such an attempt to "shovel a glimpse into what each one
> means" is doomed from the start. Like Dylan, half the fun is
> that these songs are literally meaningless, though their
> urgency and self-belief connect on some deeper level alto-
> gether, as do the instruments – and instrumentalists – chosen
> to carry them. Again, like Dylan, Elvis will also write in his
> earlier, more direct style, when the political or emotional
> need arises – 'Hurricane' or 'Tramp The Dirt Down', 'Love
> Sick' or 'I Want You'. (Hinton 1999: 192)[4]

This goes too far. For Costello, four or five lines of "gibberish" don't equal
all-out meaninglessness, literally or not: the principle, such as it is, seems
to be to surround the occasional glimpse of sense with filler lines, lines that
may be the result of pressure to meet a studio deadline. But it is also a
question of how one sets about the task of interpretation: the gibberish may
be as significant or open to interpretation as the seemingly sensible lines.
Both Gouldstone and Hinton find the key to meaning in these situations in
the accompaniment: Gouldstone in Nieve's piano, Hinton, at his "deeper
level altogether", carried by "instruments and instrumentalists". An exercise
for the reader: *without* referring to the sound of the record, what were those
lines of gibberish Costello identified? The final verse begins with the line
"You talk in hushed tones, I talk in lush tones" and ends with the line "More
like a hand job than the hand jive"; the section is heard at 1'35–2'06.

First, the lines are there partly to rhyme, but in unpredictable, inconsistent
ways. "Hushed tones" bounces within the line to "lush tones", "Italian" to
"valium"; then trisyllables "larceny" and "chastity", their openings corresponding as present participles (thinking/smoking); "staying alive" (*Saturday
Night Fever*?) and "hand jive" (without Willie). After hearing the sounds of
words, *we* can try to make sense. The narrator is chatting to someone at
a party: she talks quietly, he's drunk ("lush"). Everyone tries to look cool
and "Italian", but the records being played are soporific: "musical valium".
His mind wanders off, "thinking of grand larceny", while she smokes deliberately to thwart his advances. The final three lines seem to describe the fate

© Keith Morris/Redferns

Elvis Costello (and glasses): from the period of *Goodbye Cruel World* (1984)

of shop workers ("cute assistants") living for the weekend, but finding it ending only in a "hand job", capitalist time strict enough to organize weekends as well as workdays. Returning the lines to the recorded track reinforces the sense of forced, oppressive enjoyment, the claustrophobic sound-space of the track evoking the party. "Please send me evenings and weekends," said the Gang of Four in 1981, the year of *Trust*: "the problem of leisure: what to do for pleasure?"[5] I am going to move on to look at some of the more overt "meanings" of the songs now, but the point I would make is not to shy away from "gibberish".

One writer has a theory to encompass every song from *My Aim Is True* through *Painted From Memory*.[6] Larry David Smith's approach is grounded in the words abstracted from music, presenting six songs as exemplars in one chapter: the words are set out as poems on the page and examined as such.[7] Each song is given an attribute according to what it depicts: its situation, story, or emotion. The key distinction appears to be between personal and "impressionistic" songs, with a further division of the former into songs of the self and songs directed at others, incorporating in turn socially directed observation. In order for a song to qualify as impressionistic, there needs to be a lack of clarity in the addressee of the song: the key question in this respect is "Can you, in any way, discern who is doing what to whom?", as asked of 'Accidents Will Happen' (248). A small subset of impressionistic songs consist entirely of wordplay.[8] However, there are very many subsets to the personal songs, depending on the type of presentation made of the self, or the form of address made to another person; traditional poetical genres are at times invoked, such as satire or elegy. Songs of society vary according to their specific (societal) or universal (moral) remit.

The attribution is Smith's decision, and there is no reason to mistrust him. One might quibble with his confidence in assigning each song a *single* attribution: 'Secondary Modern' (*Get Happy!!*) was a song I expected to be a societal complaint, its title referring to a type of school in Britain to which supposedly less academic pupils were dispatched at the age of eleven, the song being about such injustice. Seeing Smith file the song as one of "three love 'warnings' that feature some sort of relational decision" (175) sent me back to the words of 'Secondary Modern' to find that it could be described as *a bit of both*.[9] The societal aspect belongs to the first and second verses, the "you and I" relational aspect (an odd reference to condoms) to the latter part of the song, with the chorus balanced between them: this points to the occasional importance of song-form divisions for the character of words.[10] Be that as it may, songs hang around for a strict time and, once established, a theme will often occupy the song in its entirety.

Smith's study is thorough, if limited by or to the moment of attribution. External information is kept to a minimum, with only two songs, 'Veronica' and 'Any King's Shilling' (*Spike*), thought to rely upon external information. 'How To Be Dumb' (*Mighty Like A Rose*) is seen as a political song, rather than the attack on Bruce Thomas that it is understood by others to be (Hinton 1999: 340; Thomson 2004: 278), while 'Riot Act' is divorced from the context of the "Columbus incident", since Smith has already dismissed race-derived reading of *Get Happy!!* with the single-word sentence "Remarkable" (177).[11] Smith defines auteur study in ways that suggest it can mean slightly different things: at p. 165 it consists of biography, artistic philosophy, creative impulse and stylistic tendency; at p. 257 biography, artistic philosophy, creative influences, and songwriting strategies; and, at p. 283, biography, creative influence, artistic philosophy and stylistic tendency. Creative influence is a major topic, as we have seen, but Smith restricts his range of reference to comparisons with the songwriters who are his other published topics of study: Springsteen, Townsend, Mitchell and, particularly in Costello's case, Bob Dylan (as at 234–5 and 257). Since Smith's method is an "objective" manner of attribution, there is no immediate follow-through to value judgement, so that it is peculiar when value judgements do appear, negative ones for *Punch The Clock, Blood And Chocolate* and, to a lesser extent, *Goodbye Cruel World.* By and large, the tone is positive, however, and the claim made of *Trust* might surprise the reader: "the practice of songwriting does not get any better than this" (178).

Smith's method is certainly useful for viewing the career as a whole. As an exercise, we can map his categories onto two examples where Costello set out to plan a series of "stories" through the album. (I shall return to these in looking at songs as novels, at pages 137–45) The three songs that completed the first vinyl side of *Mighty Like A Rose*, a group labelled "Cold War Nostalgia" by Costello (*Mighty Like A Rose* n02), bring together three of Smith's types: 'Invasion Hit Parade' is a "societal complaint", 'Harpies Bizarre' a social commentary with an "anti-Clubland theme" (271), and 'After The Fall' a "relational commentary". The separate sides of *Girls Girls Girls* offer another point of cross-reference and I have integrated Smith's categories in an analysis of the different versions of the compilation (Table 3.8), to which I will return in examining Costello as a novelist *manqué*. The fourth side of both vinyl and cassette, featuring Costello's political songs, predictably attains retrospective confirmation of Smith's method, made up of societal complaints, interrupted only by the wordplay of 'Sunday's Best' and the "narrative impressionism" of 'Tokyo Storm Warning'. The "first side" consists of societal or relational complaints. The "second side" introduces more songs characterized by "narrative impressionism", as well as another example of wordplay. The "third side" is most impressive in terms of confirming Smith's method, however, focusing strongly on the relational complaint or elegy, across different albums and different-sounding songs. In summary, Smith's book is highly commended to serious readers of Costello's songs.

The main drawback of Smith's method is the lack of mediation between the words and their musical presentation. Again, we cannot escape the problem of quantity: the sheer number of words either needs time for thorough consideration or demands selectivity. That said, the building blocks of Costello's words are familiar ones of the popular song and, to some extent, of poetry in general, be they the sonic correspondences (rhyme, wordplay) or the way the words carry social meaning. In this brief discussion, I want to focus on just two elements, line and rhyme, and use them as the basis for examining 'Tokyo Storm Warning'.

Line

I am first interested in how the words fill out the space of the musical line,[12] their "syllabic density", to use Leonard Cohen's term.[13] The line ties in what can be said about the words to their musical appearance, through factors such as speed, rhythm, and the musical cadence. *Verbal space* preserves the idea of *line* from poetry as something almost visible in the song.[14] *Speed* is crucial in defining the length of line, and there may even be a further relationship between the speed of singing and the speed of speech: John Lennon's line "My independence seems to vanish in the haze" in 'Help' (1965) is *sung* on the Beatles' record close to the pace of ordinary *speech*.[15] Once the songwriter has decided on these basic elements, he or she is effectively locked up in Leonard Cohen's 'Tower of Song'.[16]

'Oliver's Army' is a simple case of "art concealing art", as revealed by the relationship of words and beats (see Table 3.2). All these details are *charming*, charmed forces: the verbal space of "Don't start" is shortened for "My mind"; "talking" rhymes with "sleepwalking", two syllables to three, but at a distance and with different emphasis; "while I'm" sits happily alone; and the space of "talk all night" doubles syllabically for "putting the world to right". The second verse imposes the constriction of following the first verse, but is also a freedom, and here Costello loads up on *detail*: memorable little things like Checkpoint Charlie, the Murder Mile, one itchy trigger, one more widow and the white nigger. The bridge section has serious ideas in a pop song, through the names of places: Hong Kong, London "full of Arabs", Palestine, a Chinese line, and the three rivers for Liverpool, London and Newcastle. 'Oliver's Army' illustrates basic elements that we take for granted, and I now look at salient exceptions and systematic expansions.

Costello occasionally uses *silence* as a trick of verbal space. During the fast 'Radio Radio', the voice is left to occupy the musical space by itself (at 1'35–45), spotlighting words, while the slow 'God's Comic' (*Spike*) includes an extended silence (at 3'27–31) for comic effect. The drama of

Table 3.2 'Oliver's Army' (*Armed Forces*, 1979): 0'14–26

1	2	3	4
	Don't start me	tal-	-king
5	6	7	8
	I	could talk all	ni--ght
1	2	3	4
	My mind goes		sleep- -walking
5	6	7	8
	while I'm	putting the world to	right

3'46–50 of 'God Give Me Strength' (*Painted From Memory*) depends partly on silence as part of the musical phrasing at that point. At least three songs begin with the voice alone setting out an intimation of the pace and verbal space of the song to follow: 'No Action' (*This Year's Model*), 'Accidents Will Happen' (*Armed Forces*), 'I Hope You're Happy Now' (*Blood And Chocolate*).[17] The effect of speed on words can be heard when Costello performs a cover of Sam and Dave's 'I Can't Stand Up For Falling Down' (originally 1967, on *Get Happy!!*) at a considerably faster pace than the soulful original. However, although the second version of his own song 'I Hope You're Happy Now' *sounds* faster in the *Blood And Chocolate* version when compared with a demo (extended *King Of America*), this is due to the rhythmic activity of the instrumental accompaniment, and Costello's speed of enunciation is similar in both versions.[18]

Songs with empty lines

A spotlight now falls on the words of 'Almost Blue' (*Imperial Bedroom*) simply due to the slow pace of the song, but there are many subtleties to observe. The two lines of the bridge (heard at 1'10–25) increase the syllable count of the lines of the verse, so that, for the song as a whole, the syllabic limits for occupying a two-bar space are three ("almost blue") and eleven ("Not all good things come to an end now it is") or twelve ("It named me as the fool who only aimed to be"). The lines of the verse include varied correspondences in the way words sound. The most important group consists of "almost" followed by: blue, you, do, and true. A form of first-syllable-correspondence rhyme with "almost" constitutes another group: "always true", "almost me", "almost you", and even the phrase "all the things"; "almost" and "always" also appear alone. These examples can vary between being the start and end of a phrase: thus, "*All the* things that your eyes once promised", then "There's a part of me that's *always true*". Finally, note that the two verse sections rhyme or correspond with each other: blue/blue, do/do, you/true, All the things/Not all good things, hers too/chosen few, crying/couple. The bridge is a contrast in harmony and an increase in syllabic density, but still closely rhymed: "became me/aimed to be" and, possibly, "disaster/as the (fool)". This is a careful song, attending to a small collection of words, allowed to expand only a small distance from the title's core phrase.

Subtle as 'Almost Blue' is in highlighting its words against the slow space of the music, there seems to me a further leap to the technical control of 'Country Darkness' (*The Delivery Man*).[19] The piano's chords fall into a lopsided rhythmic progression, two three-beat bars clustering activity on the final beat of the first bar. The first is a richly harmonized progression away from and back to the tonic chord (I–IV–V–I). "Country" is announced in the piano immediately by the "crushed" second rising to the third (the 'acciaccatura' of music theory). The second of these two bars forms a "hole" which proves essential for the voice and its words.[20] The opening progression repeats three times, before the voice enters, at the third time. For the first sung line, a small asymmetry is introduced, two added beats. Harmonically, the music settles on chord iii, C# minor (0'26): this bass third, C#, divides the space between A and E, but the resulting dominant (E) is in its second inversion (0'29), a rich B in the bass leading, like a hymn harmonization, to the dominant, E (0'31). The title of the song is repeated as chorus over a softer pair: Bm7 to E (0'34–37, 0'40–43). This is summed up in Table 3.3. Against this sequence, its small and gentle instability, Costello's words are precise, syllabically accurate. In all three verses, each line occupies six syllables (for example, "This tattered document", "Suffer little children"), apart from one seven-syllable line at the end of the first verse ("Flies buzzing around the bulb"). There are some rhymes: document/filament, train/refrain, blade/maid. With the "hole" of the music supplying the "space" for the

Table 3.3 Harmony and phrase structure of 'Country Darkness' (*The Delivery Man*, 2004)

Introduction:	((2 + 1) +3) × 3: A
Verse:	((2 + 1) + 2 + 3): E (note the extension); ((2 + 1) + 3): C#m; ((2 + 1) + 3): perfect cadence (I 6/4 – V7) to E
Chorus:	((2 + 1) + 3): Bm7–E; ((2 + 1) + 3): Bm7–E

words, the start of each line is clearly heard. The bridge section builds up to a dissolve led by piano, an asymmetrical 4 times 3 beats (first at 1'40–44: C–F–Dm–E).[21]

What is subtle in 'Country Darkness' is a combination of its carefully controlled unpredictability alongside iron control of stripped-down detail. It makes it seem both precise and improvisatory, tight and loose. It seems to me a real advance, and comparisons can be found elsewhere in Costello's contemporaneous work. 'Radio Silence' on *When I Was Cruel* sees Costello do several things: find an interesting subject; use his vocal range to great effect, almost structuring the flow of the verse sections; and again vary bar-counts just slightly. In fact, the more stable contrast sections come as something of a let-down, recurring three times. Closer to 'Country Darkness', we can turn to a song for which Costello collaborated on words: 'Narrow Daylight' on Diana Krall's *The Girl In The Other Room* of 2004. This is another track that announces its success from the word go, that soft piano (Elton John's style, perhaps). But again it is a combination of predictable pop phrasing and less predictable verbal space that does the trick. The listener might compare the more settled pop phrasing of the section, "I stepped out on a sunlit grove" (at 1'15), the music reminiscent of a classic, soft-soul progression found in, for instance, Whitney Houston's 'The Greatest Love Of All' (1985). Then cut back to the verses near the start and you'll notice the subtle difference: "narrow daylight", four syllables, in its own empty space, but the same space as "I walked through halls of reputation", nine syllables, the latter beautifully phrased in the voice. The remaining lines come and go, some slightly fuller, some slightly emptier. Expression consists partly of these controlled, microscopic attentions.[22]

Songs with packed lines

Here too I want to pick up from different phases of Costello's work, two examples from *Punch The Clock* and an extended example from *When I Was Cruel*. I take 'The Greatest Thing' (*Punch The Clock*) to be the first case where Costello starts to subdivide verbal space so that he has to produce a great number of words and syllables. At the start of the track drums, then drums and bass, mark out the space available to the words. The song then traverses an extreme range of ways of filling the space, between three syllables (a: "punch the clock", "you'll be young", "it's OK") and 16 (b: for instance, at 0'50), occupying the same space and, at 1'38, a remarkable 17, by the addition of an extra syllable in the third beat (c) (see Table 3.4). By the time of the second example, even the backing vocals add to the wordiness with an answering phrase: "Since then times have been changing."

'King Of Thieves' (*Punch The Clock*) contains a lengthy line of 21 syllables, at 2'11 during a bridge section. This is a multi-sectional song, full of Abba-like pop detail and piano flourishes, and the line contains some odd emphases: "Blow the whistle on the whole design as they find my name in that fatal mailing list."

'Episode Of Blonde' (*When I Was Cruel*) displays a superb control of verbal space, built on a lively chord progression with salsa piano flourishes. The terrific first line – "I spy for *The Spirit of Curiosity*" – establishes an eleven-syllable "norm" for the tempo. By the time of the line beginning "a tornado dropped a funnel" (0'24), we're used to the idea of two syllables per beat. The chorus occupies 16 bars between 0'55 and 1'24, its lines working out as a syllable count of 13, 14, 16, 16 (59 in all). The next section is the one to home in on, a kind of rap between 1'24 and 2'09, occupying 24 beats, eight more than the chorus, all in groups of four. Here the syllable count rises dramatically to encompass lots of wordy detail, to 15, 13, 11, 13, 11, 16, 10, 15 – 104 in all (and that's the same space as the 59 syllables of the chorus) – followed by the extension with 15, 14, 19 (48 in all), making the rap 152 syllables in total. That's a lot of words! Table 3.5 demonstrates the unpredictability in both the quantity of words and their position in relation to the music's regular beat, indicated by beat numbers. The first two lines (at (a) in the table) are heavily stressed, with two syllables to the beat and the seventh beat emphasized in both as the final word. The next couplet (b) compresses the first phrase, then runs the words

Table 3.4 'The Greatest Thing' (*Punch The Clock*, 1983)

(a) 0'22–24			
Punch the	clock		
X	X	X	X
(b) 0'50–52			
Girls like that a-	-bove described are	not to be so	easily bribed
X	X	X	X
(c) 1'38–40			
Nights were long and	days were olden	woman to man has	been beholden
X	X	X	X

over the break, ending at the fifth beat of the next line. At (c) the words remember to dance along with the music, especially for the word "bandeon". But this is a momentary respite before the word–music relationship is again made unpredictable, at (d). Note that the greater quantity of words allows a range of grammatical type: adjectives like "wounded", "tiny", "petty"; past participles like "pinned, fixed and fastened"; and more precise and lively description ("blaring, blasting"; "lonely, likely"; "petty crime-coats shadow panic drunkards").

Two other tracks on *When I Was Cruel* can be mentioned here. Dramatic contrasts in verbal space are found in 'When I Was Cruel No. 2', between 4 ("here come the bride": 1'02), 5 ("when I was cruel": 1'47) to 14 ("the entrance hall", etc.: 3'26), 15 ("who turned out", etc.: 3'32) and 16 ("the ghostly first wife", etc.: 3'49). All these different occupations of space are made easy to hear by the repeated vocal sample signalling the eight-beat space. 'Soul For Hire' contains two of Costello's most outrageous occupations of space. In exactly the same space occupied by, for example, "I see every human kind" (1'02), with seven syllables, he manages to pack in, at 1'29, the 22 syllables of "Streams of ink and piles of paper: what are the breaks? Jump out of the window? Parole? Escape?" and, at 2'09, the 21 syllables of "Streams of ink and piles of paper to hand them over to dopers and kiddie-rapers".

An interesting final example is found in 'You Believe In Me', one of two covers of songs from the Beach Boys' *Pet Sounds* (1966) on *For The Stars* (2001), Costello's collaboration with Anne Sofie von Otter. At 2'11, Costello

Table 3.5 'Episode Of Blonde' (*When I Was Cruel*, 2002): 1'24–2'09

	1	2	3	4	5	6	7	8
(a)	Revolving	like a	jeweller's	figure	on a	music	box	
	Spangled	curtain	parted	and a	night club	scene	un-locks	
(b)	Pinned,	fixed and	fastened	in a	follow spot,		arms thrown	out to
	Everyone,	she's	giving	all she's	got			(To the)
(c)	To the last	gasp of a	wounded	ban-	-de-	-on		(A)
(d)	A tiny man	im-	-ploring	to the	ceiling	fan this	stolen	feeling
	Ampili-	-fied up	through the	busted	speaker	blaring,	blasting,	
	Ad- -ver-	-ti-sing,	distorted	beyond	rea-	-son		
	Into the street where	petty	crime-	coats	shadow	panic	drunkards	
	Half out	of the	taxi cab		the barker	seized my	elbow	He
	thought I	was an-	-other	lonely,	likely		pilgrim	
	Looking	for	Saint	Tel-	-mo			

as second voice adds a sung line that fills the space of the melody with words. While the words sound like rap to our contemporary ears, the overall effect may be closer to an ensemble number in a Mozart opera.

Rhyme

Having examined line, consider these figures: the first five songs of *Imperial Bedroom* (1982) contain 68 rhymes, the first five songs of *When I Was Cruel* (2002) contain 70, give or take a couple in both cases, averaging 14 per song. If ever Costello admitted to weariness or exhaustion with song as form, the sheer quantity of rhymes might give credible cause.[23] However, there are two great and transhistorical benefits, for producer and perceiver, as Brogan suggests:

> The testimony of poets is clear that the search for a rhyme opens up new possibilities for shaping lines that would never have been thought of without the pressure of finding a rhyme. Rhyme may thus seem the object of displaced fixation in consciousness which frees the subconscious mind for more creative wordcraft ... The intellectual appreciation of a rhyme: its difficulty, surprise, ingenuity, or wit, as well as the sheer pleasure of its euphony. ("Rhyme", in Preminger and Brogan 1993: 1060)

The topic remains under-researched: Brogan points out that in terms of "extensive collections of data ... for English, we have effectually *nothing at all*", and that "all these questions are still unanswered" (Preminger and Brogan 1993: 1061).[24] Scott begins *The Riches of Rhyme* (1988) with a "startling barrage of queries". With song, too, patient observation of rhyme loses out to the more obvious kind of discussion of meaning arising from the words, comparable to tensions in literary theory where, as Brogan argues:

> While theory construction is essential to progress in any intellectual discipline, postmodernist literary theory has privileged social activism and sought to suppress the kinds of research necessary to generate the detailed facts which would validate critical judgement about texts. But it is facts which

> are the chief means of validating or disproving any theory at
> all. The collection of useful data itself requires an acute grasp
> of theory – i.e. critical intelligence. (*ibid.*)

Brogan presents a taxonomy of "12 criteria for the analysis and categorization of rhyme types", which I summarize in a note.[25] Elsewhere, commenting on the words of songs, I took examples from NWA (rhyme's plenitude), Jackson Browne (full rhyme), Chris Difford of Squeeze (half-rhyme), Lou Reed (no-rhyme), Mark E. Smith (alliteration), concluding with a comparison of examples by Elvis Costello and Rickie Lee Jones (Griffiths 2003: 48–54).[26]

The rhyming technique of *When I Was Cruel* differs from *Imperial Bedroom* in that two of the songs ('Tear Off Your Own Head', 'Soul For Hire') use rhyme more sparingly, while in *Imperial Bedroom* rhyme may have been an automatic compositional technique. Two examples are included to suggest further work that could be done.

'Shabby Doll' (*Imperial Bedroom*) has a total of 24 rhymes: this figure assumes that each rhyming term starts from one originating word, in the presentation of the rhyme, although, of course, every word rhymes additionally with every other. The simplest rhyme in this song is the following, with the same syllable count (one) and the same lexical category (both nouns: "the gag" and "the bag"):

> **Gag**/bag (1 rhyming term)

The next group contributes to the bridge of the song (at 2'29–46), and also consists of close rhyming terms: "toy", "boy", "joy", with the addition of "enjoyed":

> **Toy**/enjoyed/nancy boy/no joy (3 rhyming terms)

Finally, the following collections include some element of disjunction: number of syllables, the avoidance of full rhyme, or "lexical category". As a result, there is an internal "push" to them that belongs to the words:

> **More**/what for/before/elevator door (3 rhyming terms)
> **Facing**/situation/assassination (2 rhyming terms)
> **This dress**/distress/possessed/undressed (3 rhyming terms)
> **Used to be**/sympathy/you and me/bribery (3 rhyming terms)

> **Whore**/before/claws (2 rhyming terms)
> **Joking**/unspoken/soaking/broken (3 rhyming terms)

The chorus (first at 0'59–1'20) has this interesting run of pararhymes and other sound correspondence, including the repetition of "you know in your heart":

> **Doll**/putting you off/putting you on/swearing upon/gone
> (4 rhyming terms)

'When I Was Cruel No. 2' (*When I Was Cruel*) has a total of 21 rhymes and one alliteration. However, as we have seen, what distinguishes *When I Was Cruel* is the density and number of words, and these in turn affect rhyme's position in the line, or the temporal distance between the rhyming terms (Brogan's tenth category). Of the rhymes in this track, one is the blunt rhyme of "much" with itself, but its phrase can be extended back to the pararhyme of "changed" and "paid": changed that much/paid too much. The alliteration is the pair "floor/fall".[27] In terms of syllable count, word category, and full rhyme, its closest correspondences are the following:

> **Glare**/air (1 rhyming term)
> **Four**/door (1 rhyming term)
> **Spouse**/house (1 rhyming term)
> **Drown**/gown (1 rhyming term)
> **Talkers**/walkers (1 rhyming term)
> **Scene**/Queen (1 rhyming term) [this one is a quotation from Abba]
> **Plug**/thug (1 rhyming term)

More disjunct sets are found in the following:

> **Rarefied**/bride/aside/snide (3 rhyming terms)
> **Better**/met her (1 rhyming term)
> **Yawn**/born to it (1 rhyming term)
> **To me**/melody (1 rhyming term)
> **Carnation**/creation/elevation (2 rhyming terms)
> **Ushers**/crushes (1 rhyming term)
> **Friends**/extend (1 rhyming term)
> **Sneaks**/week (1 rhyming term)

You/eighty-two (1 rhyming term)
Report/retort (1 rhyming term)
Changed that much/paid too much (1 rhyming term)
Floor/fall (alliteration)

As Brogan suggests, there is a *lot* more that can be done in the taxonomy of rhyme with an output like Costello's. What would further work tell us? It would indicate change or consistency in a particular aspect of Costello's songwriting technique, and offer a platform from which to compare that of other songwriters. At present the answer to such questions is that nobody knows, which is slightly different from the question of whether anybody notices or cares. For now, I shall put line and rhyme together as the basis for a reading of one song.

> "There was never any sense of a *raid* on the marketplace, that you should come up with a hit and get out. That kind of sensibility did not take root in my mind until very recently. [*Laughs*] I think maybe it's a nice idea but it's not going to happen when you write seven-minute songs." (Leonard Cohen, in Zollo 1997: 348)

> When the two strongest songs on a pop record run over six minutes apiece, we're talking sustained vision.[28]

'Tokyo Storm Warning' (*Blood And Chocolate*) is one of a small line-up of Costello songs with lots of words over deliberately limited harmony, the others being 'Pump It Up' (*This Year's Model*), 'Lover's Walk' (*Trust*), 'The Deportees Club' (*Goodbye Cruel World*) and 'Bedlam' (*The Delivery Man*). It was co-written with Cait O'Riordan and is distinguished by its prolixity.[29] The track lasts 6 minutes 24 seconds, with no variation in speed (not the chops and changes of 'Bohemian Rhapsody'), which is not "merely slow" (as is 'Hey Jude' with its extended coda): the start is similar to the middle or end, and the track fades rather than coming to an end. Table 3.6 presents an outline of the track's form. The basic harmonic pattern is the 12-bar blues, towards completion of which 12 bars the verse is two-thirds of the way: $8 \times D/4 \times G/4 \times D$. However, verses 5 to 7 double the time spent on the first chord: their formula is $16 \times D/4 \times G/4 \times D$. The chorus intervenes: 4/4/4, where each set of four bars is divided into a call and response (the title of the song) of two bars each. Finally, as an abrupt climax to conclude the chorus, there is a switch of one bar each through F# to B minor, before settling back on D for two bars. So the chord progression gradually *squashes*, verse through chorus to climax, before the whole thing starts up again. Studio tricks contribute variety and, after the fourth verse, the chorus is replaced by a guitar solo.[30] Pace is all-important, since it mediates the time of the track, the rhythm of the music, and the space available for words. It lasts 6'20 at 148 crotchets to the minute (according to the score), or 24 beats per 10 seconds, while the number of beats per line (in the song) is 16. The line shown in Table 3.7, for instance, could in theory be performed, badly, as one syllable per beat.

Nevertheless, there is a 16-syllable "norm" found in the verses, the 16 answered by a shorter line (13 or 14). Many individual lines begin with a correspondence in words to the musical anacrusis or upbeat, a good point to observe fecundity of detail: little phrases like "Well the", "So you", "So the". Next, the song establishes rhyme patterns: ABAB at the first verse, generally AABB thereafter, extending to AABBCC in verses 6 and 7, and AAA at the chorus.[31] Taken together, this constitutes a demonstration of Costello and O'Riordan's technique under the pressure of rhyme:

Verse 1 scenery/hotel/refinery/hell
Verse 2 you are/in the bar/Montgomery/holiday
Verse 3 sunrise/hi-rise/suggestions/questions
Verse 4 Rimini/facsimile/Broadway/hard way
Verse 5 Malvinas/between us/Juanita/Margarita/sauciest/
         naughtiest/Buenos Aires/lingerie
Verse 6 fortunes/Martians/pensioners/mention us/stamps/day
Verse 7 arses/hearses/purse/mercy/cried/collide[32]
Chorus   joke/poke/bloke

Many rhymes show a degree of disjunction. This couplet from verse 5 includes the inner run "cheap in", "Malvinas", "Argentina", "between us", as well as keeping the sound of the "h" running through "holidays", "Hotel" and "hardly":

Holidays are dirt cheap in the Costa del Malvinas
In the Hotel Argentina they can hardly tell between us

Table 3.6 'Tokyo Storm Warning' (*Blood And Chocolate*, 1986): 6'20

Introduction	drums 0'00, plus keyboard 0'03, full band 0'12	
Verse 1	0'18	"Well the sky"
Verse 2	0'48	"So you look"
Chorus	1'12	"What do we care?"
Verse 3	1'36	"The black sand stuck"
Chorus	2'01	
Verse 4	2'25	"So they flew"
Guitar solo	2'49	
Verse 5 (extended)	3'01	"Holidays are dirt cheap"
Chorus	3'37	
Verse 6 (extended)	4'01	"Japanese God Jesus"
Chorus	4'37	
Verse 7 (extended)	5'01	"We brave the cold"
Chorus	5'38	
Sound effect	6'02, second guitar solo 6'06, vocalise 6'11, fade 6'20	

The end of verse 6 is a non-rhyme at the line end (stamps/day) but "stamps" rhymes internally with "dampen" in "dampen down the day".

The song has a dense and varied *dramatis personae*: verse 2 has the Ku Klux Klan in Montgomery, verse 3 the barefoot girl from Naples or Barcelona, verse 4 some dead Italian tourists; verse 5 brings on Teresa, the waitress also known as Juanita, verse 6 some Japanese God–Jesus robots; and an undertaker appears in the final verse. Places vary widely: Italy, Spain, Japan, Alabama, Argentina (Malvinas), Venezuela (Puerto Margarita), Korea, and Paris (the *Folies Bergère*); Broadway might be in New York, but "the Broadway" could be in a number of locations. Verse 6 has several groups of people: pensioners, protest singers, bullies and louts.

Costello and O'Riordan play with shifting narrators. A firm "I" appears initially, four times in the one line: "I knew I was in trouble but I thought I was in hell." Verses 2, 4 and 7 feature "you" alone. First and second person are gathered for the "we" of the chorus, reappearing in verses 5 and 7 as "us" and "we", respectively. The first two references to "you" seem like general types ("you know"), but the "you" of the final verse is more

Table 3.7 'Tokyo Storm Warning' (*Blood And Chocolate*, 1986): 0'48–54

1	2	3	4	5	6	7	8
Look	a-	-round	the	ti-	-ny	room	and
9	10	11	12	13	14	15	16
you	won-	-der	where	the	hell	you	are

pointed. The seventh and final verse has "we" and "you" together, introducing a male third-person voice, with an air of romance and mystery: "How you loved him and you hated him and made him cry for mercy." The listener wonders whether Costello the singer is "I" or "he", a "bloke" like Death.

This is a vision of hell (sung like hell at 0'42–45), prompted by impending mortality, its one conclusion the repeated line, "we're only living this instant", echoing the finality of Philip Larkin's line in "Aubade", "Most things may never happen. This one will" (Larkin 1988: 209). The chorus makes light of things, giving the world a big poke and recognizing Death as a big bloke, but keeps getting dragged back to the swamp of the verses. The band play like footsoldiers on forced march, while the minimalist guitar solo sounds like the Byrds in Eastern mode (the whole-tone F#–E–D–C, G crushing onto the F#); mixed low, the backing vocals of the chorus holler like sirens, while the tiny "ba ba ba" ending sounds nastier and more desperate than its pop roots. The track is like a big slab of stone but shows how much could be achieved with the song form, where words contribute by sound and rhythm as well as providing narrative detail.

Politics

'Tokyo Storm Warning' is one of the many Costello songs that bring together political and personal themes. The best academic writer on these issues, John Street, having set out to examine music and politics, usually concludes by collapsing the distinction: "they are intimately linked, and it is impossible to separate them" (Frith, Straw and Street 2001: 253), while "judging popular culture is a political act", and "these arguments are not just *like* politics, they are *about* politics" (Street 1997: 197, 198). Thurschwell notes that 'Less Than Zero' (*My Aim Is True*) and 'Satellite' (*Spike*) feature personal lives through the mediation of television:

> More a cranky Frankfurt School theorist than a postmodern
> celebrator of commodification, Costello maintains the
> category of the human as an index of what is dangerously
> disappearing under capitalism ... [and] maintains that the
> forces of commodification invade subjectivity in ways that
> make politics a necessity for the outside world as well as the
> inside, that if the two can't be separated then neither can
> either side of the equation be ignored. (Thurschwell 1999:
> 288)

Costello's key period of direct engagement in British politics coincided with the prime ministership of Margaret Thatcher and her Conservative governments. The fact of her repeated success in elections is an important background: first in 1979 and again in 1983 and 1987.[33] Costello's engagement was direct enough for the single 'Pills And Soap' to be tied closely to the date of the General Election of 1983 (Thomson 2004: 197; *Punch The Clock* n03): this was an engagement in *electoral* politics, verging on *party* politics, and the wider sense of parties representing political *positions*. 'Shipbuilding' (1982) was an allegorical lament for Thatcher's war over the Falkland Islands in the South Atlantic.[34] 'Peace In Our Time' (1984) is an anti-war single, directed more towards US president Ronald Reagan, whose "Star Wars" policy is referred to. Costello was prepared to comment through songs on issues in British party politics, and also – imagine him turning the pages of a broadsheet newspaper – ready to engage in various ways in *international* affairs.[35] He produced and contributed vocals to 'Nelson Mandela' (1984), a commentary on South African politics, an issue for the international left of the day, some songs about Ireland that I'll consider presently (on pages 125–7), and a group of songs on *Mighty Like A Rose* which engaged in the consequences of events in the Soviet Union and Eastern Europe in the late 1980s. 'I Thought I'd Write To Juliet' (*The Juliet Letters*) is a song which arises from a letter sent to Costello during the first Gulf War. These tracks are directed towards particular themes, but create a general sense of "where he's coming from": no songs about the environment, for instance, trade unions or devolution of political power to the Celtic nations of Scotland and Wales.

Costello's 1980s political engagement can be set alongside the debates among the British left usually referred to as "New Times", in which the central figure was the cultural studies theorist Stuart Hall. A good starting-point, *in medias res*, is "Blue Election, Election Blues", Hall's analysis of Thatcher's victory in 1987. This election had a certain added significance for pop music at the time (Costello not included), since Red Wedge[36] existed in order to increase the chances of victory of the opposition Labour party, led by Neil Kinnock. The campaign was unsuccessful in that respect: the Conservatives returned to power with 42.3% of the vote (376 parliamentary seats) to Labour's 30.8% (229 seats), with the Alliance of the Liberals and Social Democratic Party (SDP) claiming 22.6% (but a mere 22 seats) (Morgan 2001: 491).[37] Hall attempted to analyse Thatcher's mesmeric grip on the British public, attributing her success to her grip on the imagination of the majority – imagination rather than material well-being. "People make identifications symbolically," he wrote, "through social imagery, in their political imaginations ... Material interests matter profoundly. But they are always *ideologically defined*" (Hall 1988: 261). Being swayed by slogans and images reflected not the irrationality of the mass of voters, but rather the belief that "they can't intervene with much hope of success, *in detail*, into policy matters, nor can they affect the fine-tuning of economic machines" (*ibid.*). High-minded distaste for image and slogan as the trivialization of politics was misguided because, he suggests, "images are *not* trivial things. In and through images, fundamental political questions are being posed and thought through" (*ibid.*). Hall's analysis, written at the time for the journal *Marxism Today*, inspired considerable debate.[38] The dichotomy he posits, between a politics that appeals to people's social imagination and one that appeals to their material interests, can be seen as options then available to the political pop song. To commemorate the next General Election in 1992 (which Labour also lost to the Conservatives, this time without Thatcher), *NME* published a chart of its favourite anti-Thatcher songs, the "Iron Maiden Fourteen":[39]

1. The Beat, 'Stand Down Margaret' (1980)
2. The Soft Boys, 'Brenda's Iron Sledge' (1979)
3. Elvis Costello, 'Tramp The Dirt Down' (1989)
4. Morrissey, 'Margaret On The Guillotine' (1989)
5. Crass, 'How Does It Feel To Be The Mother Of 1000 Dead?' (1982)
6. Sinead O'Connor, 'Black Boys On Mopeds' (1990)
7. Momus, 'Sex With The Disabled' (1986)

8. Microdisney, 'People Just Like To Dream' (1987)
9. The Not Sensibles, 'I'm In Love With Margaret Thatcher' (1981)
10. The Specials, 'Maggie's Farm' (1981)
11. The Blow Monkeys and Curtis Mayfield, 'Celebrate' (1987)
12. Simply Red, 'She'll Have To Go' (1990)
13. The Waterboys, 'Maggie, It's Time For You To Go' (unrecorded)
14. The Fatima Mansions, 'Mario Vargas Yoni' (1991)

The chart gathered together a variety of musical styles and poetic stances. Musical style ranged from the punk noise of Crass through the British ska of the Beat and Simply Red's white soul to the sound of closely recorded voice and acoustic guitar in Sinead O'Connor and Morrissey (singer as confessor, listener as priest). The poetic stance was also diverse: irony (the Not Sensibles), fantasy (Morrissey, Elvis Costello), agitprop (the Beat), and rant (Fatima Mansions). Agitprop songs like 'Stand Down Margaret' represent Hall's material or realist axis, while Elvis Costello and Morrissey represent the imaginary or symbolic. Costello refused to participate in Red Wedge (1986–7) but had been part of the earlier British political pop movement, Rock against Racism (RAR: 1976-81).[40] Analysing these two movements as a pair, Simon Frith and John Street point out that RAR had a broader aim, that of racial harmony, which was easier to promote than the specific target of Red Wedge, that of getting Labour elected (Frith and Street 1992: 78). However, RAR inherited a model of rock authenticity, close to the Costello of *Get Happy!!* and *Almost Blue*, soul and country music, reflecting in turn roots shared with pub rockers like Nick Lowe, Graham Parker and Dr Feelgood:

> For RAR, the value of a musical form lay in the proletarian authority of its performers: soul and RnB expressed the Afro-American working class; reggae expressed the Afro-Caribbean working class; punk the white working class. Music without such roots was worthless. (*ibid.*: 76)

By contrast, "two genres were prominent in Red Wedge shows: folk and '60s/'70s soul" (*ibid.*: 77). However, both *Punch The Clock* and *King Of America* have elements of those styles too. The point of separation between Costello and Red Wedge might be that, as Frith and Street say, such "aesthetic judgements" strayed into the "less politically familiar territory" of "what the music meant, and how those meanings were conveyed" (*ibid.*).

That is to say, however "imaginary" or "materialist" the song, real life forms a backdrop to political engagement where biographical factors can be germane: it was quite unthinkable for Costello to have played a concert in South Africa, for instance, or to have revealed that he was casting his vote for Thatcher. An underlying tension in evaluating Costello's political engagement arises from the sense that art and life are disjointed: high ideals in the studio, different stories on the road. Brian Hinton's biography includes an expressive juxtaposition of anecdotes from 1981. A journalist infiltrates the security cordon around Costello, but is discovered and beaten up. Hinton then refers to the letter sent by Costello's manager, Jake Riviera, to the biographer Krista Reese: "If this matter goes any further I shall pop in for a visit when I am next in New York." Immediately following,

> On 5 May, Elvis showed his compassionate side, performing a solo concert to patients at the MENCAP Rural Training Centre, Lufton Manor. He played five songs including 'Little Sister' that were to be screened at the "Year of the Disabled" gig. (Hinton 1999: 216)

There's something in that juxtaposition that gets to a rotten core in rock celebrity: low-level nastiness in the marshalling of public perception, alongside at least the possibility of low-level sincerity, at the start of a period in which "career aid" was going to become a theme. Another uneasy juxtaposition is found in Costello's liner note to *Kojak Variety* (n04), describing events in 1990. By the *end* of the note, Costello is chatting over lunch in Hampstead with Larry Adler and George Martin, listening to their yarns and concluding that "there is really no rush with music". At the *start* of the note, however, it's a different matter. An unnamed "American" is the "second engineer" for the *Kojak Variety* sessions (second, presumably, to Kevin Killen). This shadowy figure does two things: he recites a line from a pop single (by Timbuk 3) referring to his wearing of sunglasses, and he imitates the gestures of an actor on the nostalgic TV sitcom, *Happy Days*. Costello says, "I fired him on the spot. I hadn't come to Barbados to fool around, even though I was bidding a light-hearted farewell to a group of musicians with whom I'd recorded and toured for the previous five years." Again, it's the juxtaposition that rankles: clichés of good-naturedness ("really no rush with music", "a light-hearted farewell") and the seeming brutality of getting "fired ... on the spot". "Pop music hasn't the patience to slog through sub-committees and lobbying and making orderly demands," said Simon Reynolds (1990: 20): the nameless technician has no recourse to the job description, his track record as second engineer, since there was a free-market side to the musical world where those things count for little. "I fired him on the spot."

One marginal event that might help illuminate Costello's relationship to music and politics, following Red Wedge, is something that didn't concern the invention of material as such: his curatorship of the Meltdown Festival in 1995 (Thomson: 313–25). There Costello the "pop" figure was drawn into the world of policy and funding: the Southbank Centre (the collective name for the Royal Festival Hall, National Theatre and the other venues grouped on the south bank of the Thames) and the various organizations which help put on events (the Arts Council, local and national government). I say "pop" figure because this was the original peculiarity in the choice of Costello, the annual festival having been previously curated by two figures from the "contemporary classical" world (Louis Andriessen and George Benjamin), although Costello was followed by further left-field "pop" people like John Peel, Robert Wyatt, and Nick Cave. From Costello's perspective, curatorship of Meltdown was a clear success: he appeared to have worked tirelessly on the festival's behalf, has never failed to recall and celebrate the programme he helped devise, and followed the festival with several projects and collaborations. What's interesting is that the project inspired no songs, no titles like 'Public Funding (Gets A Good Job Done)' or 'Tax And Spend (Gotta Be A Good Thing, Babe)'. Why not '(Nothing Funny 'Bout A) Minimum Wage', after Labour's election in 1997? If Irishness could serve Costello's purpose as lament, what's to stop it appearing at, well, *better times*: reconciliation, compromise, 'Peace In Our Time: The Ulster Mix', however precarious? What's *with* these bitter left-wing guys? "If you do have to leave me," Costello asks in 'It's Time' (*All This Useless Beauty*), "who will I have left to hate?" In my view the key music-political figures in Britain in the 1980s, alongside Costello, were Jerry Dammers and Robert Wyatt, who together issued 'The Wind Of Change' in 1985, in the style of 'Nelson Mandela' and another terrific track. Wyatt continued to produce genuinely political pop music. Tracks like 'Free Will And Testament', 'Left On Man' and 'Blues In Bob Minor' have continued the lineage, even the promise, of some of the Costello tracks of the 1980s.[41] In addition, Costello found much to admire in Joni Mitchell's political work of the North American 1980s, gathered on her compilation *The Beginning Of Survival* (2004).

'Sleep Of The Just', a relational complaint, or elegy, in Larry David Smith's typology, always struck me as a political song, albeit one which confused the international politics of Britain and Ireland with everyday lives. The track closes *King Of America*, giving its second vinyl side the same sense of ending that 'I'll Wear It Proudly' gave to the first: dignified slowness, the boom and swish of Jim Keltner's drums alongside Mitchell Froom's non-percussive keyboards (Hammond organ and "doctored piano"). Costello describes the song's origin in the sleevenote to *Girls Girls Girls*:

> Songwriters sometimes take secret revenge on people who piss them off by making them the villain in a song. I finished this song on the bus to Letterkenny after a curt exchange of views with one of "our brave lads" at the border with what we laughingly call "our country".
>
> "It's a construction from an actual event. The opening verse happened to me, but not the rest. It's just a little story about morally superior prigs. This one – a soldier, *by coincidence* – thinks he's better than his nude model sister. It's a parable about pride, about pomposity." (in Kelly 1986)

"Mad Ireland hurt you into poetry," Auden said of Yeats, and something similar seems to have happened here, in Letterkenny, a border town in County Donegal. Born in London and raised between London and Liverpool, later living for a time in Dublin, Costello has Irish roots, and he may have felt sympathetic to the cause of the Catholic minority in Ulster. The charge levelled at the British soldier in the chorus, "I suppose you need the sleep of the just", I understand as: "I suppose, that is, since you are unlikely to sleep well,[42] and don't deserve to, as you are engaged in an unjust cause." It's only during the first verse that the soldier appears; the second verse takes us to an apocalyptic scene with a metaphorical and literal fire brought into play; the bridge and final verse take us to a rather sordid scene involving a "girl" and soldiers, either gazing at a model in photographs or a rape scene.[43] The effect of the bridge and final verse is unsettling: perhaps the moral dubiety of the soldier carries through to his personal life, but also perhaps it simply adds to the ongoing sense of the song. The song is slow and words have time to register. It is debatable whether the phrase "immaterial girl", closing the bridge, benefits from the allusion to Madonna's 'Material Girl' (1985). But what interests me further is how the song evokes its Irishness, and here I have in mind the suggestion of Rene Bookmens:

> This translating ability can be seen as the core of pop aesthetics and derives its power not from the lyrical contents of pop songs in the first place, but from the power that lies in the direct and undifferentiated use value of the *sounds* of a pop song, of which the lyrics are only a part. (2004: 73)

By "translating ability" Bookmens means the way that pop music enables the interaction of local and global musical languages. 'Sleep Of The Just' has "folkiness" coded in voice and guitar, whereas its Irishness is more subtly part of the melodic line, its achievement of the high octave twice in the verses, and four times in the bridge section, reminiscent of a song like 'The Last Rose Of Summer', and even the singer John McCormack.[44] It is the music that leads us to hear the song as a beautiful but dark criticism of the British military presence in Northern Ireland, reminding us of Derek Mahon's great line (from 1973) that "a good poem is a paradigm of good politics" (Longley 1986: 185).

'Tramp The Dirt Down' (*Spike*) is a very different affair, addressing Margaret Thatcher with no holds barred: the title is a fantasy of what should happen at Thatcher's burial. Casting Thatcher as the metaphoric "madam" of England's whorehouse, the bridge section derives from a song called 'Betrayal', first performed at the end of the miners' strike of 1984–5. 'Betrayal' was a dreadful song, "underwritten and diluted by a detour into personal matters" (*Punch The Clock* n03), but included the line "I hope that you sleep well at night". By the time of its reappearance in 'Tramp The Dirt Down', the stab at Thatcher is a contrasting section which uses a different musical theme (now "I hope that *she* sleeps well at night"). There are references to real events: Thatcher kissing a child, a father killing his son, and a war ("boys on both sides being blown to bits or beaten and maimed"). Hinton says the track "can still move me to tears", and sympathizes with the stance taken towards Thatcher (Hinton 1999: 323), while Costello has described it as containing "an unreasonable argument ... not intended to be a balanced, liberal view" (Irwin 1989), and songs lack time for differing perspectives in the manner a good political film or novel might. That said, I still have a problem with the track: not the occasional clunkiness in correspondence of words and music (at "avarice" and "punishment"), not the overwrought voice, not that the record lasts 5'40, not even that the melodic line of the verse is repeated twenty times in all (in the sequence: 7 times, 10 times, 3 times).[45] My problem is there right at the start, in the track's immediate Irishness: harplike descending guitar, moody mixolydian mode, swoony Celtic flute and, rather than a generalized Celtic, Irishness is the specific sonic *topos* of the instrumental arrangement for the song. I think that what Costello intends by that is the archaic sense of lament which the arrangement captures. But my modern ears insist on projecting Irishness upon the political theme of the song. Thatcher's period in power did little to resolve the Irish issue, although the very beginnings of the road to the Good Friday Agreement of 1998 may have happened under the Tory Secretary of State for Ireland, minister Peter Brooke (in John Major's government) in 1991 (Mulholland 2002: 131). These fantasies of mortality – Costello's tramping on Thatcher's grave, Morrissey's gazing upon her ascent to the guillotine – had been close to reality when her hotel was blown up by an Irish Republican Army bomb in Brighton in 1984.[46] Irishness seems to me to carry too much baggage for the song's purpose, as sounds arrive with cultural conditions attached. "Poetry makes nothing happen," Auden had said of Yeats, [47] and it was not music or musicians that deposed Thatcher but her own former colleagues like Michael Heseltine, Nigel Lawson and Geoffrey Howe: by the time 'Tramp The Dirt Down' appeared, Thatcher's political career was at an end (Morgan 2001: 503–5).

A footnote to Costello's political pop, and a first *boundary* to the subject matter. If Costello felt able to intervene in national or international affairs, the one clear boundary to his political songwriting was race, following the Columbus incident of 1979. The dispute forms a backbone to Franklin Bruno's book (2005: 65), and Costello has commented on the matter at length (*Get Happy!!* n03), revealing that 'Riot Act' on *Get Happy!!* was a direct response to the controversy, though the reference is hidden and indirect. As with the absence of songs celebrating left-liberal gains, this is a shame since there must have been a more direct song there somewhere. Britain in the 1970s had a whole thesaurus of racist comment alongside the residue of World War II nationalism or patriotism, and change has been a long time coming: as late as 1999, a British police force was identified as "institutionally racist".[48] 'Rednecks', 'Sail Away', 'Roll With The Punches': part of Randy Newman's thematic range remained closed to Costello.

> "You know, I keep writing these race things, as you know. I've written so many times about it. It doesn't seem to have done any good. [*Laughter*] I mean, I think I'm done, and then I write another one. But I think it's a big thing. I don't think I've written too much about it. I think there's more to say." (Randy Newman, in Zollo 1997: 286)

Romance and feminism

The demonstration and final recording of 'Satellite' (*Spike* 1988 and 1989) differ in one tiny respect. The demo has for one line (at 1'30–37), "As he undressed her with his eyes his weakness was her talent", whereas the final version (at 1'45–54) has "As he undressed her with his eyes her weakness was his talent". Weakness and talent shift between the unnamed male and female of a song that studiously avoids grounding "he" and "she" into first and second person (though the satellite blesses "us" at the very close). If one projects authorial presence into the *recording*, then Costello is the male narrator, while Chrissie Hynde's backing vocal adds something, but nothing so fundamental as the gender splits of records like 'I Got You Babe',[49] or Costello's own 'There's A Story In Your Voice' (*The Delivery Man*). Were Chrissie Hynde to sing the song herself, a switch of association would occur. The question with songs like these is whether we choose to associate them with biographical detail relating to Costello as its songwriter, issues which would not arise in the same way were the song to be covered by another singer. His or her weakness, her or his talent: does it matter? The line is vague, and becomes part of the general run of words to do with romance. Although 'Satellite' is characterized by Larry David Smith as a "societal complaint" (2004: 202, 236), the subject matter of romance is a key element of his study where, like the calling of spades, a relational assault is a relational assault, transcending time and place, much as Smith positions Costello and Joni Mitchell in a history that encompasses both the torch song and medieval troubadours (*ibid.*: xiii–xvii). However, I want to suggest that a cluster of issues lies at the heart of Costello's relational songs: the *subject position* of songs, inevitably focused on Costello as singer-songwriter, and leading towards complications in *confession*; the *relationship to women*, allowing that all relationships can include *confrontation* as well as *agreement*; and *women* themselves, against the background of *feminism*. That last one is especially important, since it points towards a period of *change* rather than *continuity*.

Writing in 1981, the time of *Trust*, Simon Frith was able to put Costello at the forefront of the love songs of his age, as well as tying in the "technical" matter of wordplay:

> The best contemporary pop song writer, Elvis Costello, writes as a man who grew up on pop and has had to cope ever since with a world in which romantic male fictions don't work, in which women don't play the same game. For Costello what is at stake is the language of love. He is obsessed with puns because they represent the possibilities, the ambiguities, the confusions of sex – "your mouth is made up, your mind is undone". (Frith 1988: 161)[50]

An important section of *Music for Pleasure* maps the period from 1979 to 1985, ending in the year between *Goodbye Cruel World* and *King Of America* (*ibid.*: 151–70). In addition, Frith's first book *The Sociology of Rock* (1978), revised as *Sound Effects* (1983), had included a section on "rock and sexuality" (Frith 1983b: 235–48), and an article with that title, jointly written with Angela McRobbie, was published in 1978 (Frith and Goodwin 1990: 371–89); for Greil Marcus's collection *Stranded*, in 1979, Frith chose *Beggars Banquet* (1968) by the Rolling Stones (Marcus 1996: 29–39). Frith and McRobbie identified "cock rock" and "teeny bop" as male and female alternatives, while analysing differing messages in songs by female singers (Tammy Wynette and Helen Reddy). Costello also identified two models that in his early years he tried to avoid: not only Frith and McRobbie's "cock rock" but an attitude he identified on the part of other, *male* singer-songwriters:

> "I mean that 'masochist' accusation I keep getting is only relevant for two or three tracks. On 'I'm Not Angry' it's there, plus 'Miracle Man' – but it's an interesting point because, as

far as I can see, those are the only two songs in the rock idiom
where a guy is admitting absolute defeat – taking all this
sexual abuse, say – without either doing the old James Taylor
self-pity bit or coming on all macho with the whole revenge
bit." (in Kent 1994: 195)

"There were two types of rock'n'roll that had become bank-
rupt to me. One was 'Look at me, I've got a big hairy chest
and a big willy!' and the other was the 'Fuck me, I'm sensitive'
Jackson Browne school of seduction." (in Flanagan 1990: 235)

In Frith and McRobbie's schema of 1978, singer-songwriters (Leonard Cohen,
Cat Stevens and Jackson Browne) belonged to "sixth form and student
culture" where "just as much as in teenybop culture, girls are expected to
be passive, as they listen quietly to rock poets". At the same time, however,
it provided "the one success route opened to women", albeit sold in terms
of "sensitivity, passivity, and sweetness" (Joan Baez, Judy Collins, Sandy
Denny); Joni Mitchell and Joan Armatrading fall outside the schema by
avoiding industry games, and getting labelled "awkward" as a result (Frith and
Goodwin 1990: 376, 377). In Frith's "Confessions of a Pop Critic" of
1985, Costello seems to lose touch with the agenda: through what was
called "the New Authenticity movement" (Costello's *King Of America* about
to appear) he was liable to be left with a combination of "rutting, romantic
men, mysterious, deceptive women". This was the period of Culture Club
and Frankie Goes To Hollywood, rock in its "modernist, formalist stage",
and Patti Smith showing the "link between modernism and post-modernism,
punk and beat, sexual liberation and sexual play" (Frith 1988: 165, 166,
168). Every word counts in the title of Simon Reynolds and Joy Press's
1995 survey, *The Sex Revolts: Gender, Rebellion and Rock'n'Roll*, but one
type left behind in all of its chapters, all its options for men and women to
have *explored*, is the expressive male singer-songwriter. Costello may have
disliked the hunched warblers of songs like 'Fire And Rain', 'Fountain Of
Sorrow', and 'Moon Shadow' but he was firmly of their number. An earlier
alternative, British glam rock, encompassed pop acts with cross-dressing,
memorable songs and records: David Bowie and Bryan Ferry, Mick Ronson
and Ian Hunter, Gary Glitter, Marc Bolan and Sweet, Elton John and Freddie
Mercury, and (of all people) the Roy Wood of Wizzard. Although "glitter

rock altered and confused the debate concerning authenticity/commercialism" (Cagle 2000: 127), this must have passed Costello by, who saw the Band in terms of age, boys and men:

> "I liked The Band because they had *beards*. They didn't look pretty and they weren't *boys*. [With] The Band, the sexuality was taken for granted, they were *men*, and yet they weren't dressing up as cowboys or anything, it wasn't phoney." (in Hoskyns 1993: 210)[51]

Costello convinced himself that a male *persona* ready to affect impotence would escape the twin dangers of showing off or using confession as seduction. However, his songs continued to rely on the singer-songwriter's key assumption, that the first person could be aligned with the singer. Confession is one of the major themes of Costello's liner notes, as the following extracts demonstrate; note that Costello is aware of the various comparisons: detection, talking cures, and the Catholic confessional.

> There was as much imagination as experience in the words of this record. Whatever lyrical code or fancy was employed, the words came straight out of my life plain enough. I hadn't necessarily developed the confidence or the cruelty to speak otherwise. (*My Aim Is True* n95)

> I never really understood the accusations of misogyny that were levelled at the lyrics of *This Year's Model*. They clearly contained more sense of disappointment than disgust. In any case, most of these songs were works of imagination rather than products of experience. The temptations and distractions of the touring life would soon enough add the more cynical and guilty edge found in 'Little Triggers', 'Pump It Up' and 'Hand In Hand'. (*This Year's Model* n02)

> Personal and global matters are spoken about with the same vocabulary; maybe this was a mistake. (*Armed Forces* n02)

> You don't have to be a detective or a psychiatrist to work out what is going on. (*Imperial Bedroom* n02)

Listening again to the raw and ragged early takes, demos, and rejected songs, I am not sorry to have employed just a little restraint and reserve in the final draft ... The record is not exactly easy listening as it is, but I trust that it isn't just the experience of one person ... It sounds like music rather than confession. (*Imperial Bedroom* n02)

In truth I didn't need a producer. I probably needed a nurse (or a priest). (*Goodbye Cruel World* n95)

This is not the time for me to speak specifically about some of the personal events behind some of this album. These are pretty plainspoken songs. (*King Of America* n05)

A pissed off thirty-two-year-old, divorcé's version of *This Year's Model*.[52] (*Blood And Chocolate* n95)

There were a lot of things that I wouldn't have to do again, like messing up my life just so I could write stupid little songs about it. (*Blood And Chocolate* n02)

This record says the world we are making is grim, and I believe that it is. We are cruel to each other, we lie and manipulate until the unworthy encounter a love to which we must surrender. It may come in the shape of a man or a woman or it may not. It's just some songs that I wrote. (*Mighty Like A Rose* n03)

If this record ended up just a little closer to the truth than these songs sometimes get it was almost by accident. What do you want? This isn't confession. This is pop music. I found myself playing in a rock and roll band again. If this did not require forgiveness, then it did assume some small understanding of anger and when to let it go. (*Brutal Youth* n02)

On the other hand, Paul Simon is more decisive: "I'm not committed to telling the truth. I'm committed to finding what the truth is in the song. But that's not a commitment to telling everyone what's going on with me" (in Zollo 1997: 104). Costello seemed never so sure of the exact role of confession in songs, whether "plainspoken" extracts of reality or material for production; women are caught between social representation and songwriting premise, neither of them comfortable roles. In occupational terms, Costello inhabited a typical version of the man's world (band, producers, management, road crew), where women appear in recorded performances as supportive vocalists: Caron Wheeler and Claudia Fontaine (*Punch The Clock*), Chrissie Hynde (*Spike*), Cait O'Riordan (*Blood And Chocolate*), Lucinda Williams and Emmylou Harris (*The Delivery Man*).[53] The questions to put to Costello's commitment to singing about romance are: which man? which woman? The charge is that both sexes remained consistent while in the real (or even the art-real) world both changed, and dramatically. Costello's women never got jobs, gave birth, got promoted to posts in senior management: they spent all day and every day getting involved in scrapes and flings and dangerous liaisons. Costello ensures that bitterness and recrimination are to hand:[54] adapting the words of Aimee Mann's 'The Other End Of The Telescope', he "felt that the text needed to be more accusative before I could really make it my own" (*All This Useless Beauty* n01). Interviewed by a men's style magazine in 1994, Costello comments on how he has been represented as an observer of relationships between men and women:

> "I've always had to put up with people saying I hate women. And I really don't. I really hate men! I think men are the guilty parties a lot of the time … People don't listen to the words properly. The point is that, if you're a faddish sort of singer you can act away with all kinds of stuff and people think you're great. Rod Stewart can sing all of these evil things about women and people say what a chap he is! The Stones wrote 'Stupid Girl' and they are, like, heroes. I wrote 'This Year's Girl', saying that fashion is a trap, a much more compassionate song, and everyone said I was a misogynist. Work that one out. I can't. The moral judgement, if any, is against men who create the situations. I've always thought the songs could be seen as feminist." (in Hill 1994: 184)

Smith agrees with the thrust of this claim: "this is the guy *everybody* deemed a misogynist. Just consider the evidence and you will quickly see just how *wrong* those people were" (2004: 271). Depicting confrontation, Costello positions men as the more deceiving, to adapt the terms of Philip Larkin's poem (Larkin 1988: 32). Even 'White Knuckles' (*Trust*), for all its visceral imagery ("white knuckles on black and blue skin") is *verité*, social-realist drama, vignettes of working-class life: mum and sister, "the boys". But where does the violence come from? "Something to do with violence/A long way back", says Larkin in 'Love Again' (*ibid.*: 215). As Christopher Ricks observed of Robert Lowell, violence has a way of seeping into ordinary language (1984: 256–73): phrases on *Imperial Bedroom* like "giving you what for always worked for me before" and "the hit man" in 'Shabby Doll', "I even slapped your face and made you cry", in 'Boy With A Problem'. Wordplay can distance subject matter, so that a comic rhyme, "you don't look so glamorous/whenever I feel so amorous", is uncomfortable in a song with punches and knock-outs – 'TKO (Boxing Day)' (*Punch The Clock*). 'Kinder Murder' (*Brutal Youth*) is a rape song, an extremity of men and violence towards women, so that for a man critically to confront that issue takes courage: compare Tori Amos's 'Me And A Gun' or 'The Boiler' of Rhoda Dakar with the Special AKA.[55] For me, the sonic image of men making nasty music and the over-expressive male vocal correspond to the problem that the reflection is intended to cure. By contrast, Graham Parker's 'You Can't Be Too Strong' was a male abortion song, as slowly paced as Costello's 'Alison', but beautiful in its hopeless misunderstanding ("did they tear it out?"), resistance ("go see the boys"), and final submission ("it gets dark down by Luna Park, but everybody else is squeezing out the sparks").[56] And for 'TKO (Boxing Day)', by contrast, Morrissey's 'Boxers' (1995) shows feminism's effect on masculinity registered by a "weary wife", mentioned only to be led gently away, leaving three crummy blokes united by failure: the feckless boxer, Morrissey observing and, "still true", the magical word "nephew" – not son but "nephew", useless at boxing and no progeny.[57] 'So Like Candy' (*Mighty Like A Rose*), on the other hand, has Costello and Paul McCartney gazing at Candy: pop memories of the Velvet Underground and Jesus and Mary Chain. But what does she actually do, day to day? Concerned with looks and clothes and kept going by tablets, she's dumped her boyfriend; upset, he digs up old photos; she finally scratches his records, uninterested in music and (says the music) a bit scary.

With *Spike*, however, things "loosened up". There is a more distanced approach to characters on *Spike* and *Mighty Like A Rose*, as in writing songs for others (the album for Wendy James by Costello and Cait O'Riordan, songs on *All This Useless Beauty*), and working collaboratively on songs presented as letters in *The Juliet Letters*. *All This Useless Beauty*, *When I Was Cruel* and *The Delivery Man* continue to suggest a variety of subject positions. But in a final twist, unlike the track 'Uncomplicated' (*Blood And Chocolate*), *North* is uncomplicated. Building on *Painted From Memory*, the album returns to lyric as the point where words and music meet, [58] the outpouring of emotion directly to the beloved, with two female protagonists, one lost, one found: "I want someone, I lost someone". We find nature ('Fallen'), witty rhymes ('I'm In The Mood Again'), and the female figure addressed and included by intimacy ('Still'). For Costello, *North* represented in some ways his greatest personal struggle, clarifying the relationship between truth and confession. This is an odd point to have reached, since it is in some fundamental sense the simplest, as these two songwriters remind us:

> "The subject of popular songs has been the same forever. And if you put it in the right setting, that is the subject matter of popular songs. People need it. They never get tired of hearing … songs about love. It's one of the big things that we think about, and this is one of the areas where we can express it." (Paul Simon, in Zollo 1997: 117)

> "I think that songs are primarily for courting, for finding your mate. For deep things. For summoning love, for healing broken nights, and for the central accompaniment to life's tasks. Which is no mean or small thing." (Leonard Cohen, in Zollo 1997: 348)

A second *boundary* is songs about or for children. Costello once tried his hand at a Disney song, eventually issued both as a solo demo (expanded *Spike*) and a prettier rendition on an album by bass player Rob Wasserman (available on the expanded *Mighty Like A Rose*). Costello's note mentions mice, men, and mercy:

> 'Put Your Big Toe In The Milk Of Human Kindness' is a demo of a song originally written for a Disney movie. Mercifully, the Mouse declined the tune, and I was able to cut it a few years later with Rob Wasserman and Marc Ribot for Rob's album

> *Trios.* It now sounds to me as if I was attempting to write
> something like the Cahn/Van Heusen song 'High Hopes'. The
> closest I ever got was 'God's Comic'. (*Spike* n01)

Not quite a brilliant mistake, the song is both delightful and comically bad
at the same time. Costello is characteristically aware of precedent, and I want
to select a couple of others too, without making the more obvious suggestion that in order to gauge the competition, you should try *Disney's
Greatest Hits*. 'High Hopes' because Costello says so,[59] 'Magic Moments'
because Costello was to work with Bacharach,[60] and 'You've Got A Friend
In Me' because its composer Randy Newman became the great measure of
the singer-songwriter who could turn his hand to any old product required
by the Disney corporation.[61] Costello's song has a chord sequence that
supports lovely guitar and bass duets in the *Trios* version. The music sounds
to me like 'If I Were A Bell' from *Guys and Dolls*: try the line, "You take
the Himalayas, you'll take Manhattan's finest mountain top", simple I–iii–IV–
V, followed by IV to minor iv. There's a nice, comical 5–1 descent in the
bass, beloved of doo-wop, although maybe the descent is repeated a few
times too many. Maybe it lacks a contrast section and, compared with the
other examples, the wisdom of including actual children ('High Hopes') or
whistling ('Magic Moments') are not to be underestimated. Costello suggests that the best he could do in this mode was 'God's Comic' (*Spike*),
one of a trio of jokey songs about mortality, heaven and hell: in 'Damnation's
Cellar' (*The Juliet Letters*) and 'This Is Hell' (*Brutal Youth*). All three rely
on the same gag, that hell includes music and other artworks that demonstrate poor taste: Andrew Lloyd Webber's *Requiem* in 'God's Comic';[62] in
'Damnation's Cellar' all sorts of references, including a bad joke about
confusing Nijinsky the dancer and horse; and in 'This Is Hell' including a line
about the superiority of John Coltrane's version of 'My Favourite Things' to
Julie Andrews's. The joke about Lloyd Webber is lightest and funniest of
the three.

Cahn, David, and Newman all have greeting-card lines, lines to embarrass
any serious person. 'High Hopes' is full of them, notably, "Whoops, there
goes another problem, ker-plop". 'Magic Moments' has perfectly constructed
lines (◡◡◡/, ◡◡◡/, ◡◡◡/, ◡◡◡//) with rhyming runs (and inner half-
rhymes) like these:

The way that we *cheered* whenever our *team* was scoring a *touchdown*,
The time that the *floor* fell out of my *car* when I put the *clutch down*,
The penny *arcade*, the games that we *played*, the fun and the *prizes*,
The Halloween *hop* when everyone *came* in funny dis*guises*.

With simple line construction, Randy Newman achieves easy lightness: "When the road looks rough ahead/And you're miles and miles from your nice warm bed/Just remember what your old pal said:/ 'Boy, you've got a friend in me'." Set next to these, 'Put Your Big Toe In The Milk Of Human Kindness' tries too hard, caught between attempted simplicity and over-complexity, with words too tough and obscure. What do you suppose this couplet means, kids? "You take the Himalayas, you'll take Manhattan's finest mountain top/ He wouldn't change his whiskey sour for any bitter crop." A section beginning "But always so contrary" and ending "unhand your mind" presents a mixture of theology and complex line construction. Metaphors mix: "fly", "toe", "milk"; "belief" dangles, unrhymed; and there is the odd phrase, "unhand your mind". Plus, alongside Father Christmas, who invited *the Virgin Mary* to the party? Given that going on at length about a throwaway song is unfair, there seems nevertheless to be something in lightness of subject and verbal construction that eludes Costello.

Jokes, now they're a different thing, and there are real song-based laughs: the "insult to the pig" in 'Swine' (*The Juliet Letters*), those "ugly children" in 'I Thought I Had A Weakness' (*The Juliet Letters*), and 'God's Comic' (*Spike*). Costello's spoken voice-over for *The Right Spectacle* (2005) is informative and entertaining; when, in a gloomy video for 'So Like Candy', he shares the limelight with an up-and-coming piglet, it's hilarious.

Novelist *manqué*

"Don't tell me you don't know the difference between a lover and a writer," says Costello in 'Everyday I Write The Book'. In its attention to the objects of writing, the pen and electric typewriter, the track recalls Squeeze's 'Black Coffee In Bed' ("there's a stain on my notebook"), which features a hearty backing vocal from Costello at the coda, and is found on the Squeeze album following *East Side Story*, which Costello had produced.[63] The idea of romance in chapters resembles a song by John Hiatt, 'The Way We Make A Broken Heart', beautifully covered on Ry Cooder's *Borderline* (1980). The metaphor may be expressive of that generation of pop musicians self-consciously regarding themselves as writers, and points us towards a way of seeing Costello's words as those of a novelist *manqué* rather than poet.[64]

"The way a writer names his characters provides a good index to the way he sees the world – to his reality-level, his responsiveness to the accidental humour and freakish poetry of life" (Amis 1987:1).[65] No mean namer himself, Martin Amis goes on to praise the names invented by Saul Bellow for the characters of his novels. There are many fictional characters in Costello's songs, indicating his occasional use of the single song as a type of short story, more so than the themed album. The names he has invented for songs include the great quartet Natasha and Elsie, Gus and Alfie ('Chelsea'), the eponymous Veronica, Mr Misery, Betty Felon, Charlie Sedarka, Mr Getgood, Candy, and Joe Porterhouse. *The Delivery Man* appears to be a theatre piece in the making, with a set of names evoking the American South: Abel, Geraldine, Ivy, Vivien. 'Little Atoms' (*All This Useless Beauty*) is a short essay on the subject, based around personal names that correspond to flowers and fruit (Marigold, Iris, Cherry), an attribute (Victor), or virtues (Faith, Hope, Charity). *All This Useless Beauty* is a great namer, including elsewhere Chopin and Atlas.

Where I think he's even better is in his sense of naming places and, for these, it is helpful to refer to a distinction made by David Lodge, who saw literature acting in a "metonymic" or "metaphorical" way (Lodge 1997).[66] To adapt, metonymic place names are characterized by realist precision, the metaphoric ones are places of the mind or of the imagination. '(I Don't Want To Go To) Chelsea' is a terrific example of the former, named precisely for its parenthetical avoidance. Rotherhithe in 'New Amsterdam' was somewhere I had to look up on a map, and was impressed by its being both representative (of London the metropolis) as well as obscure. 'New Amsterdam' may be a more metaphorical name, given the possibility of its recalling Holland as well as the USA, as the original name for New York, a double-take also found in Billy Bragg's 'New England'. On the other hand, Montgomery in 'Tokyo Storm Warning' seems to act as a place that spurs connection in the mind, to the era of Civil Rights and Martin Luther King, especially since the KKK is in town. I suggest the "metonymic" place names include the two already mentioned, Liverpool and London (also in 'New Amsterdam'), the Hammersmith Hotel ('Fish 'n' Chip Paper', *Trust*), Southampton ('American

Without Tears', *King Of America*), and the great trio of "the Mersey and the Thames and the Tyne" in 'Oliver's Army'.[67] Düsseldorf, in 'Chewing Gum' (*Spike*) is realistic, as opposed to the creepy, metaphoric Düsseldorf of Randy Newman's 'In Germany Before The War' (1977). The chorus of 'This Town' (*Spike*), nowhere named, has all the makings of Lou Reed and John Cale's 'Small Town' (on *Songs For Drella*, 1990): somewhere to leave in a hurry. 'My Dark Life' (*All This Useless Beauty*) pins its places with adjectives: Texas, Tennessee, Missouri and England are, respectively, ugly, nameless, peculiar and heartless. In addition to Montgomery, there are some suggestive metaphoric places: Bedlam (*The Delivery Man*), Hell as in 'This Is Hell' (*Brutal Youth*), Caracas and Idaho (Idaho in the middle of nowhere in 'American Without Tears'). In 'Tramp The Dirt Down', England's metaphoric status is indicated as much by the stylized music as by the words.[68] 'Times Square' in 'The Bridge I Burned' (*All This Useless Beauty*) feels cinematic.

As we move from the individual song to the album, good examples of Costello's story-telling are found in his curious decision to issue the retrospective selection *Girls Girls Girls* (1989) in four different format versions: CD, cassette, vinyl and DAT (digital audio tape). I've never seen the latter and don't have access to its listing, so will limit discussion to the three more familiar formats: Table 3.8 enables the reader to reconstruct each side. No cover versions were included (nothing from *Almost Blue*), ensuring that the key singer-songwriter issues, authorial presence and authentic self-expression, are germane. Costello's purpose for the different arrangement of tracks by format was that each side would "tell a number of different stories" (*Girls Girls Girls* n89). The smaller subdivisions of the vinyl and cassette versions, as well as the greater compression of the vinyl version, offer pointers. All formats begin side one with 'Watching The Detectives' and 'I Hope You're Happy Now', a side that seems to concern itself with surveillance and mistrust, the observation of other people. Those first two tracks also set out the temporal span, Costello's earliest recording in 1977 as well as a track from his last album in 1986. Side two has a consistent run of four tracks – 'Man Out Of Time', 'Brilliant Mistake', 'New Lace Sleeves', and 'Accidents Will Happen' – and seems to be more self-observation, with a tendency towards fracture and disorientation. Side three seems to be about betrayal and guilt, always starting with 'Alison', and containing 'Almost Blue', 'Riot Act' and, notable both for its effect and the time it takes, 'I Want You'. Side four is set apart as the public or political story, 'Oliver's Army' and 'Shipbuilding' acting as its bookends, apart from on cassette where 'Clowntime Is Over' is added to conclude. The vinyl version curiously interpolated 'Stranger In The House' into the fourth side. Table 3.8 is a guide to the various versions for further study, and includes Larry David Smith's categories for each song that his book discusses.[69]

Another example of a self-contained sequence is found on *Mighty Like A Rose*, a group of three songs that concluded what was the first side: 'Invasion Hit Parade', 'Harpies Bizarre' and 'After The Fall'.[70] The three songs form a suite which Costello has called "Cold War nostalgia", exploring the consequences of the break-up of Communist Eastern Europe around 1989. A fictional man in the first song finds himself bombarded with Western trash; the second and third songs explore the fate of a fictional woman (*Mighty Like A Rose* n02).

Novel in song: 'American Without Tears'

This is the single track which I think best sums up Costello's novelist tendency: it appeared first on *King Of America*, but the listener should track down 'American Without Tears No. 2 (Twilight Version)', originally a B-side (to 'Blue Chair', 1987), then on *Out Of Our Idiot*, and finally on an expanded *Blood And Chocolate*. The combination of both tracks, alongside 'Tokyo Storm Warning' (*Blood And Chocolate*), might illustrate Costello's ability to deliver convincing prolixity in songs, something that would put him in select company with this aspect of the work of Bob Dylan, Joni Mitchell, and Leonard Cohen.[71]

The song is a waltzing three-time, phrased in fours with extensions to five, or six in the chorus. Pace is all-important, since it enables the song's details to register: the original is about 144 crotchet beats (or 48 bars) to the minute, the "cover" a more sprightly 180 (or 60 bars to the minute), possibly a touch too fast. Harmony is nearly always a clear diatonic major, with the one minor at the chorus ("don't speak any English") and again at the coda; a change of key from G to A provides uplift for the final verse in both versions. The twilight version has a slightly different, "descending chromatic bass" chord for the start of the chorus and, interestingly, varies the harmony for one line, lending it significance: "Just like me she found out what true love is all about" (2'25–30). Arrangements differ greatly, the *King*

Table 3.8 *Girls Girls Girls* (1989): tracks included on different formats and Smith categories

CD order	Original album	Cassette	Vinyl	Smith categories
		Track numbers		

CD order	Original album	Cassette	Vinyl	Smith categories
		CD1		
'Watching The Detectives'	*My Aim Is True*	A1	A1	R1
'I Hope You're Happy Now'	*Blood And Chocolate*	A2	A2	R2a
'This Year's Girl'	*This Year's Model*	A3		S1
'Lover's Walk'	*Trust*	A6	A4	R2b
'Pump It Up'	*This Year's Model*	A5	A3	S1
'Strict Time'	*Trust*	A4		R1
'Temptation'	*Get Happy!!*	A7	A5	WP
'Chelsea'	*This Year's Model*	A12	A7	S1
'High Fidelity'	*Get Happy!!*	A13	A8	R1
'Lovable'	*King Of America*	A9	A6	R1
'Mystery Dance'	*My Aim Is True*	A11		I1
'Big Tears' (1978)	*Ten Bloody Marys*	A14		
'Uncomplicated'	*Blood And Chocolate*			R2a
'Lipstick Vogue'	*This Year's Model*	A15	A9	R2a
'Man Out Of Time'	*Imperial Bedroom*	B1	B1	N1
'Brilliant Mistake'	*King Of America*	B2	B2	R1
'New Lace Sleeves'	*Trust*	B3	B3	S1
'Accidents Will Happen'	*Armed Forces*	B4	B4	N1
'Beyond Belief'	*Imperial Bedroom*	B12	B8	N1
'Black And White World'	*Get Happy!!*			R1
'Green Shirt'	*Armed Forces*	B8	B6	WP
'The Loved Ones'	*Imperial Bedroom*	B6		N1
'New Amsterdam'	*Get Happy!!*	B10		R1
'Red Shoes'	*My Aim Is True*	B11	B7	R1
'King Horse'	*Get Happy!!*	B7	B5	S1
'Big Sister's Clothes'	*Trust*			R1
		CD2		
'Alison'	*My Aim Is True*	C1	C1	R1
'Men Called Uncle'	*Get Happy!!*	C5		R1
'Party Girl'	*Armed Forces*		C3	R1
'Shabby Doll'	*Imperial Bedroom*	C2		R1
'Motel Matches'	*Get Happy!!*			R1
'Tiny Steps' (1978)	*Ten Bloody Marys*			

Table 3.8 – *continued*

| | | Track numbers | | |
CD order	Original album	Cassette	Vinyl	Smith categories
'Almost Blue'	*Imperial Bedroom*	C6	C4	R1
'Riot Act'	*Get Happy!!*	C7	C5	R2a
'Love Field'	*Goodbye Cruel World*			NI
'Possession'	*Get Happy!!*			R1
'Poisoned Rose'	*King Of America*	C9	C6	R1
'Indoor Fireworks'	*King Of America*		C2	R3
'I Want You'	*Blood And Chocolate*	C10	C7	R1
'Oliver's Army'	*Armed Forces*	D1	D1	S1
'Pills And Soap'	*Punch The Clock*	D3	D2	S1
'Sunday's Best'	*Armed Forces*			WP
'Watch Your Step'	*Trust*	D6		I1
'Less Than Zero'	*My Aim Is True*			S1
'Clubland'	*Trust*	D8	D4	S1
'Tokyo Storm Warning'	*Blood And Chocolate*	D9	D5	NI
'Shipbuilding'	*Punch The Clock*	D10	D6	S1

		Cassette only		
'Honey, Are You Straight?'	*Blood And Chocolate*	A8		R2B
'Girls Talk' (1980)	*Ten Bloody Marys*	A10		
'Poor Napoleon'	*Blood And Chocolate*	A16		R1
'Home Is Anywhere'	*Blood And Chocolate*	B5		R1
'Turning The Town Red' (1984)	*Out Of Our Idiot*	B9		
'Sleep Of The Just'	*King Of America*	B13		R1
'Our Little Angel'	*King Of America*	C3		R1
'The Long Honeymoon'	*Imperial Bedroom*	C4		R1
'Crimes Of Paris'	*Blood And Chocolate*	C8		NI
'Jack Of All Parades'	*King Of America*	C11		RC
'Little Palaces'	*King Of America*	D2		S1
'Night Rally'	*This Year's Model*	D4		S1
'American Without Tears'	*King Of America*	D5		R1
'Suit Of Lights'	*King Of America*	D7		NI
'Clowntime Is Over'	*Get Happy!!*	D11		NI

		Vinyl only		
'I'll Wear It Proudly'	*King Of America*		C8	R3
'Stranger In The House' (1977)	*Ten Bloody Marys*		D3	

Key to Smith categories

Code	Category
I I	'Role issue' editorial (p. 238)
R I	Relational complaint or elegy (pp. 240–2)
R2a	Relational assault: childish, physically violent, mean-spirited, diabolical (pp. 242–4)
R2b	Relational warning: includes him-or-me confrontations, threats of revenge, relational danger signs, philosophical pronouncements, advisory commentaries (pp. 242–4)
R3	Various relational topics: commentary, struggle, fantasy, plea, pugilism (pp. 244–6)
RC	Relational celebration (p. 240)
S I	Societal complaint (pp. 235–6)
NI	Narrative impressionism (p. 244)
WP	Pure, unadulterated wordplay (p. 247)

Of America band in the original at its supportive best, the cover played entirely by an overdubbed Costello, with a marvellous, rasping harmonica at the chorus's tail. The original has a sweet introduction as well, starting "too low" in F and giving immediate uplift and, maybe, the sense of a story already under way; the cover cuts in immediately, after two grand Gs in the piano, with the sense of "As I was saying ...". Both versions have extended fades, Costello noodling without words in the original with a touch of Van Morrison. Costello has told of the song's circumstances: *King Of America* n05 recounts how he met two former GI brides in Florida who told him their "tale of exile and escape", adding that the song is "as close as this record comes to having a theme".

The two versions are full of detail (1 for the original, 2 for the second version):

> *Song titles:* 'It's Too Late' (Carole King, presumably, 1) and 'A Fool Such As I' (Elvis Presley, 2)

> *Places:* New Orleans, Nottingham, Southampton, America (1), Caracas, Miami, Coventry, Idaho, Havana, Florida, New Orleans (2)

> *Names:* Hitler, Sheriff of Nottingham and Little John, Costello's grandfather (1), Arnie LaFlamme, Sammy Davis Junior (2)

> *Other detail:* Revlon and Crimplene, chewing gum and fine nylon hose (1), The Voice of America (2)

In the first version, one thing that enables the sung line to approach the prose sentence, as a consequence of the line's musical length, is the frequent use of "and" to create a small listing, helping to sharpen precision: "freezing and unkind", "Revlon and Crimplene", "piano and cocktail murderess", "crying for years and for years", "beauty queen and the other was her friend", "rogues and rascals and showbiz impresarios", "chewing gum and fine nylon hose", "I'm the Sheriff of Nottingham and this is Little John", "the cold facts and lies", "suspenders and young girls' backsides", "I'm in America and running from you", "I open my mouth and I can't seem to talk". As well as that literal device, occasional sentences include phrases that run across lines and provide continuity:

> While the boys were licking Hitler, they had something to defend from men armed with chewing gum and fine nylon hose.

> Though he wasn't tall or handsome, she laughed when he told her, "I'm the Sheriff of Nottingham and this is Little John."

> At the dock in Southampton, full of tearful goodbyes, newsreel commentators said, "Cheerio, GI brides!"

The second version is more plot-led, as though it was a potential film script, and perhaps loses the delicacy of the original as a result. But there's a nice list at one point: "dowdy, down and miserable". *Blood And Chocolate* n95 explains that:

> The new edition of the story is told from the perspective of the vanished husband of one of the women in the *King Of America* version of the song. He tries to pluck up courage to return from his South American exile but in the end he becomes cynical and loses his nerve. Some of the locations have also slipped in a "Twilight Zone" way. This is alluded to in the sub-title and the electric guitar part.

Surely this is a film script, and note that it is from the same time as Costello appeared in and provided music for *Straight to Hell,* Alex Cox's 1986 film. Mention of film seems appropriate since, taken as a pair, 'American Without Tears' comes close to being a small-scale, pop-song equivalent to a narrative film or fat novel: describing the "extra verses" Costello also describes the possibilities as "a continuation of the story or even a sequel" (*Blood And Chocolate* n95). It is a shame that the second song didn't get beyond the demo stage, or that both versions don't appear concurrently on the one album, but they form an interesting pair.

Costello's "collected prose"

For a course of study entitled "words and music", Costello could appear many times. Most of his recorded output takes the form of songs which bring together words and music, and our final chapter will examine the words of critics about Costello's words and music. Between these familiar topics, a third area: Costello's own writings about his own words and music. In the bookshop, the songs would be Costello's *Collected Poems,* filed under the author's name, with criticism filed under author criticism, and here we have Costello's *Collected Prose.* I am of the view that Costello's collected prose is a substantial exercise in authorial, critical mediation, to be set alongside Henry James's prefaces and the Stravinsky conversation books; as James Perone says, several times, "Costello's liner notes should be considered essential material" (Perone 1998: 107, 113, 114).[72] To date, Costello has written on his own work, but he might in future write essays on others; commenting on his own cover versions, he often makes penetrating remarks about other musicians and songwriters. The publishing context of the liner notes is important, as Costello controls the prose pieces, their content as well as, presumably, the time taken over them. While it is possible that they were spoken by him and transcribed by someone else,[73] there are convincing signs that this is not the case; *Kojak Variety* n04 includes this reminiscence:

> What follows is the original sleeve note for this album. It was my first rock and roll record to contain such notes. I thought that the disc could stand something that tipped a hat to the likes of Tony Barrow, whose liner notes for the Beatles I had

> pored over for many hours, as reading them again and again
> would reveal more story.

Costello's initial inspiration thus seems to have been the notes that were commonly to be found on records during the early 1960s: *The Freewheelin' Bob Dylan* (1963), for example, included an essay in criticism by Nat Hentoff, with entries for all thirteen songs and commentary by Dylan himself, presumably extracted by interview. The other model is the programme note of classical music: reissue notes are retrospective, while the classical notes (for *Il Sogno*, for instance) are prescriptive. The immediate spur to the production of these notes was CD itself: the notes became part of the effort that went into what was a field day for the record industry, when old or formerly abandoned tracks were presented as new. Liner notes were written mostly by journalists or academics with a particular specialism: some artists contributed, if only small commentaries and memoirs. It is characteristic of Costello that he went about his task in such a thorough and helpful manner, and key evidence of how much interest he takes in the enjoyment and engagement of his listeners. Costello has produced many commentaries on his recorded output, which are listed in Table 3.9.

The first liner notes are those for *Girls Girls Girls* in 1989. This is complicated by the fact that there were four different versions of the compilation, for CD, cassette, vinyl, and DAT. The latter adds no song (and note) found elsewhere, however; otherwise, all formats include at least one unique song (and note). *The Juliet Letters* (1993), *Kojak Variety* (1995), *Extreme Honey* (1997), and *Bespoke Songs, Lost Dogs, Detours And Rendezvous* (1998) all appeared with original notes during or after the first set of reissues on Demon. "Classical" works like *The Juliet Letters*, *For The Stars*, *North* and *Il Sogno* could be considered separately in that they follow the tradition of the classical programme note. In fact, *Il Sogno* and *North* have brief informative notes, and Costello's contribution to *Il Sogno* is a detailed synopsis including analytical notes, while the introduction is written by Vaughan Sinclair with interview input by Costello. *The Juliet Letters* note was reprinted as an introduction to the published score,[74] evidently unedited, since the last paragraph concerns technical aspects of the recording. The two television soundtracks, *GBH* and *Jake's Progress*, did not include commentary by Costello. *The Right Spectacle*, a DVD compilation of music videos

Table 3.9 Inventory of Costello liner notes, indicating dates at which they were included

Album	Date	Notes with original reissue	Notes with Demon reissue	Notes with Edsel/Rhino reissue
My Aim Is True	1977		1993	2001
This Year's Model	1978		1993	2002
Armed Forces	1979		1993	2002
Get Happy!!	1980		1993	2003
Trust	1981		1993	2003
Almost Blue	1981		1993	2004
Imperial Bedroom	1982		1994	2002
Punch The Clock	1983		1995	2003
Goodbye Cruel World	1984		1995	2004
King Of America	1986		1995	2005
Blood And Chocolate	1986		1995	2002
Girls Girls Girls	1989	1989		
Spike	1989			2001
Mighty Like A Rose	1991			2002
The Juliet Letters	1993	1993		2006
Brutal Youth	1994			2002
Kojak Variety	1995	1995		2004
All This Useless Beauty	1996			2001
Extreme Honey	1997	1997		
Bespoke Songs	1998	1998		
Painted From Memory	1998			
For The Stars	2001	2001		
When I Was Cruel	2002			
North	2003	2003		
The Delivery Man	2004			
Il Sogno	2004	2004		
The Right Spectacle DVD	2005	2005		
My Flame Burns Blue	2005	2005		
The River In Reverse	2006			

North and The River In Reverse include accompanying DVD material. The Live In Memphis DVD (2005) also includes filmed documentary material. Notes accompanied neither the compilations Ten Bloody Marys & Ten How's Your Fathers (1980) and Out Of Our Idiot (1987) nor the soundtrack albums GBH (1991) and Jake's Progress (1996). The note for The Juliet Letters is dated as having been written in 1992.

(2005), does include printed notes to the bonus tracks, but also, in keeping with the format, "director's cut" banter in the commentary to accompany each video. *North* and *The River In Reverse* both include bonus DVDs with Costello speech: at the time of writing, this was a new mode, mixing aural CD and visual DVD. The first column of Table 3.9 indicates albums that, for these various reasons, contained liner notes at their original release.

The second and third columns of Table 3.9 show liner notes included as part of the two separate reissue programmes: Demon (1993–5) and Edsel/Rhino (2001–6). The first five Demon reissues form a set: they are all laid out within quotation marks, as though derived from an interview, and contain differently formatted sections, as though a commentator intervenes to provide information. Word count is fairly low, with a separate section in each case for the bonus tracks added at the reissue. With *Almost Blue*, the note expands in length, the device of commentator intervention is all but dropped, but the quotation marks remain. *Imperial Bedroom* is also a lengthy essay, but preserves the quotation marks, if only as part of its visual design. With *Punch The Clock*, both intervention and quotation marks have gone, albeit with an occasional italicized section seemingly for variety of font; bonus tracks continue to have their separate section. This pattern held good for the remainder of the Demon reissue programme, so that *King Of America* was a particularly extended essay, *Blood And Chocolate* slightly less so. When the Edsel/Rhino reissue series commences (2001), the question arises of whether to reprint the Demon version, rewrite the note altogether, or something in between: all three solutions are found. Note too that the latter reissues do not make a separate section of their bonus tracks. As might be expected, the first five records all have substantial rewrites from their limited models: *My Aim Is True* is a good example of substantial increase. With *Almost Blue* and *Imperial Bedroom*, where the initial Demon reissue was already more substantial, the Edsel/Rhino reissue contains both replication and new material, even referring back to the earlier note (*Almost Blue* n04: "I have previously described this album as ..."). The same holds for *Imperial Bedroom*. With *Punch The Clock*, we reach the obvious consequence: simply to reprint the 1995 note while adding a scene-setter opening and "postscript 2003" on the bonus tracks. However, *Goodbye Cruel World* really is a complete rewrite, including reference back to the 1995 version. *King Of America* and *Blood And Chocolate* have new essays, the one on *King Of*

America again more substantial, close to being a full critical autobiography. From here on, all of the rock albums – *Spike*, *Mighty Like A Rose*, *Brutal Youth* and *All This Useless Beauty* – receive notes for the first time, of varying lengths. *The Juliet Letters* and *Kojak Variety* were both issued originally with liner notes in 1993 and 1995: for *Kojak Variety* the 2004 reissue reprints the original with a preface and postscript for bonus tracks; *The Juliet Letters* has an extended postscript covering aspects of the work's reception and notes for the bonus tracks. This leaves *Extreme Honey* and *Bespoke Songs*, similar to *Girls Girls Girls* as compilations including notes, with *Extreme Honey* taking the form of a diary covering 1988–97. One feature of the second series of reissues is that, with the possible exception of *Spike*, each album begins with the "scene-setter" opening (*Spike* seems to lack one), a device Costello describes at one point: "I have begun each note accompanying this programme of re-releases with an anecdote in hope [*sic*] of capturing something of the moment in which the album was made" (*Punch The Clock* n03).

To examine just one example, both sets of notes for *King Of America* (1995 and 2005) are substantial, the latter the peak of the liner notes *in toto*. Both start with the Coward Brothers tour, the 1995 version as objective observation. Costello then encapsulates his approach to producing the Specials and Pogues, and follows with a joke, referring to Cait O'Riordan of the Pogues: "After that, I pretty much gave up producing other people's records. You can only marry the bass player once." Both the Coward Brothers yarns and the description of the Presley TCB band naturally turn into a carnival of references: George Jones, Bobby Charles, Leon Payne, Hank Williams, Dale Hawkins, Ricky Nelson, Elvis Presley, Randy Newman. References continue to appear throughout the note. Even the first recording as a band for *King Of America*, 'The Big Light', is referred back to their TCB performance of 'Mystery Train'. Note that Costello knew this band more from their Gram Parsons connection (stories familiar from the *Almost Blue* note). The *King Of America* note is very much musician territory, with references galore and technological detail. The entry of jazz musicians Earl Palmer and Ray Brown bring by osmosis a set of references bordering on the popular-sacred (Dizzy Gillespie, Charlie Parker, Duke Ellington, Little Richard), and there's a genuine sense from Costello of being in exalted company, and even out of his depth, describing himself as "some kind of crazy limey millionaire who went round hiring my jazz and RnB heroes on a whim". Costello's descriptions of these sessions are filled with wonder: the players at one point are in a semicircle, "in support of the singer", "live", with the musicians making "wonderful use of this extra space". Comparison with the Attractions is inevitable:

> This was just the kind of detail that was impossible to isolate in my recordings with the Attractions (although that does not mean that you cannot hear such fine playing). It is just that you would have to listen a little harder due to the claustro-phobic nature of our sound (*King of America* n95).

An honest account follows of difficult sessions for *King Of America* with the Attractions, "my sullen and estranged band"; nevertheless, Costello rates their recording of 'Suit Of Lights' as "one of the most passionate recordings of the Attractions". This leads to a wise consideration of British and American musician attitudes: "virtues in both approaches". The note is concerned mostly with production details. References to song meanings are less plentiful: there's a dip into confession for 'Indoor Fireworks' ("romantic obituary") and 'Suit Of Lights', "a song about work and respect", which arose from watching his father "sing of experience and tenderness to an uncomprehending rabble of karaoke-trained dullards". The note ends with a footnote, mainly music-industry gripes in the USA and UK. It turns out that "brilliant mistake" was a phrase Costello "accidentally stumbled" upon while talking to David Weiss.[75] Costello considers the 1995 *King Of America* the record's "first serious release".

The 2005 essay also opens with the Coward Brothers escapades, now in cheery detail: in fact, a photograph adds Jimmy Reed and the Everly Brothers to their reference list. Note that, in this version, Costello meets Bret Easton Ellis, the author of the novel *Less Than Zero*, "an uneasy moment". Turning back to the record at hand, there is immediately a note of confession, and a point about songwriting technique: "Several songs employ a narrative form to make the private details seem less self-regarding." 'American Without Tears' is now related to "my grandfather's travels to New York in the 1920s", while the theme of "exile and escape" in the 1995 note now becomes: "The theme of exile and a simultaneous attraction and repulsion to an ideal. That is why the album is called *King Of America*. It is inherently contradictory."

The note then reproduces the 1995 version, almost verbatim. It is with the discussion of the Attractions as "my sullen and estranged band" that Costello stops off to provide an answer to "the most absurd slander" made by Bruce Thomas (not named) concerning Terence Donovan's striking photograph for the album cover, which had not been discussed in the 1995 version.[76] Costello gives vent to his pique at Thomas's comments, insisting that he, Costello, ordinarily had to take responsibility in many areas other than musical performance, "while everyone else was on holiday or in the bar". He also comments on his "vengeful geek" persona, drawing attention to his deed-poll change to "Elvis Costello", but now wishing to reclaim his birth name. It is then back to 1995 material, those notes now described as a "serious attempt to locate and address the audience for *King Of America*". Lengthy extended-play notes follow, opening with the theme of change from initial idea to final recording as a way of introducing demo versions. An important section of the note is Costello's discussion, arising from the track 'Deportee', of "the idea of America as a place where dreams and ideals are as easily misplaced as they are realized", which for the first time in the liner notes quotes from older songs ('New Amsterdam' (*Get Happy!!*) and 'Kid About It' (*Imperial Bedroom*)): in fact, the extract from 'Deportee' quoted here had already appeared in *Goodbye Cruel World* n04. In the midst of Americana, Costello gets back to Britain for discussion and quotation of 'Betrayal', the root of 'Tramp the Dirt Down' (*Spike*), and the miners' strike of 1984–5. He then describes the Spectacular Singing Songbook tour with the Confederates: lots of cover versions. A detailed review of all the various band members from this time and their subsequent appearances on Costello albums follows: the one for Ray Brown includes current reference to Diana Krall and *North*. The note ends with an affectionate memoir of the "Black and White Night" for Roy Orbison, including a fan-like reference to John Lennon at Shea Stadium. An earthquake occurs in LA but, presumably in the light of appearing alongside so many musical idols, "it would have been a decent way to go out".

What sort of book would we have if all liner notes were reprinted together? True to Costello's musical world, the book would be characterized by diversity, with examples of these writerly modes: aesthetic statement;

influences and musical reminiscence; explanations of musical derivation and interpretations of words; commentary on production and arrangement; value judgements; aspects of autobiography: diary, development of artistic sensibility, confession, anecdotes, family, friends, and lovers; and, finally, comments on reception. Costello's *Collected Prose* would be a book primarily for music-lovers, with big record collections, interested in the identity of players, fascinated by stories about how records were made, charmed by knowing connections between different pieces of music. But they go further, in two useful directions: into a statement of aesthetic intent or attitude, and into a mode of autobiography.

* * *

This chapter began with the question of whether songs allow endless possibilities of subject matter or arrive with built-in limitations. It has covered a variety of subjects: a lengthy vision of Hell, some political pop songs, songs that explore human relationships at a time when feminism made a great impact, comic songs and the equivalent of a novel. A few boundaries were also suggested: songs about race and songs for children. While there is no necessary limit to the words of songs, their musical material – chords, melodies, voice and instruments, recording, form and temporal duration – will always structure and check those possibilities. It is that rather technical relationship between music and words that holds the key. Meanwhile, Costello's "collected prose" offers an essential contribution to understanding his considered views on many subjects.

4 Criticism

"I don't think it's very good for a serious songwriter to pay attention to what [critics] say. It's just too hard. And it's not informative. They don't know what they're talking about. And *can't* know what they're talking about, by definition. Unless you write songs and make records, you just really can't know what it's about." (Paul Simon, in Zollo 1997: 115)

Every author, so far as he is great and at the same time *original*, has had the task of *creating* the taste by which he is to be enjoyed: so has it been, so will it continue to be. (Wordsworth [1815]1984: 657–8)

"It's a desperate business. It's a desperate business. They're not musicians, rock critics, for the most part. So they have to write about words. And there's nothing to write about." (Randy Newman, in Zollo 1997: 282)

I think I shall be among the English Poets after my death. (Keats 2002: 151)

Very few friendships can survive your saying, "I like you but I don't like your poems." Much better to say: "I don't like you but I like your poems." Yes, that would have been OK. (Hamilton 2002b: 10)

Delegated to decide which old poems should be kept,
And which destroyed, to lessen the excess baggage of time,
In a bad mood, hungover, he burns scroll after scroll,
Hugging his own works to his heart and crooning.[1]

"I had found myself being taken too seriously and over-analysed from the very outset of my recording career" (*The Juliet Letters* n06), says Elvis Costello, who in 1977 had a "little black book he carries around with him, full of the names of folk who have crossed him up, so to speak" (Kent 1994: 189–90). Costello allows the critic autonomy but keeps a close watch on what's being

Elvis Costello (and glasses): from the period of *Brutal Youth* (1994)

said. He had a fine analogy for the purposelessness of writing about music, "like dancing about architecture" (in White 1983: 52).[2] But dance and architecture are odd things, which do concern abstract form as well as bodies and bricks. A fascinating gloss on Costello's comment can be found in Wimsatt and Brooks's history of criticism:

> The Abbé du Bos' *Réflexions critiques sur la poésie et sur la peinture* of 1719 says a good deal not only about painting and poetry but also about sculpture, engraving and music, and in the English translation of this work in 1748 the word *Music* is added to the title. This was one milestone. But to the Abbé Charles Batteux, in his *Les beaux arts réduits à un même principe* of 1746, seems to go the credit of having first defined and rationalized almost exactly the modern category. The common principle was "imitation of beautiful nature", and the arts included were music, poetry, painting, sculpture, and the dance. Succeeding writers, notably the encyclopaedists (Montesquieu, Diderot, d'Alembert) took up and broadcast the ideas of Batteux, substituting for the dance architecture – and the grouping most often encountered today was established. (Wimsatt and Brooks 1957: 263)

In this final chapter, I guide the reader towards the types of writing that constitute Costello's reception. The handover from *taste* to *value* is crucial in determining whether an artist makes it to the canon.[3] All judgements are concerned with time: taste is personal and immediate (*de gustibus non est disputandum*); a canon confronts us at birth and is likely still to be there at death; in between, value is under constant review, resulting in what Leonard Cohen calls "an interesting game":

> "So it's very difficult to see what the verdict is going to be about a piece of work. And the thing that really makes it an interesting game is that each generation revises the game, and decides on what is poetry and song for itself. Often rejecting the very carefully considered verdicts of the previous generation." (in Zollo 1997: 337)

Towards the end of his life, the poet and critic Ian Hamilton set himself the task of reprising, for twentieth-century poets, Samuel Johnson's survey, *Lives of the Poets* (1781). Apart from the "greats" (Shakespeare, Milton, *et al.*), many of Johnson's poets had disappeared from view; in fact, some survived "simply *because* they had appeared in Johnson's *Lives*" (Hamilton 2002a: x). Hamilton, on the other hand, left out Hardy, Yeats, Eliot and Auden, stating that, for this quartet, "oblivion presents no threat" (*ibid.*: xvi). His selection then includes forty-five poets, from Rudyard Kipling to Sylvia Plath, each given an essay and a small selection of poems. Hovering over them is Hamilton's dark comment on most of the poets in Johnson's book: "not even Johnson's hospitality had been sufficient to protect them from the final darkness" (*ibid.*: x). If a similar exercise were carried out on singer-songwriters, how would Costello fare: already there with Bob Dylan, Joni Mitchell, Randy Newman, Paul Simon? Or is he in need of advocacy?

I examine three types of information: the first are summaries of various "quantitative" evaluations: critic ratings, end-of-year critical positions; secondly, I'll focus on some specific writers as a way of "reading in" the way that Costello's reception is progressing; and finally, I shall consider Costello's musical influence. Reviewing Larry David Smith, Keith Negus thinks that we should pay more attention to ordinary listeners and, although the thoughts of fans can be enlightening, I have more faith in professional critics (Negus 2005: 456).[4] What may strike the British reader as curious is Larry David Smith's use of reviews from the music critics of regional and metropolitan newspapers in the USA (the *Oakland Chronicle*, *Dallas Morning News*, and so on); in the UK, for much of Costello's career, rock criticism was firmly in the hands of the *music* press, and it is still unusual to find any attention to the British regional, as opposed to the national, press.[5] Since Costello has been "at it" for so long, he has survived great changes in the music press: the young Costello would have considered the demise of the *Melody Maker* (in 2000) as unlikely as the British Communist Party being elected to government. Costello has featured in many different sorts of music publication: style magazines (*The Face*, *I-D*), style magazines for men (*GQ*, *FHM*), music magazines (*Record Collector*, *Q*, *Mojo*), genre-based music magazines (*Wire*, *Gramophone*, *Folk Roots*, *No Depression*, *Jazz News*), the fortnightly music magazines at the height of Britpop (*Select*, *Vox*), more broadly based magazines of music and culture (*Uncut*, *Word*). The one survivor among the

Table 4.1 Positions in 'albums of the year' lists (UK magazines)

Album	Year	NME	MM	Sounds	Q	Mojo	Uncut
My Aim Is True	1977	3/30	no list	9/20			
This Year's Model	1978	3/30	1/1	8/20			
Armed Forces	1979	6/40	14/20	–/10			
Get Happy!!	1980	2/50	+/12	20/20			
Trust	1981	7/50	2/5	–/20			
Almost Blue	1981	20/50	3/5	–/20			
Imperial Bedroom	1982	2/50	no list	6/20			
Punch The Clock	1983	1/50	–/17	6/20			
Goodbye Cruel World	1984	12/50	–/16	no list			
King Of America	1986	14/60	5/30	+/50	–/50		
Blood And Chocolate	1986	13/60	3/30	–/50	+/50		
Spike	1989	10/50	20/30	27/50	+/50		
Mighty Like A Rose	1991	–/50	–/30		–/50		
The Juliet Letters	1993	–/50	–/40		+/50		
Brutal Youth	1994	–/50	–/40		–/50	19/25	
Kojak Variety	1995	–/50	–/50		–/50	30/35	
All This Useless Beauty	1996	–/50	–/50		–/50	19/40	
Painted From Memory	1998	–/50	–/50		+/50	18/40	+/40
When I Was Cruel	2002	–/50			–/50	33/40	–/70
The Delivery Man	2004	–/50			–/50	8/40	34/70
The River In Reverse	2006	–/50			92/100	–/50	–/50

+ = included in ungraded list; – = not included in list.
Sounds ceased publication in 1990, *Melody Maker* (*MM*) in 2000.
Vox (1990–97) and *Select* (1990–2000) never included Costello.

British weekly magazines is the *NME*, rather than the four when he started, including *Melody Maker, Sounds* and *Record Mirror*. Costello also saw changes in attention from the British press, the daily and Sunday broadsheets: again, it would have been quite unthinkable for that young Costello to have been featured in the *Daily Telegraph*.

First, let's see how Costello is faring in various critical charts and judgements, included as Tables 4.1 to 4.3 and Appendices 4.1 to 4.3. One of the features of reissue programmes that followed the shift to CD was the great emphasis placed on music writing as consumer guide. Robert Christgau had taken this approach for many years (Table 4.2),[6] but stars and grades and marks out of five or ten became the currency of summary value judgement. There are at least three common time-scales to critics' judgements: the rapid

Costello collaborated with Allen Toussaint on *The River In Reverse* (2006), but they first worked together in 1983.

review at the album's release, end-of-year reviews (Table 4.1), and occasional charts that attempt to gauge historical importance (Table 4.3 and Appendix 4.1), the last of these approximating to an emerging canon, in which case the rarity of the exercise may be a gauge of reliability. The time taken in judgement is important, and a critic has to concentrate on first hearing, with little sense of what others think. The summaries, especially the long-term ones, pick up lots of baggage along the way: the views of others, sales, the weight of "classic" status. Another issue is which and how many people vote: in my view, critics are the most consistent; artist contributions are interesting but may include genuflections to friends and fellow musicians; as for listeners, they are irredeemably locked in the present and recent past: my album of the year is inevitably album of that autumn and winter.

Costello's position in end-of-year polls in the British weeklies and the newer monthlies presents a dramatic story, in which he is cast into the outer darkness for the 1990s (Table 4.1).[7] Poor *Mighty Like A Rose* (1991) bears the burden of failure, disappearing in the year of Nirvana's *Nevermind*, Massive Attack's *Blue Lines*, U2's *Achtung Baby*, Primal Scream's *Screamadelica*.[8] *Brutal Youth*'s return to rock roots was of no avail. With the arrival of monthlies and their older demographic,[9] things start to pick up, and even *Painted From Memory* makes it into a *Mojo* chart, while *The Delivery Man* sees Costello back in their top ten. Up to and including *Spike* in 1989, most Costello records made it into the top twenty of the weeklies; who would have predicted *Punch The Clock* as album of the year in the *NME* for 1983? The British peaks seem to have been the *NME* critics' poll of 1985, with five albums in the list, and the *NME* readers' poll of 1988, with five albums in the list: *Imperial Bedroom* has had great impact, and listeners are still reeling from *King Of America* and *Blood And Chocolate*. The *NME* nods off in the 1990s, while only *Imperial Bedroom* and *This Year's Model* mark a presence in the monthlies.[10] *The River In Reverse*, the 2006 collaboration with Allen Toussaint, saw Costello return to a position in the "pazz and jop" poll in the USA (Table 4.2). With individual writers, there is more variety in the judgements, as Table 4.3 suggests. Covering huge spans for their histories, both Donald Clarke and Robert Palmer pass Costello by; where Costello has been included in summative histories of pop and rock music, frequently written by American authors, he is positioned as representative of punk or the new wave (Appendix 4.2). Authors of monographs on Costello offer preferences, St. Michael's "damning judgement" of *Imperial Bedroom* a notable exception (Appendix 4.3).

Some individual critics

The breakthrough article: Nick Kent

Nick Kent's 1977 *NME* interview-based article seemed to have set the agenda for Costello's critical position.[11] Although the essay is suffused with emergent punk attitude, more striking at a distance is how much it evokes Romantic themes, and I shall read the article alongside Robert Pattison's undervalued study, *The Triumph of Vulgarity* (1987), as well as Simon Reynolds and Joy Press's *The Sex Revolts* (1995). Kent's italicized words in this passage proved to be influential:

> "The only two things that matter to me, the only motivation point for me writing all these songs," opines Costello with a

perverse leer, "are *revenge* and *guilt*. These are the only emotions that I know about, that I can feel. Love? I don't know what it means, really, and it doesn't exist in my songs." (190)

Taken as a package – no to love, yes to revenge and guilt – the attitude evokes a strain of Romantic misogyny; projected onto models schematized by Simon Reynolds and Joy Press, the comments begin in "fear and loathing" and reach over to "abjection" (Pattison 1987: 116–19; Reynolds and Press

Table 4.2 US records of the year list from *Village Voice*

Album	Year	Critics	RC	RC grades
My Aim Is True	1977	2/30	–/30	B+
This Year's Model	1978	1/30	6/30	A
Armed Forces	1979	5/40	40/40	A–
Get Happy!!	1980	7/40	–/40	B
Trust	1981	3/40	3/60	A
Almost Blue	1981			B–
Imperial Bedroom	1982	1/40	–/59	B+
Punch The Clock	1983	11/40	–/70	B+
Goodbye Cruel World	1984			B+
King Of America	1986	2/40	19/58	A–
Blood And Chocolate	1986	9/40	14/58	A–
Spike	1989	7/40	–/58	B
Mighty Like A Rose	1991			C+
The Juliet Letters	1993			dud
Brutal Youth	1994	31/40	–/60	one-star honourable mention
Kojak Variety	1995	–/40	–/71	two scissors
All This Useless Beauty	1996	–/40	–/64	dud
Extreme Honey	1997			two scissors
Painted From Memory	1998	18/40	–/82	three-star honourable mention
When I Was Cruel	2002	13/40	–/91	
The Delivery Man	2004	–/40	–/77	three-star honourable mention
The River In Reverse	2006	32/40		three-star honourable mention

'Critics' refers to the annual 'pazz and jop' critics' poll in the *Village Voice*, RC to Robert Christgau's own estimation of Costello in that poll. Christgau offers both at www.robertchristgau.com. The final column refers to the grade that Christgau gave the album at initial appearance (his consumer guide).
'Veronica' was 16/24 in critics' singles, 1989. Christgau graded two further compilations: *Taking Liberties* as B in 1980, and the 1985 *Best Of Elvis Costello* as A–.
+ = included in ungraded list; – = not included in list.

Table 4.3 Three individual judgements

Dave Marsh, *The Heart of Rock and Soul: The 1001 Greatest Singles Ever Made* (Penguin, 1989): no. 203 'Less Than Zero' (p. 142), no. 588 '(What's So Funny 'Bout) Peace, Love and Understanding?' (pp. 385–6), no. 642 'Psycho' (pp. 416–17), no. 750 'Oliver's Army' (p. 479), no. 754 'Alison' (pp. 482–3).
Note that only three of these are Costello songs, one a country cover and one by Nick Lowe. Costello-produced, Special AKAs' 'Nelson Mandela' is at no. 781 (p. 499).

Colin Larkin, *The Virgin Encyclopaedia of Popular Music* (Muze, 1999), gives stars out of 5:
5: *This Year's Model, Imperial Bedroom*
4: *My Aim Is True, Get Happy!!, Trust, King Of America*
3: *Armed Forces, Almost Blue, Punch The Clock, Blood And Chocolate, Spike, Mighty Like A Rose, The Juliet Letters, Brutal Youth, All This Useless Beauty, Painted From Memory*
2: *Goodbye Cruel World, Kojak Variety*
Larkin included the TV soundtracks (with Richard Harvey): *GBH* (2/5), and *Jake's Progress* (2/5).
Live records: *Deep Dead Blue* with Frisell (1995) and *Costello And Nieve* (1996) get three stars.
Compilations:
5: *Girls Girls Girls* (1989)
4: *Ten Bloody Marys & Ten How's Your Fathers* (1980), *The Man* (1985), *The Very Best* (1994), *Extreme Honey* (1997), *Bespoke Songs* (1998)
3: *Out Of Our Idiot* (1987)

Martin C. Strong, *The Great Rock Discography* (Canongate, 2002) gives marks out of ten:
9: *My Aim Is True, This Year's Model, Armed Forces*
8: *Get Happy!!, Trust, Imperial Bedroom*
7: *Punch The Clock, King Of America, Blood And Chocolate*
6: *Brutal Youth*
5: *Almost Blue, Goodbye Cruel World, Spike, Mighty Like A Rose, The Juliet Letters, All This Useless Beauty, Painted From Memory*
4: *Kojak Variety*
Out Of Our Idiot scores 5, (presumably) the 1999 *Very Best* compilation 8.

1995: 19–32, 85–101). In a memorable vignette, the *female* representative of Island Records sidles over, only to be met with teenage levels of tight-lipped contempt and seething disregard. Kent's role as ready accomplice is not to be underestimated, ever ready to supply withering observations. "Then she opens her mouth", full stop. "A bourgeois glamour victim who thinks she's the cat's pyjamas". "She's the classic 'Natasha who looks like Elsie'." Kent's farewell is a magnificent writerly put-down:

> Getting nowhere with her enquiries, the girl [*sic*] finally gets up from her seat, feigning extreme boredom with a low farting noise issuing derisively from her lips to register her full disgust. As she retreats back to her noisy friends well away from our table, Costello's face has a menacing glow to it. (192–3)

Though we're not told why Island Records were in any sense a bad thing, they're still set up as the enemy within, the "cheap hood's bargain with the world" that Pattison traces far back to William Godwin (1756–1836) (Pattison 1987: 142–3). There are some unexpected religious references. "I had to be either Catholic or Jewish now, didn't I?" asks Costello (191); then comes this detail, evoking the intensity of Pinkie in Graham Greene's *Brighton Rock*:

> His eyes stare coldly out from behind the horn-rims and our El quietly digs his hand into one of his four jacket pockets to produce an enormous bent steel nail, something ideal for pinning whole limbs to crosses at a crucifixion. (193)

Finally, the familiar Romantic yearning for young death: "rock and romanticism share an aesthetic appreciation of death as the ultimate form of excess" (Pattison 1987: 123). "I'm never going to stick around long enough to churn out a load of mediocre crap like all those guys from the sixties ended up doing. I'd rather kill myself. I mean, [Gram] Parsons's exit was perfect" (193). Among the purveyors of "mediocre crap" may well have been the people who wished to "die before I get old".[12] "I'm deadly serious about this," says Costello, his adverb evoking his final end. "I'm not going to be around to witness my artistic decline" (194).

Was this article about Costello or really about Nick Kent? It is the textbook case of how music benefits from, and even needs, the writer's mediation. Who can forget the "opinionated old geezas hunched around a spittoon" (193), Costello the "mousy figure, all insect anonymity" (196)? That he was a fine writer would have been no news to Kent, who proudly parades his inclusion in a Costello song, critic and artist on equal terms: "even *I* am in a Costello song" (189).[13]

Marcus, Costello and the punk world-view

As a writer, Greil Marcus is difficult to categorize: cultural historian, culture-critic, maker of music-derived and music-informed ideas. Marcus is Lennonishly something to be, impossible to become, and a Master's in Marcus would involve too many bits and bobs. He finds ideas lurking in unexpected places: *Mystery Train* found the spirit of America in a variety of music centring on Elvis Presley, while, during his discussion of *Invisible Republic*, the *Basement Tapes* of Bob Dylan and the Band "rank with the most intense outbreaks of twentieth-century modernism" (Marcus 1997: xiii).

Punk is one of Marcus's major themes: *Lipstick Traces* (1989) was a "secret history of the twentieth century", discovering a line that linked Dada, the Situationist International, and the Sex Pistols. A compilation on Rough Trade (1993) was a soundtrack to the book, bringing together punk bands such as the Buzzcocks, Slits, Adverts, the Mekons and Gang of Four, alongside extracts from Guy Debord and Dada figures like Tristan Tzara and Richard Huelsenbeck, and tracks like Joe Strummer goading the audience in 1976 or the sound of the audience at the Roxy ballroom in 1977. Obscure and unexpected, Marie Osmond's reading of a short Hugo Ball poem was the collection's gem, eliciting from Marcus (in the liner note) this typical observation:

> As host of a special show on sound poetry, Osmond was asked by the producer to recite only the first line of Ball's work; incensed at being thought too dumb for art, she memorized the lot and delivered it whole in a rare "glimpse of freedom".

In appreciating Costello, Marcus was quick off the mark, including both *My Aim Is True* and *This Year's Model* in the first edition of *Stranded* in 1979 (Marcus 1996: 264). Costello was subsequently placed dead centre in a book that gathers together Marcus's writings on punk, the word being employed for a wide range of tasks (Marcus 1993):[14]

> I wrote about a good deal *as* punk that to other people was not punk at all, stuff that sullied the very purity of the concept … not because to me punk is an attitude more than a musical style, but because I think it is infinitely more than a musical style, period. (6)

This introduction, written in 1992, goes on to position two Costello records alongside another seemingly unlikely candidate for punk status, Bruce Springsteen's album *Nebraska* of 1982:

> Costello and Springsteen work as parallel figures in these pages: one always nibbling at the boundaries of the mainstream, the other seemingly at home nowhere else. In the 1980s, under Thatcher and Reagan, they were headed towards the convergence of Springsteen's *Nebraska* and Costello's 'Pills and Soap' and *King Of America*. They were three of the quietest punk records ever made, and three of the truest – negotiations as complete and unflinching, in their way, as hard and cruel, as any of the explosions in 'God Save the Queen'. The Sex Pistols' first achievement was to burn rock'n'roll down to essentials of noise; if punk ever really ended, it was in the middle of its tale, when two singers from whom most punk chroniclers would withhold the name burned punk down to something close to silence. (*ibid.*: 7)

Marcus had been inspired by Costello's reference, during his 1977 interview with Nick Kent, to "revenge and guilt", referring to it in six of the collected articles in the book.[15] Reading Marcus, one is often led to material that is not strictly about Costello, including the ideas of Christopher Lasch (34), Bernard-Henri Levy (38), Hannah Arendt (249), Susan Sontag (250) and Walter Benjamin (251). Fascism is evoked at various points, especially in the reviews of *Armed Forces* (33–8), *Taking Liberties* (136–7) and 'Pills And Soap' (249), the latter chapter providing the title for the book. Pills and soap are to be found "in the fascist bathroom" (250), and this is extended to mean the reduction of people "to utensils, to their social and economic function" in "the Thatcherist or Reaganist project" (252).

The literary or political references are nothing compared to those that Marcus can hear musically, and these have been referred to in an earlier chapter (page 16). Marcus can discern a "melody and arrangement (pretty much Billie Holiday's 'Strange Fruit')" (259) in 'Pills And Soap', a song that "begins to sound like something Peggy Lee might sing" (251). "Detached from rock, country, or R&B rhythms", *Goodbye Cruel World* tends toward "cabaret, Billie Holiday, Frank Sinatra" (259). 'Our Little Angel' (*King Of*

America) displays "the cadences of an ancient Irish anticonscription ballad" (313).

Marcus is attentive to words, as his review of *Armed Forces* demonstrates by chunky quotation (35–8). Of 'Pills And Soap' (1984), "poetry is necessary, and in the case of Elvis Costello – a family man interested in all public affairs – this means wordplay, puns, diverted homilies, distorted slogans" (250). But words rely on their delivery by the voice, and Marcus observes, of the same track, "Costello's insistence on singing to the music, not to the words" (250) and later finds "the only moment where Costello sings to the words, not the music" (252). As observed in another earlier chapter (pages 82–3), Marcus has much to say of the voice, his critical view perhaps summed up as ambivalent. The Attractions, meanwhile, appear to improve. In 1977, "the band, punk in looks and to a fair degree musically, is weak" (26), but by 1979 is "tight and tricky", "anonymous but not impersonal, drawing on the mid-sixties tinniness of the British Invasion while insisting on late-seventies punk intensity" (34). By *Goodbye Cruel World*, a problem lies "in the bass-drums-keyboard accompaniments and the way Costello fits his guitar into them", "in the arrangements – arrangements which don't shape the songs but muffle them" (258), and which "don't carry the ironies (let alone question them), they underscore them, thus killing them" (259). *King Of America* "dropped the ornamented orchestrations and clogged melody lines" of *Goodbye Cruel World* and *Imperial Bedroom*. However, Marcus devotes some space to consideration of the electronic handclaps in 'Pills And Soap' (249–50).[16]

In critical judgement, Marcus appears to favour *Armed Forces*, *Punch The Clock* and *King Of America* over *Taking Liberties* and *Goodbye Cruel World*. Indeed, "the super *Punch The Clock* … should have won the 1983 Pazz and Jop poll but didn't come close" (258). Two critical truths Marcus delivers with respect to Costello, one from Walter Benjamin (251): "the tendency of a literary [we can say 'aesthetic'] work can only be politically correct if it is also [aesthetically] correct".[17] The second (of 'Tramp The Dirt Down', 1989) was made perhaps with reference to events such as Live Aid of 1985 or the Nelson Mandela concert of 1988: "To make true political music, you have to say what decent people don't want to hear; that's something people fit for satellite benefit concerts will never understand, and that Costello understood before anyone heard his name" (367).

The repercussions of Marcus's capacious conception of punk are felt nowhere more clearly than in Larry David Smith's book on Costello, where the word "punk" is employed, often as adjective, for a remarkable array of both musical and personal aspects. Costello's career is analysed as three phases, in the second of which (*Imperial Bedroom, Punch The Clock* and *Goodbye Cruel World*) he is the "punk tunesmith", followed by the "punk composer".[18] That *Get Happy!!* was "punk soul" (175) might have made sense at the time, but it takes a leap of the listener's imagination to hear:

> a punk roots record (*King Of America*),[19] two punk pop albums (*Spike, Mighty Like A Rose*), a punk chamber music record (*The Juliet Letters*), a punk lounge album (*Painted From Memory*),[20] and a punk techno project (*When I Was Cruel*). (145)

Elsewhere, Costello is "without question, the musical world's original punk torch singer" (219). Two summary statements encapsulate the argument:

> Whether he employs the sounds of chamber music, pop standards, rock and roll, or roots music, the auteur brings a punk attitude to his subject matter.

> I guess this all proves a simple, yet compelling, point – You can take the auteur out of the punk genre, but you can't take the punk out of the auteur. (183)

In words or attitudes, punk can mean a lot of different things: "punk introspection" ("What a thematic innovation!") (183), "listless punk wallowing" (192), "Cosmopolitan Punk" (209, of *The Juliet Letters*), "punk empathy" (236), "punk lover" (249). Virtuosic as it is, punk can yet be intensified by italic: "a driving *punk* attitude" (167), "a systematic, coherent, *punk* attack" (237). Described as "an aggressive, irreverent, melodramatic artistic worldview" (167) or "an artistic attitude" (172),

> the ever-present punk worldview and its melodramatic imperative fuel a relentlessly aggressive exploration of loving relations and their perils. His response may feature anger, remorse, "revenge and guilt", acquiescence, or a host of other

emotions, but it is always aggressively melodramatic. (226–7)

"Revenge and guilt" is from Nick Kent, of course, and Smith also picks up from Kent the "bent nail" in Costello's pocket, making it a repeatable reference and, indeed, concluding a chapter with the summary sentence: "Elvis Costello is more than a punk lover – he's Billie Holiday with a bent nail" (249).

In an earlier chapter (pages 45–6), I urged restraint in characterizing Costello as musical punk, and confess to some scepticism towards its ready use as cultural concept. Marcus's characterization of *King Of America* deflects from what is apparent in the record: themes of exile to America and the "new authenticity" sound that brought along its own agenda. Quite apart from what it says about punk or punk rock, Smith's wide-ranging use of the term has the corrosive effect of reducing the variety of musical innovation or critical intelligence on Costello's part.[21]

Christgau's appreciations and objections

The "Dean" of rock journalism, Robert Christgau pioneered rock criticism as consumer guide and, eventually, the vast majority of rock criticism caught up with him. For the internet, he has supplied a rich and usable resource of his collected reviews. His critical judgement can never be doubted for sincerity, fairness, wisdom and, if those terms sound like they belong to the generation of Lionel Trilling, F. R. Leavis and Raymond Williams, this appears to be from where they derive.[22] Worth appreciating is the brevity of the consumer-guide reviews, capsule summaries that put great pressure on the writing. Small wonder that a distinguished "tribute album" already exists with a song-derived title: *Don't Stop Til' You Get Enough* (Carson, Rachlis and Salamon 2002).

Christgau has not so much a blind spot for Costello as an appreciation, born of admiration, that zooms in on let-downs and failings with precision. He is consistent in his attention to the relationship of words to music in song, with a keen sense of both their necessity and peril (Eisen 1969: 230–43). He was sceptical of this aspect of Costello's work from the start: *My Aim Is True* shows an "overconcentration on lyrics", whereas *Armed Forces* "needs words because they add colour and detail to his music"; Costello is a "phrasemaker" rather than "an analyst or a poet". The punchline arrives with *Trust*: "I said he wasn't much of a poet: all wordplay as swordplay and puns for punters", with a "punderous construction" on *Punch The Clock*.[23] On *Get Happy!!* "tropes and hooks abound: why deny lines like 'You lack lust you're so lacklustre' or 'I speak double Dutch to a real double duchess'? On the other hand, why bother digging them out?" His response to *Imperial Bedroom* is ambiguous: in this short passage Christgau opens with a back-handed compliment to the lyric sheet, which had arranged the words as unpunctuated runs of words as capital letters, and carries the highest praise as well as the sign of a fatal criticism:

> I admit it – I love the lyric sheet. Helps me pay attention, though not always, and persuades me absolutely that 'The Long Honeymoon' and 'Kid About It' are as great as songwriting ever gets. But it also shores up my impression that he can be precious lyrically, vocally, and musically, and gnomic for no reason at all – in short, pretentious.

With *Punch The Clock* there is "an elusive feeling that's half pinned down by the words because that's all the grasp he's got on it". The words are always liable to elicit a prickly response: on *King Of America* "wordplay is still too private", *Spike* shows "obsessive wit", and 'The Other Side Of Summer' on *Mighty Like A Rose* is simply "a song with a lot of words in it".

The words rely on voice for delivery, and Christgau seems to regard Costello's voice as generally a good thing, and more dependable than the words, summed up by a phrase used of *Trust*: "he makes the music make the words". A serious joke, made of the same record: "Who ever said he was not much of a singer? Was that me? No." Early again, Christgau had spotted a key element, hearing a "relentless nastiness of instrumental and (especially) vocal attack" on *Armed Forces* and finding on *This Year's Model* "his snarl more attractive musically and verbally than all his melodic and lyrical tricks". Of *Armed Forces*, another familiar point: "While I'm glad he's got soul, too often he invests emotion in turns of phrase he should play cool"; and of *Blood And Chocolate*: "He's just voicing his pain, and the world's, in that order, as usual."

Like Marcus, Christgau is sympathetic to the moment of punk music: on *Taking Liberties* Costello is described as "a punk fellow-traveller, and he'll be missed". However, this aspect is tied more closely to explicitly political engagement through music-making, so that Christgau approved of "the sociopolitical tenor" of *This Year's Model* and, as late as *Mighty Like A Rose*, saw that "its theory of life is that fascism has a great deal in common with songs you don't like on the radio". *Pace* Marcus, Christgau reads *King Of America* less as punk music as such but as the sign of a shift towards studio musicians who "collaborate with their paymaster on that incommensurable token of collective creation, a groove." But in so doing, one key indicator of punk virtue is finally abandoned:

> The Attractions always betokened Elvis's punk integrity – his commitment to collective creation, his rejection of the International Pop Music Community's expedient playing around. And the last time they were fully equal to his music was on *This Year's Model* in 1978.

Indeed, the role of arrangement has been a running theme through Christgau's Costello. Only having heard *My Aim Is True* and a Stiff compilation, Christgau saw that "overconcentration on lyrics can be cured by a healthy relationship with a band", so that on *This Year's Model* the "bite and drive of the backup" was to be admired when compared with the "well-played studio pub-rock of *My Aim Is True*". The arrangements on *Mighty Like A Rose* are also drawn into an extraordinary sentence which manages to say a lot about Tom Waits and Randy Newman: "The Mitchell Froom-produced arrangements here are stuck between Tom Waits as Kurt Weill and Tom Waits as Jackson Browne – Randy Newman is beyond them."

One comment on Costello's albums as albums: "Never expect a perfect compilation from somebody who essays a perfect album every time out" (*Best of Elvis Costello*, 1985). Finally, as someone who reviewed records professionally almost his whole life, Christgau has a panoramic sense of musical history and, discussing *Spike*, he presents Costello's musical diversity in these terms, with an unexpected but fascinating comparison to hand:

> Paul Whiteman was a bigger star, and though my jazz friends may cringe, I doubt he was as good. But like Elvis C., he made the mistake of applying his refined taste to what he knew was the music of the future: hiring fine players, commissioning

Ellington and Copland, emphasizing the danceability of an
orchestra too grand to be called a band, he honoured the
classics. Who knows which of Costello's virtues will seem
equally irrelevant 40 or 10 years hence: his obsessive wit?
his precise arrangements? his respect for musical history?
Unless I'm mistaken, though, he's doomed to be remembered
as fatally self-conscious. And doomed as well never to convert
the unconverted again.

Biographies and studies

The published biographies of Costello follow a pattern by which earlier
examples take bearings from pop models, guided by visual imagery as much
as information or analysis: Mick St. Michael's biography published in 1986
was described as "illustrated" even though the visual material was confined
to the standard inserted section of photographs.[24] Krista Reese appeared to
get there first in 1981 with her "completely false biography based on rumour,
innuendo and lies", St. Michael followed in 1986, Tony Clayton-Lea two
years later. All three relied on interviews, with St. Michael strong on
Costello's early years as a musician, Reese good on the sense of "being
there" characteristic of early picture-driven biographies. A step-change
occurs for Brian Hinton in 1999 and Graeme Thomson in 2004: both were
able to refer to Costello's liner notes to varying degrees, and to call upon
more interviews; Hinton's star turn is Bebe Buell, Thomson has Allan Mayes,
Bruce Thomas and many others. Thomson ignores previous biographies. Both
expend more effort on reception via print articles and reviews in both the
music press and, increasingly during the 1990s, daily and weekly newspapers;
over time, websites begin to act as archives for some but not all such
material. Both make considerable reference to Pete Frame and Kevin Howlett's
1992 BBC radio series and the many published interviews, the two-part
interview with Peter Doggett in particular (Doggett 1995). Both are keen
listeners, Hinton going the extra mile into bootleg material.

Studies that are not biographical are less readily found, and this book
takes its place among them. David Gouldstone's *Elvis Costello: A Man out
of Time* is perhaps surprising in its rarity as a monograph on Costello's work
with no claims to providing a biography, although his approach is chronological: my chapter on words makes reference (on page 102) to Hinton's
criticism of Gouldstone's book. I have made reference throughout the book

to academic articles, and the most fecund of these appear in David Brackett (1995: 157–98). Perone points out that Brackett's was the first case of Costello being part of a doctoral submission, which then became *Interpreting Popular Music*. His chapter on Costello is one of four case-studies, along-side Billie Holiday and Bing Crosby, Hank Williams, and James Brown, and focuses on the track 'Pills And Soap'. As we saw in the first chapter, Brackett has also published a paper on 'It's Time' (*All This Useless Beauty*), which continues the music-cultural approach of the earlier book. Other peer-reviewed academic publications on Costello include contributions by Pamela Thurschwell, Peter Horton-Taylor and Rene Bookmens.

The relationship between music journalism and academia has been uneasy. A conference held in New York in 1997 attempted to bridge the divide,[25] but one of its convenors, Evelyn McDonnell, found that

> The squabbling was as much intra- as inter-disciplinary, as ideological debates turned into rock-critic ego wars – a room full of bespectacled men muttering to themselves, it's not a pretty sight … I learned long ago that rock criticism is a petty and competitive field, that there's no one we like to dis as much as each other – and the academics were failing to lead us to a higher ground. These are people who have made their failure to fit into "normal" society a moral crusade, who can turn the pleasures of pop into taxonomies of categories and ratings, who can make a matter of personal taste a criminal judgement. (Kelly and McDonnell 1999: 13)

If the journalists were the bad boys of that occasion, at a previous conference academics were deemed to have misbehaved (*ibid.*: 12). Believing that "it's a snobbism to think that people who rock don't think; it's anti-intellectual to think that people who think don't rock", McDonnell insists on being "anti-pseudo-intellectual: against the virtuosic use of language to bewilder meaning" (*ibid.*: 14).[26]

It is interesting that neither Hinton nor Thomson made it his business to cover David Brackett's analysis of 'Pills And Soap', suggesting that both saw their "home ground" in journalistic debate. Thomson is the active, "jobbing" journalist, while Hinton occupies the interesting position of freelance writer: "It's a lonely job, writing!" he declares at one point (Hinton 1999: 7).

Hinton elsewhere sets out his understanding of these issues. "Proved True with Time", Nick Kent's 1977 article, discussed above, is "the finest flowering of rock journalism, anywhere" (*ibid.*: 129). Kent, with Paul Williams, Allan Jones, Pete Frame, Mark Williams, and Steve Burgess (each connected by "and") "will always remain closer to my heart. Enthusiasts all, yet with a wonderful sense of irony. Just like Costello's music, in fact." Closer, that is, than Jon Savage who provides "the kind of writing you admire rather than love". Savage in turn represents "cooler, varsity educated writing – cue Barney Hoskyns and John Rogan – which has since spread into the posh Sundays and the media mainstream, followed by an unspeakable raft of dry academics, from Simon Frith downwards" (*ibid.*). The last point was not so in chronological terms,[27] but the schema seems to assert distinctions between journalists, and to preserve the distinction between journalism and academia, in ways that ultimately say more about Hinton's own taste. Hinton and Gouldstone share the similarity of being readers of twentieth-century poetry as well as careful students of Costello's words: Hinton compares Costello with Thom Gunn, T. S. Eliot and Ted Hughes (*ibid.*: 88, 296, 358), Gouldstone with Philip Larkin (Gouldstone 1989: 92). Gouldstone presents a clear sense of relative value among the albums; Hinton makes judgements in terms of individual songs rather than albums.

David Hepworth: tranquil recollection

It is possible to argue that Costello brings out the best in a certain kind of writer, that his music finds the ideal writer as mediation. There were times when David Hepworth would have seemed an unusual person for Costello to give one of his best interviews, as Hepworth's earlier magazines, *Smash Hits*, *Just Seventeen* and *Q*, might seem more the 1980s sound of *Punch The Clock* than the *NME* authenticity of *Get Happy!!* However, in 2003, Hepworth and Mark Ellen founded *Word* magazine, their *Mojo* already having pointed the way, and *Word* seemed, by curious coincidence, to provide the magazine equivalent to the Costello of recent years: relaxed and considerate, prepared to listen without undue prejudice, ready to turn to ideas in the wider culture where appropriate. Hepworth's article on Costello appeared in only the magazine's second issue, when Costello was working on *North*. For the famous keywords of the Kent article, a more optimistic set is now found: vivid, boldness, curiosity, adventure, joy, beauty (Hepworth 2003: 72).

This essay is a model of how to fill up the space of writing: like a good song, art conceals art. It is a long piece, in which Hepworth arranges things to keep us moving, as well as including a few unifying devices. For instance, Costello recounts three recent concerts recently attended: a Rolling Stones stadium concert for which Costello had opened, a tribute concert for George Harrison, and a college concert by Elton John. There are frequent and considered views on music, musicians and singers, and the music industry. On a good day, simple transcription of Costello's comments can yield results, but Hepworth is a canny transcriber and intervenes at the right points. For instance, his opening is simply to let Costello talk about the Rolling Stones, but Hepworth it is who provides the trenchant summary:

> I include that anecdote for no other reason than I thought you
> might enjoy it and there is something in the way it embodies
> the young fan's enthusiasm, the fellow pro's technical analysis,
> the critic's aesthetic expectations, the purist's preference for
> the B side and the puritan's disappointment with popular taste
> that is quintessentially Elvis Costello. (*ibid.*: 67)

Each of those is there: Hepworth is not making it up. So, the young fan's enthusiasm: "I was at school in Liverpool in '72..."; the fellow pro's technical analysis: "Charlie who is actually a swing drummer and Keith is the horn section"; the critic's aesthetic expectations: "the only thing I'd say is that [the Stones' set] doesn't accumulate ... whereas when you watch U2 on a similar-sized stage they build something much bigger than themselves"; the purist's preference for the B-side: "If I'd written 'She Smiled Sweetly' I'd play it every night ... Totally decadent things like 'Play With Fire' and 'Off The Hook'";[28] and finally, the puritan's disappointment with popular taste: "the level of comprehension at the average rock and roll show is not great".[29]

Eventually, Hepworth guides Costello towards questions of age, perhaps because this might have been a defining element for the imagined readership of *Word* magazine (*ibid.*: 72). Only four years older than Costello, Hepworth first met him at Stiff Records in 1977, and so the article looks back over a quarter-century. Costello's relationship to his audience may have mirrored Hepworth's own relationship to his readership. Earlier in the article, Costello looks back on a performance at a British rock festival in 2002 as "the longest fifty minutes of my life", confronting "all these sullen little Thatcher's children looking up and sneering because we were old".[30] But there is still room for a good joke about musical taste, spanning the day's queen of manufactured pop with the archetype of tough-listening jazz: "'Go home and listen to your Posh Spice records'. Then he smiles. 'I don't really mean that, that's not fair, they probably love everything, probably go home and listen to Cecil Taylor records'" (*ibid.*: 67).

Inside academia: Rene Bookmens

If there is a problem in the way Costello's reception is developing, my guess is that academics are free to pick up on the work of journalists, but journalists don't make it their business to cover the work of academics. However, it is the hard initial work of journalists that enables academics eventually to pay attention. The time-scales of these forms of writing are different, and academics are sometimes able to access research funds denied to journalists. The internet may break down barriers, and search engines should in theory allow access to academic material. There is good and bad work in both domains, but I think it is a pity if any writer on Costello avoids the work of David Brackett or, as an example, an article by Rene Bookmens. No regular reader of or subscriber to *The European Journal of Cultural Studies*, I came across it only via a university-based search engine, but I am glad I did. I have made reference to this article at several points in the book, but here I'd like to pull out a few themes.[31]

Drawing on an article by W. J. T. Mitchell, Bookmens observes a lack of tradition of *criticism* in writing about pop music, comparing it unfavourably with writing on "literature, painting, cinema, or serious music" (62). Mitchell had claimed (in 1989) that newer modes of criticism "studied all kinds of cultural behaviour, political issues and social or gender questions while using art works as an interpretative tool and as a helpful theoretical device" (63). Criticism in Bookmens's view is "pragmatic in the sense that it is directed at and meant for use in specific cultural practices and not destined to play an archival and monumental role in the university libraries" (63).[32] In writing about pop music, such criticism faced two problems: a populist argument (being too dependent on charts and people's choice) and a "debunking" argument, an ironic view sceptical of any claim to take pop seriously, belittling the object of study in so doing (63). It seems to me that these three key terms – criticism, populism and irony – map onto Frith's three arguments that Bookmens draws on later in the article (at 68): the art argument (autonomy and education, corresponding to Mitchell's idea of criticism), the folk argument (spontaneity and communal roots, corresponding to the populist view), and the pop argument (fun and commercial appeal, corresponding to the ironic view). Bookmens reads Costello's career as spanning two pairs of dichotomies that shift historically: high and low, and global and local. For high and low (69–70), Bookmens compares Costello's development favourably with the much more laboured attempts to break down barriers of progressive rock and heavy metal in the 1970s. Crucial in this development was the blurring of age-based boundaries which tied pop music to the category of youth and, in consequence, we experience Costello's boundary-breaking in a less charged way than before (70). Bookmens is optimistic about the second dichotomy, between global and local (70–3), seeing the development of pop music as enabling what he calls "translations" (73) between the two locations, with the result that Dutch bands can still be recognized as playing with certain musical codes, to an audience that is musically savvy enough to understand. If he is right, it would surely mean a lot for an English musician like Costello generally obsessed with America.

Many of the points that Bookmens discusses genuinely enrich the way we might think of Costello's career, and it would be a shame if the article was kept in academic confines. Writing of Frank Kermode, Clive James reflects on what he perceives as a change in the relationship between "Grub Street" and "the academy" in literary writing between 1974 and 2006. The key difference now, he claims, is that academics (Kermode, Christopher Ricks, John Carey) have become "readable", as well as respecting their roots in "scholarship". James broadens to a wider point about standards in writing in general terms, but sees this not as a charge that can be left with the university professors (James 2006: 113). "Readable" is partly in the eye of the beholder, but I'd say this was not a problem at all with Bookmens's piece.[33]

Musical influences

Considering allusion in the context of plagiarism, Christopher Ricks mentions a very interesting point made many years ago by William Walsh: "For although we are pleased to say, in our metaphorical language, that a plagiarist shines in stolen plumes, not a plume is really lost by the fowl who originally grew them".[34] In the first chapter we looked at influences on Costello's own work; by extension, one obvious way an artist "stays alive", so to speak, is through influence on the music of others. Again, this is a complex topic never predictable in the present and, for Costello, there is an additional problem: if we were right in the earlier chapter (taking a cue from Costello himself) to celebrate him as a great alluder, reference-maker, soaker-up-of-influence, there is the strong possibility that his own work acts only as a generous gateway to, and education in, other music. Costello wears the plumes, rather than being among "the fowl who originally grew them". For instance, how many British listeners of a certain age acquired a first taste of country music from *Almost Blue*, thence to country-rock, such as Gram Parsons and Johnny Cash, thence to the heartland country of George Jones and Merle Haggard? So different from the Smiths or Tom Waits, where the style seems to appear from nowhere, so that its influence works only on its own terms.[35] I have suggested that Costello picks up on Tom Waits's later signature sound – clanky, Mitchell Froom production, Marc Ribot guitar, traces in songs – but the influence surely works one way only: which Waits track demonstrates Costello's impact in return? Where I have seen acknowledgement of Costello as influence it has been couched in general terms: here Suzanne Vega pays tribute more to an attitude on Costello's part than anything specific in sound or style and, while that is not to be disparaged, there is no telling whether her music would *sound* much like Costello and, to the best of my knowledge, it didn't:

> "Although my *ideal*, and I have to say lately [1992], I've been listening to Elvis Costello, all his songs over the last ten years, and the great thing about what he does is that he still writes about love, thwarted ambition, jealousy, all these basic things in life that aren't particularly ambitious. Everybody writes about love. But at the same time he'll do it in a way that it's his and it's distinctive. He's not afraid to use long words, he's not afraid to use his vocabulary. He's not afraid to say 'I want you' and say it over and over again for five minutes. And it's still Elvis Costello. As a songwriter I need to be able to say those things that are a part of everyday life: I need you, I want you. War must end. How you get to say them without sounding like a jerk or sounding simplistic,

that's my next challenge. Because everyone says, 'Oh, she's so intellectual'. But I *am* trying to communicate. How do you say it but say it in such a way that it seems as if they haven't heard it before?" (Suzanne Vega, in Zollo 1997: 575)

The most direct influence from Costello was supposed to be the Jags:[36] Hinton hears their one hit single, 'Back Of My Hand' (1980) as "not so much a tribute as an outright plagiarism" (Hinton 1999: 193), but this is unfair. Starting with the open fifths of the Easybeats' 'Friday On My Mind', the track has a clear shape and packs plenty into its 3'14: verse, link, chorus, and a brief guitar solo at 1'48. 'Radio Radio' silences are heard at 1'46 and 3'04 to the (dead) end, and plenty of big dominant preparations. At 2'00 there is a modulation of the kind we saw with 'Radio Sweetheart' (E major to G major) but from 2'12 to 2'27 a chord progression, wrenched back to E as tonic, that was, if anything, *ahead* of Costello at the time.

Simon Frith in 1981 thought that "Costello's influence is evident in all good pop LPs these days", mentioning Squeeze, *East Side Story* (1981), which Costello produced, and the Undertones' *Positive Touch* (1981): "songs about songs, about the clichés in which lives have to be led" (Frith 1988: 160).[37]

Franklin Bruno hears the influence of *Armed Forces* in the Boomtown Rats' *Mondo Bongo* of 1982 and of 'Oliver's Army' in the track 'Another Piece Of Red' (Bruno 2005: 95). This is spot-on: the track 'Another Piece Of Red' is about the British Empire, with a reference (whistled at one point) to 'Rule Britannia' and a third verse that follows 'Oliver's Army' in presenting place names. Like the Attractions, or Joe Jackson, the Boomtown Rats often kept piano at the centre of their sound. They split in 1984, leaving Bob Geldof to go on to interesting times in the 1980s through Live Aid.

David Sheppard mentions Costello as a possible influence on Paul Heaton of the Beautiful South,[38] connecting 'Let Love Speak Up Itself' (*Choke*, 1990) to *Imperial Bedroom*, 'Pretenders To The Throne' to *King Of America*, and 'Rotterdam' (1996) specifically to 'New Amsterdam' (*Get Happy!!*) (Sheppard 2000: 131).[39] 'Let Love Speak Up Itself' may have a Costello-like touch of the macabre in its second verse, "let them take your feelings and tie them in a knot, hang them from a cleaver", but its gospel build-up sounds some distance from *Imperial Bedroom*. The hook line of 'Pretenders To The Throne', "your town is dragging me down", has cynicism but sounds too over-produced for *King Of America*. The third one works in that both refer to trisyllabic cities in Holland, and Heaton's other two place names, Liverpool and Rome, have that "metonymic" realism: the three cities must be to do with football. I imagine that what Heaton really admired in Costello was the freedom to pick and choose from the past (Al Green! Burt Bacharach! Willie Nelson!). The sustained signature of the Beautiful South was the two-voice, male–female song, as well as occasional contrast *within* the song, neither really Costello terrain. Heaton's *Under The Influence* compilation (DMC, 2004) includes 'Lipstick Vogue' (*Armed Forces*) among a Costello-like mixture of soul, gospel and country, with two Allen Toussaint songs that Costello recorded for *The River In Reverse*.[40] The sleeve notes are even closer to Costello: Heaton can hardly be contained by the sixteen recordings on the CD and includes a long supplementary list that, in its obsessive inclusiveness, reminds us of Costello's first *Vanity Fair* article, while Heaton's occasional tying of the songs to times in the day ("No better song to shave to") can be set alongside Costello's second such essay (Costello 2000, 2002a).

Even as a producer, for the terrific trio of Squeeze, the Pogues and the Specials, Costello aimed to bring out their own style as much as possible: if anything *he* picked up from *them*. "'Human Touch' was clearly made under the spell of my recent work with the Specials" (*Get Happy!!* n03), also there in both versions of 'I Stand Accused'. In his memoir, Shane MacGowan of the Pogues is unkind to Costello, who produced their *Rum, Sodomy And The Lash* (1985) (Clarke and MacGowan 2002: 173), but a more affection-ate tribute is found in their fine record *If I Should Fall From Grace With God* (1988), which picks up thematically from *King Of America* and mentions Costello and O'Riordan in 'Fiesta'.

Still, the Jags, the Boomtown Rats, Beautiful South, Squeeze, Suzanne Vega: although they all have their merits, a certain view of music might not regard them as key figures; they're not "icons of pop music". Inducting Bob Dylan into something called the Rock'n'Roll Hall of Fame in 1978, Bruce Springsteen described him as crucial ("without Bob") for the Beatles, Beach Boys, Sex Pistols, U2, Marvin Gaye, Grandmaster Flash, the Count Five and Electric Prunes (Bauldie 1992: 192). Perhaps something is out of place here: Dylan overestimated, Costello underestimated. Time may tell whether Costello's torch passed to a younger generation of singer-songwriters: Ron

Sexsmith, Joe Henry, Fiona Apple. However, the point remains: Costello the generous gateway, the vital connection, the expert imitation.

Conclusion

In this final chapter I have examined the views of Costello's critics in the interest of discovering trends in reception, and I introduced a note of doubt concerning Costello's musical influence. As a way of concluding the book as a whole, and given that I have such faith in the views of professional critics as opposed to any other informed listener, I should face the obvious question: well, what do *you* think? In order to do this, I shall briefly reinstate the album as guiding category.

I shall reveal my most contentious assertion, one I like to think has been kept well-hidden: that it would be no disaster if all five first studio albums were to disappear; *My Aim Is True, This Year's Model, Armed Forces, Get Happy!!* and *Trust,* all taken to some imaginary dump. In their place I'd set a short album of about twelve tracks: we agree immediately on the first nine ('Oliver's Army', '(I Don't Want To Go To) Chelsea', 'Radio Radio', 'Alison', 'Clubland' and so on), then descend into bitter recrimination over the last three. Such compilations have appeared from time to time, with the first of Costello's own compilations of fugitive material, *Ten Bloody Marys & Ten How's Your Fathers* (1980), still a dependable template. The cover album *Almost Blue,* like *Kojak Variety,* is a separate issue, essential for considering Costello as a vocal interpreter but, when push comes to imaginary shove, it would share the fate of the first five song-written albums: in their place, a selective, classy collection of Costello's cover versions.

Imperial Bedroom is the first album that stays, as it still works as a continuous record, albeit as two vinyl sides, and a great English record. *Punch The Clock* has been one of the surprises of writing this book, with interesting songs, although listening to them still seems a fearsome prospect. *King Of America* remains the great Costello record, both sides. Although I quibble with his over-emphasis on punk, Greil Marcus is right in seeing it as a significant album of its day, foreshadowing records like REM's *Document* (1987), Lyle Lovett's *Pontiac,* the Waterboys' *Fisherman's Blues,* and Michelle Shocked's *Short Sharp Shocked* (1988). The first vinyl side of *Blood And Chocolate* (up to and including 'I Want You') is just as good: 1986 was Costello's "good year for the roses".

Free of the Attractions and signed to Warner, a new Costello starts with *Spike*. As CDs, albums generally last too long but, taken together, Costello's work now reveals an imaginative and challenging singer-songwriter, conscious of precedent in the past. To this end we have observed: developing mastery of harmony and voice-leading that enables a wide range of the possibilities of tonal music; varied arrangements and orchestrations (reflecting essential separation from and happy reconciliation with the Attractions' line-up of instruments); arrangement and production tied to musical and expressive needs; the exploitation of a wide range of expressive vocal techniques; words that demonstrate varied occupation of verbal space and variety of rhyming practice; and a readiness to explore a wide thematic range within the song's formal constraints. Albums like *All This Useless Beauty, Painted From Memory, When I Was Cruel* and *North* invite repeated listening, containing details that become evident over time.

Recall Costello's joke that filming a video at the time of *Mighty Like A Rose* might have been a good point to end: in another sense, it was around then that he made available all of his musical, vocal and verbal resources, even if greater diversity has risked losing former devotees. Most of Costello's works are in a form that is neither music nor poetry alone, but their expressive and crafty combination. The poet Philip Larkin ended the introduction to his music criticism with the poignant thought that, had his birth date been his death date, how profound would have been his loss for never having heard the jazz he so adored (Larkin 1970: 28). The last thirty years have been all the better for Elvis Costello: here is a body of work that helps us to enjoy or to endure.[41]

Appendix 4.1 Canon formation – Costello in all-time greatest lists

NME best hundred albums 1985: *Imperial Bedroom* 31, *This Year's Model* 40, *Get Happy!!* 67, *Armed Forces* 89, *My Aim Is True* 93

NME best hundred albums 1993: *Blood And Chocolate* 39, *King Of America* 88

NME best hundred albums 2003: no Costello

NME best British albums 2006: *This Year's Model* 66

NME readers' poll 1988: *Imperial Bedroom* 14, *King Of America* 22, *Get Happy!!* 25, *This Year's Model* 53, *Blood And Chocolate* 89

NME readers' poll 2006: no Costello

NME 150 greatest singles (1987): 'Shipbuilding' (recorded by Robert Wyatt) 20, 'Alison' 119

NME best 100 indie singles (1992): 'Less Than Zero' (unranked list)

NME 100 greatest singles (2002): no Costello

Melody Maker top 100 (2000): *Blood And Chocolate* 90

Sounds top 100 (1985): *My Aim Is True* 29, *Armed Forces* 67

Sounds singles (1985): 'Watching The Detectives' 9/100

The Wire (September 1998), '100 records that set the world on fire': no Costello

Record Collector (Janury 2000), '20th Century Collection – classic albums from 21 genres' (ten albums per genre: 1950s, 1960s, 1970s, 1980s, 1990s, avant-garde, blues, country, dance, folk, hip-hop, indie, jazz, metal, pop, prog, psychedelia, punk, reggae, rock, and "soul and funk"): no Costello

Q readers' '100 Greatest Albums in the Universe' (February 1998): *Imperial Bedroom* 96. Revised version in January 2003: no Costello; 2006: no Costello

Mojo, '100 Greatest Albums Ever Made' (August 1995): *This Year's Model* 69

Mojo, '100 Greatest Singers of All Time' (October 1998): no Costello

Special editions, devoted to individual performers or genres, were issued by *NME/Uncut* (c. 25 editions, starting with the Beatles in 2002) and *Q/Mojo* (c. 30 editions, starting with the Beatles in 1999): no Costello.

Rolling Stone
100 best of 1980s (1990): *Get Happy!!* 11, *Imperial Bedroom* 38
Top 100 1967–87 (1987): *This Year's Model* 11, *My Aim Is True* 29, *Get Happy!!* 65
Top 100 (1997): *Imperial Bedroom* 30, *This Year's Model* 47, *My Aim Is True* 64

John Peel Festive 50 appearances
BBC Radio DJ John Peel (1939–2004) occupied an interesting role in British musical culture as the guardian of an idiosyncratic idea of musical good taste. The Festive Fifty was a Christmas poll of the listeners to his programme.

1978: 'Watching The Detectives' 25, 'Alison' 37
1983: Costello's 'Shipbuilding' 48
1986: 'I Want You' 40
Robert Wyatt's 'Shipbuilding' was 2 in 1982 and 11 in the All-time Festive 50 in 2000.

Appendix 4.2 Some histories

Steve Taylor, "The Seventies", includes *This Year's Model*, downhill to *Armed Forces*, just out: "By *Armed Forces* the dream was starting to fade." Not only that, but "such, one is tempted to conclude, is the voracious efficiency of rock's corporate machine. It's a little depressing' (Collis 1980: 318–19).

Originally issued in 1979, Greil Marcus, "Treasure Island", includes both *My Aim Is True* and *This Year's Model*, just out (Marcus 1996: 264).

Ken Tucker covers Costello in "The Postpunk Implosion" (Ward, Stokes and Tucker 1986: 567–9).

Charles T. Brown mentions Costello alongside Graham Parker: "They both made the transition through pub music and punk to new wave. They brought to new wave an energy that included the anger of punk and the sophistication of other musical styles." A photograph of the cover of *Trust* is included (Brown 1987: 247–8).

Donald Clarke, *The Rise and Fall of Popular Music* (1995), has 620 pages, but no Costello.

Robert Palmer has eight "unruly top tens" – roots of rock, R and B, rock and roll, modern rock, funk, punk, postmodern, planet rock – with no Costello (Palmer 1996: 294–8).

Paul Friedlander has several Costello entries, and *The Very Best Of Elvis Costello* is in the discography for the chapter on punk rock (Friedlander 1996: 326).

Reebee Garofalo includes Costello as part of the New Wave, followed by the Police and Pretenders (Garofalo 1997: 329–31).

Chuck Eddy includes *This Year's Model* in his discography for 1978 (1997: 329). *Armed Forces* is "his last worthwhile record, really" (15). Elsewhere, via "trashy organ parts", Costello is set alongside Jim Morrison and Prince: "They all peaked real early in their careers – Morrison with his first LP [*The Doors*, 1967], Costello with his second [*This Year's Model*], Prince with his third [*Dirty Mind*, 1980]. Morrison was a piddly narcissistic reduction of Dylan/Jagger nihilism in the same way Prince and Elvis C. were piddly narcissistic reductions of Johnny Rotten nihilism. And they were all primarily obsessed with trying to get laid" (162).

John Covach has Costello with the Police and Joe Jackson as "British New Wavers in America" (Covach 2006: 430–1). A photograph is included of Costello's 1977 appearance on the American TV show *Saturday Night Live*, in which a performance of 'Less Than Zero' was curtailed for one of 'Radio Radio': "for many, this was a triumphant expression of the punk attitude."

Appendix 4.3 Commentators on Costello

Mick St. Michael (1986) prefers *Punch The Clock* and *Goodbye Cruel World* to *Imperial Bedroom*. He discusses *Imperial Bedroom* at pp. 83–6, an analysis he describes as "a trifle severe".

David Gouldstone includes a ranking order, adding, with admirable precision: "if side two of *This Year's Model* were as good as side one, it would be up there along with *Trust*" (1989: 158).

> Top three: *Get Happy!!, Trust, Imperial Bedroom*
>
> Next two: *My Aim Is True, King Of America* (all five so far "extremely good")
>
> Next five (by deduction): *This Year's Model* (top of this five), *Armed Forces, Ten Bloody Marys & Ten How's Your Fathers, Punch The Clock, Out Of Our Idiot* (bottom of the five)
>
> "Definitely fail to make the grade": *Goodbye Cruel World, Blood And Chocolate*

Brian Hinton avoids rating albums, preferring to respond to each individual song in turn, and gathers critical responses to albums from reviews. However, *Imperial Bedroom* "remains perhaps his most perfect achievement" (1999: 246), and *This Year's Model* seems an assured favourite (134), while *Painted From Memory* is "as graceful and emotional a record as anything Costello had ever (co-)written" (416–17). *Mighty Like A Rose* (340–2) and *Kojak Variety* (382) are criticized more than most, while Hinton shows greater appreciation of *The Juliet Letters* than is often the case (354–6, 358–9).

Larry David Smith is generally positive, especially perhaps about *Trust* (2004: 178), *Spike* (201) and *Mighty Like A Rose* (205). He is critical of *Goodbye Cruel World* (190), damning of *Punch The Clock* (187–8), and *Blood And Chocolate* (197–8).

Graeme Thomson starts from a fan's high estimation, but allows for positives and negatives. *My Aim Is True* is "extraordinarily fresh" (2004: 94) and *This Year's Model* "effortlessly stands up to scrutiny" (115). However, wearing "emperor's new clothes" (133), *Almost Blue* is "only half the towering pop masterpiece it proclaimed itself to be" (134). *Get Happy!!* is "a masterpiece", but *Imperial Bedroom* is again the pinnacle: "fantastic, richly drawn pop music" (190). A dip follows: *Punch The Clock* is "thin and contrived" (200), while *Goodbye Cruel World* seems to be Thomson's nadir, "pretty desperate stuff" (207) that "makes *Punch The Clock* sound like *Blood On The Tracks*" (213). *King Of America* represents "a new lease of life in his writing" (221), while *Blood And Chocolate* "required an element of faith from the listener" (240). Another dip: *Spike* is "somewhat stilted" (261), *Mighty Like A Rose* "heavy, difficult and misconceived" (282). After this, with the exception of *Kojak Variety* ("jaded piece of work", 316), Thomson admires the later albums: *The Juliet Letters* is "triumphant and seductive" (297), *Brutal Youth* "wildly eclectic ... ambitious, melodically broad and warmer" (306), *All This Useless Beauty* is ambiguously "seductive, beguiling" but with "a certain glumness, a sullen quality" (332–3), *Painted From Memory* is "an emotionally involving document" (350), *When I Was Cruel* convincing if not "a truly *great* EC record" (379). Thomson defends the "fragile beauty" of *North* against some of its defects, identifying it as "winter time late-night early-morning listening" (388–9).

Notes

Preface

1. It was kindly footnoted in three locations: Moore 1995; Brackett 1995; Hesmondhalgh 1996.
2. Piston's work has gone through many editions; it was first published in 1941, while Mark de Voto's revision and expansion dates from 1977. My own copy of *Harmony* was published by Victor Gollancz in 1987. The "old" Princeton encyclopaedia was first published in 1965.

1 Past

1. Thomson explains the change of spelling from MacManus to McManus (2004: 9–10).
2. The album title *Day Costello Sings Elvis Presley's Greatest Hits* is given in Thomson 2004: 21.
3. This line exchange occurs towards the end of James Joyce's *A Portrait of the Artist as a Young Man* (1914) (Levin 1976: 526).
4. He credited himself as a lead guitarist on track 19 ('Grave Dance') of *Jake's Progress*.
5. And who's talking: listen to Tom Waits, 'Big In Japan' (*Mule Variations*). Costello and the three Attractions were "inducted into the rock'n'roll hall of *fame*" in Cleveland, Ohio, on 8 March 2003. (Thomson 2004: 386–7).
6. Thomson 2004: 96, 187, 259, 345. My thanks to Dave Laing for clarifying the history of some of these labels. See also the entries for "Record corporation" and "Label", many of them by Laing, in Shepherd *et al.* 2003: 632–7, 683–777.
7. See *Kojak Variety* n95. Throughout the book I shall use the abbreviation (n), to indicate the notes or essay produced by Costello to accompany the CD reissue of an earlier album, followed by the shortened year of reissue (e.g., 95). The essays are discussed in a later chapter.
8. Scary intimations can be found in Thomson 2004: 310–11. Conflict lies at the heart of Keith Negus, "The Production of Culture", in du Gay 1997: 67–118. Negus 1999 is a valuable study by someone who did talk to people in the offices of record companies.
9. "Grub Village" (1970), in Larkin 1983: 188–9.

10. *Ten Bloody Marys & Ten How's Your Fathers* was entitled *Taking Liberties* in the USA.
11. For example, see Johnson and Grant (1979) on William Blake.
12. 'I Wanna Be Loved', written by Farnell and Jenkins, was originally recorded by Teacher's Edition (1973), 'Don't Let Me Be Misunderstood', by Benjamin, Marcus and Caldwell, was first recorded by Nina Simone (1964), and covered a year later by the Animals.
13. *Almost You: The Songs Of Elvis Costello* (Bar/None, 2003), including artists such as Fastball, the Mendoza Line and Vic Chesnutt.
14. Note to "Bacchus" (1955), in Empson 1984: 104.
15. "The Real Thing: Bruce Springsteen", first published 1987 (Frith 1988: 94–101). At 101, Frith describes the tradition and iconography of American "populist anti-capitalism" that supports Springsteen, adding that "no British musician, not even someone with such a profound love of American musical forms as Elvis Costello, could deal with these themes without some sense of irony."
16. Reviewing Costello in concert in 1977, first published 1978.
17. Citizen Elvis is based on an analogy (at p. 135) with the fictional hero of Orson Welles's 1941 film *Citizen Kane*. By my count the epithet is used 120 times within the 160 or so pages of the book that concern Costello, often in the phrases "Citizen Elvis's editorials" or "Citizen Elvis's punishing observations", or at page 220: "Citizen-turned-Reverend Elvis".
18. "I see my exit as being something more like being run over by a bus," Costello said in 1977 to Nick Kent (1994: 193–4). "If I went under a bus today they'd still play 'Oliver's Army' on the radio" (Costello in 2003 to David Hepworth 2003: 67).
19. Accessed via www.youtube.com, on 12/07/2007, and derived from www.maccaspan.com
20. But see Brackett 1995: 161–2, for Costello linked to the British art schools, using the arguments of Frith and Horne 1987.
21. See Costello's comments in *The 100 Best Record Covers of All Time* (*Q* magazine special edition 2001, p. 168).
22. See Gouldstone 1989: 111. Hinton (1999: 21, 66) is terrific on Stiff Records' roots in the hippy era, including reference to earlier artwork by Barney Bubbles.
23. Brief discussion of this theme in Costello is found in Moore 1993: 179.
24. An internet contributor once heard Costello perform 'Pump It Up' with one verse from Chuck Berry's 'Too Much Monkey Business' and one from Bob Dylan's 'Subterranean Homesick Blues'.
25. The song title itself may allude to Terence Rattigan's play *French without Tears* (1936) – a standard of repertory theatres and amateur dramatic groups in the 1940s and 1950s, and filmed in 1939 by David Lean. Could

Costello have seen the film one afternoon on TV? (My thanks to Sandra Margolies for suggesting this connection.)

26. "The *idea* of genres can be way more interesting than the genres themselves" (Eddy 1997: 4).

27. www.elviscostello.info, accessed on 12/07/2007.

28. Excellent discoveries are also to be found in Bruno 2005, for example, at pp. 29, 48–9, 64–5, 147.

29. See Little Feat: *Feats Don't Fail Me Now* (1974). St. Michael describes 'Cold Cold Cold' as a cover version performed by Costello's earlier band Flip City (1986: 13).

30. See Costello's commendation on the cover of Hoskyns 1998b.

31. For Toussaint, see Costello's cover of Yoko Ono's 'Walking On Thin Ice' (*Punch The Clock* n03) and 'Deep Dark Truthful Mirror' (*Spike*).

32. By the Clash (1977), Costello (*This Year's Model*, 1978) and Nick Lowe (1978) respectively. Was it a similar fascination that lay behind Amis 1984? See also Reynolds 1991 on Costello and Martin Amis.

33. Both on *Fifth Dimension* (1966).

34. Paul McCartney has commented on 'My Brave Face' as a Beatles reference. Accessed via www.youtube.com, on 12/07/2007, and derived from www.maccaspan.com

35. Bruno 2005: 74–7, on 'I Stand Accused', written by Tony Colton and Ray Smith (*The Very Best Of The Merseybeats*, 1997). Pete Thomas described the original 'Everyday I Write The Book' in these terms on a BBC radio documentary in 1992.

36. 'All Grown Up' (0'20–34): D–**Bm–C#**–F#m–A7; 'Blackberry Way': **Em (C,C#,C)–F#**–Am–Em.

37. See Eddy 1997: 121, on Van Morrison's ululations.

38. I discuss these changes in sound quality, with reference to Suzanne Vega, some of whose work was also produced by Mitchell Froom, in Griffiths 2004a: 560–1, 568–70.

39. Compare 0'31–39 of Costello with 0'25–32 or 0'58–1'06 of Waits: the chord progression is Dm–Am–B7–E.

40. Waits and Costello were among many musicians to contribute to Hal Willner's varied record productions: Waits is on *Lost In The Stars: The Music Of Kurt Weill* (1985), while Costello performs 'Lost In The Stars' on another Willner tribute to Weill, *September Songs* (1997), as well as on *Weird Nightmare: Meditations On Mingus* (1992).

41. Film footage of Mina performing the song on Italian TV in 1965 was available at www.youtube.com, accessed on 12/07/2007.

42. Compare the melody (A–C–A–F–C, B–D–B–G–D) at 1'57 bass, 2'06 melody of Bowie with 0'35 of Costello (D–F–D, A–G–A–G–A: "nothing that you can do for you").

43. *The Best Of Detroit Spinners* (Warner, 2000).
44. The connection between the songs was also sung on the US digital TV channel VH1, in a "Storytellers" programme about Costello in 1997.
45. The B-side of 'Oliver's Army' in 1979, also on *Ten Bloody Marys & Ten How's Your Fathers* and elsewhere in reissues.
46. *Lady Day: The Best Of Billie Holiday* (Sony, 2001). Alison Moyet went on to a 1985 British hit single with a cover of Billie Holiday's 'That Old Devil Called Love'.
47. Costello performs 'My Funny Valentine', 'Gloomy Sunday' and 'Almost Blue' on *Marian McPartland's Piano Jazz* (Concord, 2005), a radio programme recorded in 2003.
48. *Imperial Bedroom* n02 describes Chet Baker's versions. And see *Bespoke Songs* n98.
49. Costello describes the film *Straight to Hell*, in which he acted and for which he provided music, as "this pastiche of a Spaghetti Western (which, I suppose, means that it was a pastiche of a parody)" (*Blood And Chocolate* n95). Pastiche and parody are discussed in Jameson 1991: 17.
50. The line at 0'41 ("from rage to anaesthesia") may be from the Hanns Eisler song 'An den kleinen Radioapparat', "adapted" by Sting as 'The Secret Marriage' on ... *Nothing Like The Sun* (1987).
51. See Fabian Gudas, "Originality" (Preminger and Brogan 1993: 869–70).
52. Discussion following "The Cultural Study of Popular Music", in Grossberg, Nelson and Treischler 1992: 183.
53. "We want to honour art school musicians for thirty years of music which has been funny, fascinating and, above all, argumentative" (Frith and Horne 1987: 180).
54. *The Great Rock'n'Roll Swindle* (1979), but recorded in 1976.
55. Elton John has a notably bad version on *Victim Of Love* (1979), like a stodgy school dinner.
56. Graham Parker, born 1950, Joe Strummer 1952, Jerry Dammers 1954, Joe Jackson and Costello 1955, Tilbrook and Difford 1954 and 1957, John Lydon 1956, Paul Weller 1958. Ian Dury was older, born in 1942.

2 Music

1. See also the commentary to 'The Other Side Of Summer' on *The Right Spectacle* DVD (2005).
2. Wolfgang Bernhard Fleischmann and J. K. Newman, "Classicism", for example, has seven options (Preminger and Brogan 1993: 215–18)
3. Wayne C. Booth, "Pluralism" (Preminger and Brogan 1993: 918–20).
4. To be pedantic, I don't know of much "early rock'n'roll" in Costello – 'Mystery Dance' on *My Aim Is True*? – if by that we mean Elvis Presley, Bill Haley, Carl Perkins.

5. But see C. A. J. Coady's entry "Relativism, epistemological": "Indeed, global relativism at the level of 'good for me' has so little to recommend it that its popularity with ordinary people is truly astonishing" (in Honderich 1995: 757).

6. Or as Alex Ross did at a concert performance of *Il Sogno*: "I got out a book and started to read." Weblog entry dated 18/7/04, accessed via www.therestisnoise.com, 12/07/2007.

7. Costello: "These musical ghettos the radio stations have created don't allow people to have a completely open interest in music." Interview with Tony Lioce for the *Providence Journal* in 1983 (Smith 2004: 152).

8. The table is basic maths, dividing the total time of the album by the number of tracks to reach an average. The CD clock made all of this more visible and germane: I don't remember totting up totals for each track in the vinyl days, even though summaries were sometimes given. Note that I use expanded versions of the first three albums, to include 'Watching The Detectives' (*My Aim Is True*), 'Radio Radio' (*This Year's Model*), and '(What's So Funny 'Bout) Peace, Love And Understanding?' (*Armed Forces*). *Blood And Chocolate* has three notably long tracks ('Tokyo Storm Warning', 'I Want You' and 'Battered Old Bird') while *The Juliet Letters* has two notably short tracks ('Deliver Us' and 'Why?').

9. Larry David Smith might note the added time as support for his idea of *Imperial Bedroom* instigating a "punk tunesmith" period.

10. Everett 2000: 269–345 is a major source for this research, as well as my roots in Piston 1987. Everett deals with formal divisions at pp. 272–8.

11. The cadence of 'Radio Sweetheart', "two plagals and one perfect", echoes the "three plagals and one perfect" that end 'Roadrunner' (Jonathan Richman and the Modern Lovers, 1975).

12. Mercer-Taylor (1995: 39) observes tonal unity across the tracks of *Blood And Chocolate*, an interesting avenue for examination not followed here.

13. Antonia King identified this allusion.

14. Everett (2000: 318) sums up passages like these as points in tonal music where "intermediate verticalities have no harmonic function, but are driven instead by counterpoint". That is to say, the music is governed by the free flow of separate parts (counterpoint), sometimes harmonized (as "intermediate verticalities") rather than the decisive and structural motion from one harmonic point to another ("harmonic function").

15. Sheila Davis refers to such a section as the "climb" (1985: 55).

16. Everett (2000: 319) has Bob Dylan's 'Simple Twist Of Fate' (1974) and 'Make You Feel My Love' (1997) as examples.

17. One listener hears reference to Paul McCartney's 'Maybe I'm Amazed' (1970), accessed via www.elviscostello.info, 12/07/2007.

18. Alan Robinson, liner note to Elvis Costello, *Singles, Volume One* (Edsel, 2003).

19. See Piston 1987: 57–9, 222–5. For mixture, see Forte 1962: 460–2.
20. "Expanded journeys to chromatically derived tonal areas" are included in Everett 2000: 307–11. In order to understand this, think of the white notes on the piano (C major): mixture enables the music to explore the black notes as tonal areas in themselves, enabling harmonic references (in C) like E♭ major, F# minor, and so on.
21. 'Is That Love?' (1981) by Squeeze, produced by Costello, is a good example of this principle as the musical basis of the song.
22. Chords: Bm–G–C#dim–F#. In the minor key, "chord ii" is a diminished chord – in this case, the notes C#, E, G. The guitar chord describes it as "C#m7–5".
23. See the cover of *A Hard Night's Day: A History Of Stiff Records* (MCA, 1997).
24. See also Bruno 2005: 57.
25. Stevie Wonder's 'I Just Called To Say I Love You' (1984) demonstrates this twice, from D flat to D at 2'57, to E flat at 3'30. At 4'16–21, what an ending! My compilation follows with the drumbeat of 'Superstition': instant forgiveness.
26. "I've never modulated a song in midstream," says Leonard Cohen (in Zollo 1997: 342). "I might find a way to do it – maybe in the middle of a line except in [*sic*] the beginning of a verse. There might be some sneaky ways to do it."
27. *Trust* n03 mentions the acquisition of a Bechstein baby grand piano in 1980, and the 2003 edition of *Trust* includes a solo piano performance by Costello of 'The Long Honeymoon'.
28. The documentary was researched by Pete Frame and Kevin Howlett.
29. "You can't beat 2 guitars, bass, drum," says Lou Reed on the *New York* album cover (1989).
30. At the time, there really were pianos in British pubs. I played them regularly, but that's a different story! See Frame (1980: 28, 30) for marvellous presentations of the pub rock scene, including the Attractions. *Naughty Rhythms: The Best Of Pub Rock* (EMI, 1996) is an excellent compilation, with sleeve notes by Will Birch (and see Birch 2000), drummer in the Kursaal Flyers. 'Surrender To The Rhythm', Nick Lowe's 1972 song for Brinsley Schwarz, sounds like a template for some of the songs on *My Aim Is True*: its "link" section (0'36–50), ending with dominant preparation for the chorus, sounds like a background to 'Pay It Back' and Sneaky Feelings'.
31. 'Talking In The Dark' (*Ten Bloody Marys & Ten How's Your Fathers*; *Armed Forces*: 0'50–1'11) has a Nieve organ solo that sounds like Rick Wakeman or Tony Banks.
32. 'Desert Island Woman' and 'Breathe A Little' from *Bongos Over Balham* (1974), and 'Friday Song' (1975). 'Breathe A Little' is jazz cocktail pastiche.

They were managed by Jake Riviera with artwork by Barney Bubbles.

33. For an earlier version of a similar moment, see Cale and Bockris 1999: 70, 74. Concluding the sleeve note to *Naughty Rhythms*, Dai Davies makes the perceptive observation that pub rock, describing a "commercial reality", allowed for greater diversity than the "musical styles" of folk and progressive rock. "In reality, the Sex Pistols were no less of a Pub Rock group than Ducks Deluxe, only a bit younger."

34. Mick St. Michael was snooty about this view in 1986, sensing the arrival of johnny-come-latelies: "Significantly, although *Imperial Bedroom* is disliked by many enthusiasts, those less conversant with Costello's music find it one of his more attractive records" (St. Michael 1986: 83). A different view is taken by Stuart Maconie: "*Imperial Bedroom* is Elvis Costello's best LP – ignore any statements to the contrary" (in Aizlewood 1994: 16).

35. No one could play it: see *Imperial Bedroom* n05 for the story of the three-man accordion.

36. Costello's relationship with Bruce Thomas eventually came to an end: see Thomas, "Preface to the new edition" (2003, not paginated).

37. Included in the Costello compilation *Bespoke Songs* (1998).

38. Perone makes a thematic connection between 'I Want You' (*Blood And Chocolate*) and Schumann's 'Ich Grolle Nicht' (text by Heinrich Heine) (Perone 1998: 6).

39. I evoke the word only in the sense of progress in the harmony book: see "Tonality in Schubert" (1928) or "Normality and Freedom in Music" (1936) (Tovey 1949: 134–59, 183–201). The progress of "progressive rock" meant different things: see Moore 1993: 56–8 and Macan 1997: 26–7.

40. The same chromatic line and transposition are found at the opening of 'Maybe This Time' in Kander and Ebb's *Cabaret*.

41. Everett (2000: 318–19) has spotted a chromatic descending *inner* line (at 0'32–37) in that "very catchy pop song", 'Veronica' (*Spike*).

42. Often explained for the benefit of Christian listeners as the "Amen" cadence, the plagal cadence is prevalent in general terms, being chord IV to chord I (so, in C, chord F to chord C). 'Hey Joe' was memorably harmonized by Jimi Hendrix (1967) as a series of interlocked plagal cadences: see Everett 2000: 323–4.

43. Following the logic of the harmony, in theoretical terms the B is more strictly C♭, leading on from D♭m. Tovey was excited by these re-spellings, for instance, in referring to the development of the first movement of Beethoven's Opus 2, No. 1 in C (1931: 25–6).

44. Tovey often made reference to this distinction. See, for instance, "Tonality in Schubert" (1928) (1949: 137).

45. I keep hearing the music for "used to be victim" from the chorus of 'Accidents Will Happen' (*Armed Forces*) at 0'13–17.

46. Are the Doors fans in the third verse, "making movies", older but equally annoying equivalents of the "Showbiz Kids" of the Steely Dan song (*Countdown To Ecstasy* 1973)?

47. The words "brutal youth" are contained in the second verse.

48. "I believe it is among the very best songs that I have been fortunate enough to write" (Costello, *Brutal Youth* n02).

49. The "emotional line" of a song is discussed and diagrammed in Webb 1998: 105–35.

50. One CD edition of *North* included a bonus track, 'Impatience', but I assume the cycle ends with 'I'm In The Mood Again'.

51. Each bar consisting of three beats: the music is "in three/four".

52. Note also the orchestral lead-in just before the downbeat at 3'52, glissandi galore.

53. For example, the harmonic adventures of the word "Alfie" in the song with that title (1966) is a lesson in itself; while 'Anyone Who Had A Heart' (1963) starts with a bar of five followed by four.

54. The published score (Chester, 1996) specifies each member's contribution: cellist Jacqueline Thomas co-wrote with Costello the music to 'Taking Your Life In Your Hands', while first violinist Michael Thomas wrote the music for 'Jacksons, Monk and Rowe'.

55. Costello interviewed by Allan Jones, *Melody Maker*, 25 June 1977 (Brackett 2005a: 327).

56. See Vaughan Sinclair, "Costello's Dream", liner note, *Il Sogno*.

57. Weblog entry dated 18/7/04, accessed via www.therestisnoise.com 12/07/2007.

58. Third in a four-part series, broadcast 14 March 1992. Transcription by Dai Griffiths.

59. Nieve is described on the sleeve of *Goodbye Cruel World* as "Maurice Worm" making a "random racket".

60. Toni Prince, 'Just To Hear Your Voice', *Country* (Vinyl Junkie, 1995) is one example among many.

61. '9th and Hennepin', *Rain Dogs* (1985).

62. Stephen Heath's 1977 translation is reprinted in Frith and Goodwin 1990: 293–300.

63. Moore thought that a variety of headings describing resonance corresponded to Barthes's grain, adding this point as two separate factors: attitude to pitch and to rhythm (Moore 1993: 43).

64. On Costello's changes of regional accent: "The Singer, on the other hand, was given to wild variations, particularly during stage pronouncements. In Liverpool, it became a thick, nasal Scouse. It was a top o' the morning, may the road rise with you, bejabbers brogue in Dublin. In London, it became a Cheltenham cockney that recalled the early Jagger" (Thomas 2003: 35).

65. Dated 1974–5 on extended *My Aim Is True*. Is that the start of Wings' 'Band On The Run' (1973) in the opening guitar riff?

66. Is that really him? The Edge from U2 also has the sort of falsetto that convinces the listener that a female voice is present.

67. Found on *Out Of Our Idiot* and the 2002 edition of *Blood And Chocolate*, and not as polished as the one on *Blood And Chocolate*. Bruno (2005: 17) refers to the backing vocals on this "bizarre version". The arrangement reminds me of a great track on Stiff: 'Free Yourself' by the Untouchables (1984).

68. At 3'00–03 of 'I've Got You Under My Skin', on *Songs For Swingin' Lovers!* (Capitol, 1956). *Desert Island Discs*, broadcast 28.2.91.

69. Ross MacManus, from a documentary entitled "In The Mood", National Sound Archive (PLN 007902A7066).

70. BBC recording, National Sound Archive (T86746). See also "Joe Loss: The Legacy" (H2707).

71. Internet research reveals a fascinating song: possibly Russian, travelling via Finland and American 1960s folk music to Paul McCartney and finally to Mary Hopkin. Gene Raskin wrote the English words.

72. An affectionate memoir of Ross MacManus is found in Stuart Maconie, "Get Happy!" (Aizlewood 1994: 17–19).

73. A demonstration record, HMV Pop 1279, can be found at the National Sound Archive.

74. From 'In The Mood', National Sound Archive, PLN 007902A7066.

75. Compare Bob Dylan: "There are a lot of spaces between the Carter Family, Buddy Holly and Ornette Coleman, but Jerry Garcia filled them all." Costello comment found in *Mojo* (Costello 2002b). Ross MacManus comments on Leslie Vinyl in "Joe Loss: The Legacy" (National Sound Archive H2707).

76. A recording found on the 2006 edition of *The Juliet Letters*.

77. On Nonesuch Records in the vinyl days: Schoenberg's *Pierrot Lunaire* and songs by Charles Ives.

78. Sting, *Songs From The Labyrinth* (Deutsche Grammophon, 2006) enables an unexpected comparison of both singers performing the same Dowland song. See James Fenton on Dowland and Sting, *Guardian*, "Review", 14 October 2006, p. 15.

79. "Online exchange with Simon Frith, part 2", accessed via www.rockcritics.com, 12/07/2007.

80. See *The Look Of Love: The Burt Bacharach Collection* (Warner, 2001).

81. William Wordsworth, "Preface to Lyrical Ballads" (1802) (1984: 598, 611).

82. For an account and discussion of the incident, see Bruno 2005: 41–8 and Costello, *Get Happy!!* n03.

83. Gouldstone thought that "much needed self-deprecating levity" would be achieved by transposing the song to A flat (1989: 143).

84. Thomas was more explicit at Thomson 2004: 121.

85. A photograph included with the reissued *Mighty Like A Rose* (2002, at pp. 22–3) seems to capture the singer "hand on heart".
86. *A Tapestry of Dreams* (Barclay, 1974).
87. Costello's version is also included on *Light Of Day: A Tribute To Bruce Springsteen* (Buffalo Records, 2003).
88. At 0'14 and 0'44 of Parsons, at 0'20 and 0'48 of Costello. Parsons's recording is in F, so the low note is B flat, Costello's is a tone higher, in G, with the low note C.
89. Originally performed by Betty Everett (1965), Sam and Dave (1967) and the Temptations (1966).
90. McCartney compares the song to moments in cartoons where devils appear to urge bad behaviour, and to moments in Beatles songs (like 'Getting Better') where Lennon would add a grumpy counterpoint to McCartney's genial lines. Accessed via www.youtube.com, on 12/07/2007, and derived from www.maccaspan.com
91. "When I made *My Aim Is True*, my favourite record was Randy Newman's first album" (Costello in Fricke, 2004).
92. *Surrender To The Rhythm: The Best Of Brinsley Schwarz* (EMI, 1991), also on *Naughty Rhythms: The Best Of Pub Rock* (EMI, 1996). Costello's version is included in expanded versions of *Almost Blue. Basher: The Best Of Nick Lowe* (Demon, 1989) included 'American Squirm' next to the Costello version.
93. Steve Earle, *Just An American Boy: The Audio Documentary* (2003). See also *Jerusalem* (2002).
94. See Dave Marsh (1989: 6–7) on the Righteous Brothers, 'You've Lost That Loving Feeling' (1964).
95. *Judy Sings Dylan: Just Like A Woman* (Geffen, 1993).

3 Words

1. Joni Mitchell said in 1985: "When Dylan sang 'You gotta lot of nerve', I thought, Hallelujah, now, the American pop song has grown up. It's wide open. You can write about anything that literature can write about" (in Russell and Tyson 1995: 53). See also Robert Christgau (2000), "Let's get busy in Hawaiian: a hundred years of ragged beats and cheap tunes", accessed through www.robertchristgau.com, 13/07/2007.
2. Should the ballad be included, in the story-telling sense? Woody Guthrie's 'Pretty Boy Floyd' (1940) begins: "Come gather round, you people, a story I will tell." On "Genre", see the entries in both *The New Princeton Encyclopaedia of Poetry and Poetics* (Preminger and Brogan 1993) and *The New Grove Dictionary of Music and Musicians* (Sadie 2001).
3. 'Dukla Prague Away Kit', a record by Half Man Half Biscuit (1985), is in fact closer to Davis's history category, telling the story of playing games as

boys; but its title has the air of fabulation. See *C86: 48 Tracks From The Birth Of Indie Pop* (Castle, 2006).

4. Hinton has 'Tread the Dirt Down'.

5. 'Return The Gift' and 'Natural's Not In It', *Entertainment!* (1979).

6. Smith 2004; subsequent page numbers in text refer to this edition.

7. Larry David Smith shows his awareness of the issue with reference to 'I Want You', a joke that backfires: "One gets chills just *reading* these lines (and if you get it bad, *never* listen to Costello sing it!)" (p. 242). Whether this is due to choice or a lack of musical ability is hard to tell, though his description of *The Juliet Letters* at p. 247 as "rhythmic snippets and orchestral meanderings" does not inspire confidence.

8. Compare the discussion of "gibberish" above. 'Strict Time' is a "relational complaint", he says twice (pp. 178, 240).

9. Smith, p. 240, allows "societal-relational hybrids".

10. At Smith, p. 203, the "relational complaint" of 'Deep Dark Truthful Mirror' "remains in the shadows (reiterated by the chorus)".

11. See Costello, *Get Happy!!* n03, but which Smith may not have had access to.

12. See T. V. F. Brogan, "Line" (Preminger and Brogan 1993: 694–7).

13. "The line of music is very influential in determining the length of a line or the density, the syllabic density" (in Zollo 1997: 341).

14. See Griffiths 2003: 39–59. One of the examples (at pp. 48–9) is 'No Action' (*This Year's Model*), which builds on the analysis in Moore 1993: 176–7.

15. The line was noted by Robert Christgau, "Rock Lyrics Are Poetry (Maybe)" (1967, revised 1968) (in Eisen 1969: 240).

16. *I'm Your Man* (Columbia, 1991). And see Cohen's conversation with Zollo (1997), *passim*.

17. The three first albums (*My Aim Is True*, *This Year's Model*, *Armed Forces*) began with voice alone.

18. There were three versions: see *Blood And Chocolate* n05.

19. It is one of those tracks that announces itself as good from the word go: slow pace (it better be good!), the piano part, a quality of recording; compare the start of Aretha Franklin's 'I Never Loved A Man (The Way That I Love You)' (1967).

20. A lovely song of Nick Lowe, 'What's Shakin' On The Hill', *Party Of One* (Reprise, 1990) also has its words "talking back" to its opening riff. "EC" is thanked on the sleeve.

21. My ears hear a similar point at 1'30 of George Harrison's 'Here Comes The Sun' (*Abbey Road*, 1969).

22. The subtleties of verbal phrasing were never better than Bacharach and David's 'Walk On By' (1964): rhyming "street–cry–meet–by", the syllable count descends, 9/5/4/3, mirroring the lovers' nervous approach to each other, ending on the three-syllable request to "walk on by".

23. St. Michael thought (of *Get Happy!!*) that "with so many sets of words to come up with, Costello plundered his past" (1986: 58).

24. "And yet it is clear that much could be learned about literary and cultural history if any prominent word were taken, *nature*, say, and the itinerary of its changing partnerships traced; or if a recurrent pair, say *justice/supplice*, were inspected against its changing verse contexts" (Preminger and Brogan 1993: 1061).

25. We may distinguish twelve criteria for the analysis and categorization of rhyme types (summarized from Preminger and Brogan 1993: 1054–8): 1. By the number of syllables (for example, single, double and triple). 2. By the morphology of the words which the rhyming syllables inhabit. 3. By the position of stress on the rhyming (and adjacent) syllables. 4. By the lexical category of the rhyming words (the use of a noun to rhyme with a verb, for example). 5. By the degree of closeness of the sound match in the rhyme (for example, the "true" or "perfect" rhyme and various forms of "near" rhyme). 6. By the semantic field of the words, for example, "As every rhyming poet knows, choice of the word for a rhyme immediately constrains the range of words available for its mate(s), hence for extension or completion of the sense" (p. 1057). 7. By the effects of further complication of sound patterning in the rhyme words (for example, assonance and consonance). 8. By participation of the rhymes in sound patterning nearby. 9. By the position in the line of the rhymes (for example, internal rhyme). 10. By the interval between the rhymes. 11. By the order of sequencing of rhyme (for example, formal patterns, rhyme and stanza form). 12. By sight versus sound (for example, eye rhyme)

26. The comparison brought together Brogan's first, fourth and sixth categories, while the review of rhyme corresponds to Brogan's fifth (with Mark E. Smith at the seventh). My source for the fourth category was Wimsatt's "classic 1944 essay" (Preminger and Brogan 1993: 1056), "One Relation of Rhyme to Reason" (Wimsatt 1954: 153–66).

27. This pair also includes assonance. See Percy G. Adams, "Alliteration", "Assonance" and "Consonance" (Preminger and Brogan 1993: 36–8, 102–4, 236–7).

28. Robert Christgau, review of *Blood And Chocolate*, accessed through www.robertchristgau.com, 12/07/2007. The other song to break the six-minute barrier on *Blood And Chocolate* was 'I Want You', though 'Battered Old Bird' falls only ten seconds short.

29. The single version, which followed an older practice of splitting a long track into two parts for the 45-rpm version, carried a striking visual image, a tabloid front page designed by Costello as Eamonn Singer.

30. The "backward guitar" at 2'50 or 6'06 may refer to 1'08 of 'Tomorrow Never Knows' from the Beatles, *Revolver* (1966), a solo that "marks an important event in the Beatles' history" (Everett 1999: 36). "It's very

simple and not original," was Gouldstone's view of 'Tokyo Storm Warning',
but he heard some useful sources: "The tune is a close relation of Chuck
Berry's 'Memphis', the rhythm guitar chugs up and down through sixths and
sevenths as in a thousand other rock songs, the riff from the Rolling Stones'
'Satisfaction' whinges away in the background (probably as an intentional
allusion), and the guitar solo sounds like one of George Harrison's out-takes
from *circa* 1966" (Gouldstone 1989: 151).

31. Note that the fifth verse adds another pair in the same musical space as
the CC of verses 6 and 7, so AABBCCDD.
32. Hinton notes the rhyme of "purse" and "mercy" (1999: 303).
33. Understandably, Smith (2004) tends to misread the political context of the
UK, tying it too much to royalty and aristocracy ("Her Majesty's United
Kingdom", "Royal Family" and "aristocratic England" are twice mentioned),
rather than to Parliament and the votes of the British electorate.
34. The Malvinas of 'Tokyo Storm Warning' is the Argentine name for the
Falkland Islands.
35. Costello's essays for reissues of *Punch The Clock* and *Goodbye Cruel World*
contain extensive sections on 'Pills And Soap', 'Shipbuilding' and 'Peace In
Our Time'.
36. Red Wedge was the name of a loose collective of musicians and other
performers, formed in 1985 with the aim of securing a Labour victory in
the 1987 election, and eventually disbanded in 1990. See Denselow
1989: 203–32.
37. Results for other general elections of the period can be found in Morgan
2001: 421–2 (1979), 466 (1983), 512 (1992) and 543 (1997).
38. See Angela McRobbie, "Looking Back at New Times and Its Critics", in
Morley and Chen 1996: 238–61.
39. *New Musical Express*, 11 April 1992, p. 14. The title was a deliberate
conflation of Iron Maiden, a prominent heavy metal band, and the Iron Lady,
an epithet often used to describe Margaret Thatcher.
40. 'Goon Squad' appears on *Rock Against Racism's Greatest Hits* (RARecords,
1980).
41. 'Free Will and Testament' and 'Blues In Bob Minor' on *Shleep* (1997), 'Left
On Man' on *Dondestan* (1998). Wyatt receives a "salutation" on the sleeve
of *When I Was Cruel*.
42. Echoes of John Lennon's 'How Do You Sleep?' (1971).
43. The odd reference to "family pride", relating to a soldier, returns in both
The Juliet Letters ('I Thought I'd Write To Juliet') and *Brutal Youth* ('Kinder
Murder'), the latter almost a sequel to 'Sleep Of The Just'.
44. One of Thomas Moore's *Irish Melodies* from the early nineteenth century:
see John Warrack's article on Moore in Sadie (2001). The Irish tenor John
McCormack (1884–1945) is quoted on the sleeve of *Mighty Like A Rose*.

See McCormack, *Songs and Ballads* (EMI, 2002), and Desmond Shawe-Taylor's article on McCormack in Sadie (2001).

45. Reviewing *Spike* for *NME* in 1989, Terry Staunton heard Stevie Wonder's 'Isn't She Lovely?' (1976) in the repeating melody. It works, and the thought of just one of Costello's earnest, gloomy lines substituting for the words "Isn't she lovely? Isn't she wonderful?" is enough for a big laugh.

46. "Five people died, several MPs were injured, and Mrs Thatcher was lucky to escape alive ... [the IRA said]: 'You were lucky this time. But, remember, we only have to be lucky once'" (Mulholland 2002: 117).

47. W. H. Auden, "In Memory of W. B. Yeats' (1939) (Auden 1978: 242). See also Sarah Maguire, "Poetry Makes Nothing Happen" (Herbert and Hollis 2000: 248–51).

48. *The Stephen Lawrence Inquiry: Report of an Inquiry by Sir William Macpherson of Cluny* (HMSO, 1999), 6.48, p. 30. See also *The Future of Multi-ethnic Britain: The Parekh Report* (Profile Books, 2000).

49. Chrissie Hynde as Cher in the 1985 cover version with UB40.

50. A similar point is made by Frith (1996: 171): Costello's songs are "not so much ... about people as about characterization".

51. In addition to his studies of the Band and country soul, Hoskyns (1998a) has written a history of glam rock, a crossover that was beyond Costello.

52. Costello has "divorcee" for "divorcé".

53. See "The Voices of Women" (Frith 1988: 155). Having made Frith "*physically* uneasy by the sense of exclusion" as one of the Mistakes, Mavis Bayton went on to complete *Frock Rock: Women Performing Popular Music* (1998), and the point I make here owes much to her book.

54. Note that Smith found only three or four "relational celebrations" across the output: 'Jack Of All Parades' (*King Of America*), 'Such Unlikely Lovers' (*Painted From Memory*), '15 Petals' (*When I Was Cruel*), as well as O'Riordan's 'Broken' (*Mighty Like A Rose*) (Smith 2004: 240).

55. *Little Earthquakes* (East West, 1992) and *Stereo-typical: As, Bs, and Rarities* (EMI, 2000). 'The Boiler' originally 1982.

56. *Squeezing Out Sparks* (Vertigo, 1979).

57. *World of Morrissey* (Parlophone, 1995).

58. See James William Johnson, "Lyric" (Preminger and Brogan 1993: 713–15) and Elise Bickford Jorgens, "Song" (*ibid.*: 1165–7).

59. Recorded by Frank Sinatra in 1961, the song by Sammy Cahn and Jimmy Van Heusen.

60. Recorded by Perry Como in 1958, the song by Burt Bacharach and Hal David.

61. *Toy Story* (1995), and also found on *Guilty: 30 Years of Randy Newman* (Warner/Rhino, 1998).

62. The *Requiem* was a chart hit in 1985, four years before *Spike*.

63. *Sweets From A Stranger* (1982).

64. Thurschwell (1999: 295–307) examines two novels that derive their titles from Costello songs: Bret Easton Ellis's *Less Than Zero* (1985) and Nick Hornby's *High Fidelity* (1995).
65. And see Daniel Karlin, "Bob Dylan's Names" (Corcoran 2002: 27–49).
66. The distinction is dramatized in the novel *Nice Work* (Lodge 1988: 154–7).
67. Bruno (2005: 97) sensibly hears the positioning of Liverpool's river in the trio as pride of place and a nod to the city's beat groups though, funnily enough, I always hear prime position going to the Newcastle river at the *end* of the line!
68. Note in passing how many of Costello's place names are trisyllabic – Rotherhithe, Liverpool – and so on, something to do with the melody, perhaps.
69. 'Watching The Detectives' is not spelled out in Smith's Chapter 8, and I deduced a category from Smith 2004: 167–8.
70. The expanded edition of *Mighty Like A Rose* (2002) added to the group 'Just Another Mystery', a strange song based on the composer Béla Bartók.
71. Interviewing Leonard Cohen, Paul Zollo observed that most songwriters might have managed two of the verses of 'Democracy' (on *The Future*, 1992) rather than the six of Cohen's recording; Cohen said, in reply: "I've got about sixty" (including presumably, among other things, sixty rhymes for the "A" of USA) (Zollo 1997: 335).
72. The present section is a summary of, and extract from, a complete survey of the liner notes to date, in which a total of 34 liner notes were examined.
73. "Everything about you sounds like it is ghost written" ('New Amsterdam'). The *NME* asked Morrissey, of all people, if he was seeking assistance in writing an autobiography. "Are you doing it yourself?" "*(splutters)* Yes. I'm not really going to hire an old *Melody Maker* journalist to help me find the dictionary" (17 April 2004, p. 23).
74. Published by Chester Music, 1996.
75. Costello was in good company. Following his visit there in 1909, Freud is supposed to have said, "America is a mistake; a gigantic mistake, it is true, but none the less a mistake" (Jones 1964: 348).
76. Bruce Thomas had described his astonishment at the *King Of America* cover on the 1992 BBC radio documentary. See also Thomson 2004: 225.

4 Criticism

1. Frank Kuppner, *A Bad Day for the Sung Dynasty*, no. 242 (Carcanet Press, 1984) (reprinted in Hulse, Kennedy and Morley 1993: 159).
2. See also Brackett 1995: 157.
3. Fabian Gudas, "Taste" and "Evaluation" (Preminger and Brogan 1993: 1266–7, 391–4) and Joseph C. Sitterson, Jr, "Canon" (*ibid.*: 166–7).

4. For the views of fans of the Smiths, see Gallagher, Campbell and Gillies 1995; also see Frith, "Confessions of a Rock Critic" (1988: 166–7).
5. This section benefits from hours of conversation with Jennifer Skellington about and around her research into music journalism in broadsheet newspapers in the 1980s.
6. On the grading, see www.robertchristgau.com. Christgau used two systems over the years. Costello's A grade in 1978 was "a great record both of whose sides offer enduring pleasure and surprise. You should own it." C+ was "a not disreputable performance, most likely a failed experiment or a pleasant piece of hackwork". In the earlier system, there was some way to go to the bottom (E-), while in the later system starred honourable mentions are sub-B+. Scissors indicate good "cuts" on a bad album. The "dud" category (for *The Juliet Letters* and *All This Useless Beauty*) was "a bad record whose details rarely merit further thought. At the upper level it may merely be overrated, disappointing, or dull. Down below it may be contemptible."
7. Most of this information derives from www.rocklist.net.
8. See the Costello-free zone that was "The 90 best albums of the 1990s", in *Q*, 159 (December 1999), p. 70.
9. *Q* was launched in 1986, *Mojo* in 1993, *Uncut* in 1997 and *Word* in 2003.
10. My apologies to publications in the non-anglophone world! It is hard to think that Costello never featured in the ratings of *Les Inrockuptibles*, since my copy of *Le Rock Anglais* (La Sirène, 1992) has Costello interviewed alongside cover-boy Morrissey, Lloyd Cole, Brian Eno, XTC, Julian Cope, the Buzzcocks, Happy Mondays, Monochrome Set and Jesus and Mary Chain.
11. The 1977 article is gathered with one from 1991 as "Horn Rims from Hell: Elvis Costello", in Kent 1994: 188–201. Page references in the text are to this edition.
12. The Who, 'My Generation' (1965).
13. Kent is depicted in the first verse of 'Waiting For The World To End' (*My Aim Is True*).
14. Page references in the text are to this edition. There are in all thirteen Costello-related references or chapters: in the introduction, dated 1992 (6–7); a review of a 1977 concert, 1978 (25–6); a review of *Armed Forces*, 1979 (34–8); a review of *Taking Liberties*, 1980 (135–7); the *Rolling Stone* interview, 1982 (221–34); a chapter on 'Pills And Soap', 1984 (249–52); a review of *Goodbye Cruel World*, 1984 (258–61); a review of Bret Easton Ellis's novel *Less Than Zero*, 1985 (288–9); a review of *King Of America*, 1986 (311–14); a chapter, "Music", comparing Costello's 'Peace, Love And Understanding' with Brinsley Schwarz's original, 1987 (357); a page on 'I Want You', performed in 1987 (358); a page on 'Tramp The Dirt Down', 1989 (367); the discography (411–12).

15. At pp. 25, 34, 135 ("his notorious, brilliantly careerist comment"), 136 ("revenge and guilt ... can be more specifically named as an obsession with love and fascism"), 137, 233 (interview question), 258 (now imagined as an ironic reference made by Costello), 357. Marcus notes the impact of his own chapter, "Elvis Costello Repents", on Bret Easton Ellis's *Less Than Zero* at pp. 288–9.

16. This is the reason for one of only two references to Marcus's review of 'Pills And Soap' in David Brackett's chapter on this track (Brackett 1995: 235, footnotes 33 and 37).

17. This is a version of a sentence from "The Author as Producer" of 1937. See Arato and Gebhardt 1978: 256.

18. Smith 2004: 165 for summary, or 167–232. Subsequent page references in the text are to this edition. The first phase, up to *Imperial Bedroom*, is "the making of Citizen Elvis".

19. "To be sure, the punk attitude remains but its articulation takes a compelling artistic turn" (196).

20. *Painted From Memory* has "punk attitude" and "the ever-present punk worldview" (226).

21. Roger Sabin is suspicious of attempts to contain punk, that it might indeed have represented "a basic shift in the zeitgeist" (Sabin 1999: 5). But he means more specific aspects of art and culture or political movements like "anarchism, green radicalism, and neo-fascism". See his introduction and the essays in Sabin 1999.

22. See Christgau, "Living in a Material World: Raymond Williams' Long Revolution" (1985). This and Christgau's reviews of Costello albums that follow were accessed through www.robertchristgau.com, on 12/07/2007. See also "Introduction: My Favourite Waste of Time" (Christgau 1998: 1–13).

23. Bruno questions whether Costello often uses puns (2005: 31).

24. See Frith (1983a) and Swiss (2005).

25. As did a conference held in Seattle in 2004, commemorated in an issue of *Popular Music* (24/3, 2005).

26. A trenchant but inspiring consideration of journalism and literary theory is found in Paulin 1996: ix–xiv.

27. In the British context alone, academic writing on rock and pop music goes back further (Laing 1969; Middleton 1972; Mellers 1973; Frith 1978); the International Association of Popular Music and the academic journal *Popular Music* were both founded in 1981.

28. 'Off The Hook' was the B-side of 'Little Red Rooster' in 1964, 'Play With Fire' the B-side of 'The Last Time' in 1965, 'She Smiled Sweetly' a track on *Between The Buttons* (1967).

29. In case that seems haughty, Costello had seen "a cartoon naked manga girl writhing on a Rolling Stones tongue" on stage, sensing that among the audience he was alone in embarrassment (Hepworth 2003: 67).

30. Compare "Do you really want me to care about the nasty little Reagan's children of the Napster generation?" (Costello, in Groening and Bresnick 2003: 282).
31. Bookmens 2004: 59–74. Subsequent page references in the text are to this edition.
32. It is arguable that the "new musicology" or "critical musicology" had helped to achieve this, though very much within the academy. Compare Bookmens with Simon Frith and Jon Savage's call for "a new language of pop culture: one derived from anthropology, archetypal psychology, musicology, which has a grasp of pop both as an industrial and as an aesthetic form" (1993: 116).
33. Bookmens has two splendid errors: the drummer Steve (for Pete) Thomas at p. 65 and lyricist Hal Davis (for David) at p. 70. On "readable" as a judgement: "Almost none of the essays has been written with a view to being read" (Hornby 2003: 18).
34. William Walsh, *Handy-Book of Literary Curiosities* (1909), cited in Ricks, "Plagiarism" (2002: 239).
35. John Peel described the Smiths as "an example – perhaps *the* example – of a band that arrived out of the blue without any apparent influences" (Gallagher, Campbell and Gillies 1995: ix).
36. Nick Watkinson and John Alder were the songwriters. The Jags produced two albums, *Evening Standards* (1980) and *No Tie Like A Present* (1981); *The Best Of The Jags* (Spectrum, 1991) is the complete works.
37. Frith misnames the Undertones album *Positive Noise*.
38. See also Pattenden (1999), who refers to Costello at pages 204 and 211.
39. 'Let Love Speak Up Itself' was on *Choke* (1990), 'Rotterdam' on *Blue Is The Colour* (1996), while 'Pretenders To The Throne' was a 1995 single found on the compilation *Solid Bronze: Great Hits* (1991).
40. Lee Dorsey, 'Who's Gonna Help Brother Get Further?' (1970) and 'Freedom For The Stallion' (1973) by the Hues Corporation.
41. I am alluding here to Samuel Johnson's review of Soame Jenyns, *A Free Inquiry into the Nature and Origin of Evil* (Johnson [1757] 1984: 536), via Philip Larkin (1970: 27).

Bibliography

Note: Unpaginated articles, marked with an asterisk, were accessed via www.elviscostello.info

Abraham, Gerald. (1964) *A Hundred Years of Music*, 3rd edn. London: Duckworth.

Aizlewood, John (ed.). (1994) *Love Is the Drug*. Harmondsworth: Penguin.

Amis, Martin. (1984) *Money: A Suicide Note*. London: Jonathan Cape.

Amis, Martin. (1987) *The Moronic Inferno and Other Visits to America*. Harmondsworth: Penguin.

Arato, Andrew, and Eike Gebhardt (eds). (1978) *The Essential Frankfurt School Reader*. New York: Continuum.

Auden, W. H. (1978) *The English Auden*, edited by Edward Mendelson. London: Faber and Faber.

Bate, W. J. (ed.). (1970) *Criticism: The Major Texts* (enlarged edition). San Diego: Harcourt Brace Jovanovich.

Bauldie, John (ed.). (1992) *Wanted Man: In Search of Bob Dylan*. Harmondsworth: Penguin.

Bayton, Mavis. (1998) *Frock Rock: Women Performing Popular Music*. Oxford: Oxford University Press.

Birch, Will. (2000) *No Sleep Till Canvey: The Great Pub Rock Revolution*. London: Virgin.

Bookmens, Rene. (2004) "Uncanny Identities: High and Low and Global and Local in the Music of Elvis Costello", *European Journal of Cultural Studies*, 7/1, pp. 59–74.

Brackett, David. (1995) *Interpreting Popular Music*. Cambridge: Cambridge University Press.

Brackett, David (ed.). (2005a) *The Pop, Rock, and Soul Reader: Histories and Debates*. Oxford: Oxford University Press.

Brackett, David. (2005b) "Elvis Costello, the Empire of the E Chord, and a Magic Moment or Two", *Popular Music*, 24/3, pp. 357–67.

Brown, Charles T. (1987) *The Art of Rock and Roll*, 2nd edn. Englewood Cliffs, NJ: Prentice-Hall.

Bruno, Franklin. (2005) *Elvis Costello: Armed Forces*. New York: Continuum.

Buckley, David. (2005) *Genesis, Q Classic: Pink Floyd and the Story of Prog Rock*, pp. 86–93.

Cagle, Van M. (2000) "Trudging through the Glitter Trenches: The Case of the New York Dolls", in Shelton Waldrep (ed.), *The Seventies: The Age of Glitter in Popular Culture*. London and New York: Routledge, pp. 125–51.

Cale, John and Victor Bockris. (1999) *What's Welsh for Zen? The Autobiography of John Cale*. London: Bloomsbury.

Carr, Roy, Brian Case and Fred Dellar. (1986) *The Hip: Hipsters, Jazz and the Beat Generation*. London: Faber and Faber.

Carson, Tom, Kit Rachlis and Jeff Salamon (eds). (2002) *Don't Stop 'Til You Get Enough: Essays in Honor of Robert Christgau*. Austin, TX: Nortex Press.

Cavanagh, David. (2001) *The Creation Records Story: My Magpie Eyes Are Hungry for the Prize*. London: Virgin.

Christgau, Robert. (1998) *Grown up All Wrong*. Cambridge, MA: Harvard University Press.

Clarke, Donald. (1995) *The Rise and Fall of Popular Music*. Harmondsworth: Penguin.

Clarke, Victoria Mary and Shane MacGowan. (2002) *A Drink with Shane MacGowan*. London: Pan Macmillan.

Clayton-Lea, Tony. (1998) *Elvis Costello: A Biography*. London: André Deutsch.

Clements, Andrew. (1995) "This Year's Muddle", *Guardian*, 20 June, p. 9.

Collis, John (ed.). (1980) *The Rock Primer*. Harmondsworth: Penguin.

Cook, Richard and Brian Morton. (1996) *The Penguin Guide to Jazz on Compact Disc*. Harmondsworth: Penguin.

Corcoran, Neil (ed.). (2002) *Do You Mr Jones? Bob Dylan with the Poets and Professors*. London: Chatto and Windus.

Costello, Elvis. (2000) "Costello's 500", *Vanity Fair*, November, pp. 60–78.

Costello, Elvis. (2002a) "Rocking Around the Clock", *Vanity Fair*, November, reprinted in Matt Groening and Paul Bresnick (eds), *Da Capo Best Music Writing 2003*. Cambridge, MA: Da Capo, 2003, pp. 277–88.

Costello, Elvis. (2002b) Comment on Leslie Vinyl, *Mojo* (March).*

Covach, John. (2006) *What's That Sound? An Introduction to Rock and Its History*. New York: Norton.

Davis, Sheila. (1985) *The Craft of Lyric Writing*. Cincinnati: Writer's Digest Books.

Denselow, Robin. (1989) *When the Music's Over: The Story of Political Pop*. London: Faber and Faber.

Doggett, Peter. (1995) "Elvis Costello", *Record Collector*, 193 (September), pp. 38–49, and 194 (October), pp. 88–96.

Du Gay, Paul (ed.). (1997) *Production of Culture/Cultures of Production*. London: Sage.

Eddy, Chuck. (1997) *The Accidental Evolution of Rock'n'Roll*. New York: Da Capo.

Eisen, Jonathan (ed.). (1969) *The Age of Rock: Sounds of the American Cultural Revolution*. New York: Random House.

Empson, William. (1984) *Collected Poems*. London: Hogarth Press.

Everett, Walter. (1999) *The Beatles as Musicians: Revolver through the* Anthology. New York: Oxford University Press.

Everett, Walter. (2000) "Confessions from Blueberry Hill, Or, Pitch Can Be a Sticky Substance", in Walter Everett (ed.), *Expression in Pop-Rock Music: A Collection of Critical and Analytical Essays*. New York: Garland, pp. 269–345.

Fitzpatrick, Rob. (2005) "Revenge and Guilt a Speciality", *Word*, 24 (February), pp. 78–9.

Flanagan, Bill. (1990) *Written in My Soul*. London: Omnibus.

Forte, Allen. (1962) *Tonal Harmony in Concept and Practice*. New York: Holt, Rinehart and Winston.

Frame, Pete. (1980) *The Complete Rock Family Trees*. London: Omnibus.

Fricke, David. (2004) "The *Rolling Stone* Interview", *Rolling Stone*, 22 September.*

Friedlander, Paul. (1996) *Rock and Roll: A Social History*. Boulder, CO: Westview.

Frith, Simon. (1978) *The Sociology of Rock*. London: Constable.

Frith, Simon. (1983a) "Rock Biography", *Popular Music*, 3, pp. 271–7.

Frith, Simon. (1983b) *Sound Effects: Youth, Leisure and the Politics of Rock'n'Roll*. London: Constable.

Frith, Simon. (1988) *Music for Pleasure: Essays in the Sociology of Music*. Cambridge: Polity.

Frith, Simon. (1996) *Performing Rites: On the Value of Popular Music*. Oxford: Oxford University Press.

Frith, Simon. (2004) "Does British Music Still Matter? A Reflection on the Changing Status of British Popular Music in the Global Music Market", *European Journal of Cultural Studies*, 7 (February), pp. 43–58.

Frith, Simon and Andrew Goodwin (eds). (1990) *On Record: Rock, Pop and the Written Word*. London and New York: Routledge.

Frith, Simon, and Howard Horne. (1987) *Art into Pop*. London: Methuen.

Frith, Simon, and Jon Savage. (1993) "Pearls and Swine: The Intellectuals and the Mass Media", *New Left Review*, 198, pp. 107–16.

Frith, Simon, Will Straw and John Street (eds). (2001) *The Cambridge Companion to Rock and Pop*. Cambridge: Cambridge University Press.

Frith, Simon, and John Street. (1992) "Rock against Racism and Red Wedge: From Music to Politics, from Politics to Music", in Garofalo, pp. 67–80.

Gallagher, Tom, Michael Campbell and Murdo Gillies. (1995) *All Men Have Secrets*. London: Virgin.

Garofalo, Reebee (ed.). (1992) *Rockin' the Boat: Mass Music and Mass Movements*. Boston: South End Press.

Garofalo, Reebee. (1997) *Rockin' Out: Popular Music in the USA*. Needham Heights, MA: Allyn and Bacon.

Gouldstone, David. (1989) *Elvis Costello: A Man out of Time*. London: Sidgwick and Jackson.

Green, Lucy. (2002) *How Popular Musicians Learn: A Way Ahead for Music Education*. Aldershot: Ashgate.

Griffiths, Dai. (2002) "Cover Versions and the Sound of Identity in Motion", in David Hesmondhalgh and Keith Negus (eds), *Popular Music Studies*. London: Arnold, pp. 51–64.

Griffiths, Dai. (2003) "From Lyric to Anti-Lyric: Analysing the Words in Popular Song", in Moore (2003), pp. 39–59.

Griffiths, Dai. (2004) "History and Class Consciousness: Pop Music Towards 2000", in Nicholas Cook and Anthony Pople (eds), *The Cambridge History of Twentieth-century Music*. Cambridge: Cambridge University Press, pp. 557–83.

Griffiths, Dai. (2004) *Radiohead: OK Computer*. New York: Continuum.

Grossberg, Lawrence, Cary Nelson and Paula Treischler (eds), (1992) *Cultural Studies*. London and New York: Routledge.

Hall, Stuart. (1988) *The Hard Road to Renewal: Thatcherism and the Crisis of the Left*. London: Verso.

Hamilton, Ian. (2002a) *Against Oblivion: Some Lives of the Twentieth-century Poets*. London: Penguin.

Hamilton, Ian. (2002b) Interview with Dan Jacobson, *London Review of Books*, 24/2, 24 January.

Hepworth, David. (2003) "Nobody Talks Like Elvis Costello", *Word*, 11 March, pp. 64–72.

Herbert, W. N., and Matthew Hollis (eds). (2000) *Strong Words: Modern Poets on Modern Poetry*. Tarset: Bloodaxe.

Hesmondhalgh, David. (1996) "Rethinking Popular Music after Rock and Soul", in James Curran, David Morley, and Valerie Walkerdine (eds), *Cultural Studies and Communication*. London: Arnold, pp. 195–212.

Hill, Dave. (1994) "Elvis Lives", *GQ*, April, pp. 112–17, 184–5.

Hinton, Brian. (1999) *Let Them All Talk: The Music of Elvis Costello*. London: Sanctuary.

Hobsbaum, Philip. (1996) *Metre, Rhythm and Verse Form*. London and New York: Routledge.

Holloway, Robin. (1979) *Debussy and Wagner*. London: Eulenberg.

Honderich, Ted (ed.). (1995) *The Oxford Companion to Philosophy*. Oxford: Oxford University Press.

Hornby, Nick. (2003) Review of Allan F. Moore, *Analyzing Popular Music, TLS*, no. 5239, 9 August.

Hornby, Nick and Ben Schafer (eds). (2001) *Da Capo Best Music Writing 2001*. Cambridge, MA: Da Capo.

Horner, Bruce and Thomas Swiss (eds). (1999) *Key Terms in Popular Music and Culture*. Malden, MA: Blackwell.

Hoskyns, Barney. (1983) *RAM*, 25 November.*

Hoskyns, Barney. (1991) "El Hath No Fury", *The Wire*, June.*

Hoskyns, Barney. (1993) *Across the Great Divide: The Band and America*. Harmondsworth: Penguin.

Hoskyns, Barney. (1998a) *Glam! Bowie, Bolan and the Glitter Rock Revolution.* London: Faber and Faber.

Hoskyns, Barney. (1998b) *Say It One More Time for the Brokenhearted: Country Soul in the American South.* London: Bloomsbury (first published 1987).

Hulse, Michael, David Kennedy, and David Morley (eds). (1993) *The New Poetry.* Tarset: Bloodaxe.

International Advisory Board. (2005) "Can We Get Rid of the 'Popular' in 'Popular Music'?" *Popular Music,* 24/1, pp. 133–45.

Irwin, Colin. (1989) "Folk Singer's Revenge", *Folk Roots,* 1 July.*

James, Clive. (2006) *The Meaning of Recognition: New Essays 2001–2005.* London: Picador.

Jameson, Fredric. (1991) *Postmodernism or the Cultural Logic of Late Capitalism.* London: Verso.

Johnson, Mary Lynn, and John E. Grant. (1979) *Blake's Poetry and Designs.* New York: W. W. Norton.

Johnson, Samuel (1984), edited by Donald Greene. Oxford: Oxford University Press.

Jones, Ernest. (1964) *The Life and Work of Sigmund Freud,* edited and abridged by Lionel Trilling and Steven Marcus. Harmondsworth: Pelican (first published 1953–7).

Keats, John. (2002) *Selected Letters,* edited by Robert Gittings. Revised edition by John Mee. Oxford: Oxford University Press.

Kelly, Danny. (1986) "The Mortician's Wax", *New Musical Express,* 1 March, pp. 18–19.

Kelly, Karen, and Evelyn McDonnell (eds). (1999) *Stars Don't Stand Still in the Sky: Music and Myth.* London and New York: Routledge.

Kent, Nick. (1994) *The Dark Stuff.* Harmondsworth: Penguin.

Laing, Dave. (1969) *The Sound of Our Time.* London: Sheed and Ward.

Larkin, Colin. (1999) *The Virgin Encyclopaedia of Popular Music.* London: Muze.

Larkin, Philip. (1970) *All What Jazz: A Record Diary.* London: Faber and Faber.

Larkin, Philip. (1983) *Required Writing: Miscellaneous Pieces 1955–1982.* London: Faber and Faber.

Larkin, Philip. (1988) *Collected Poems,* edited by Anthony Thwaite. London: Faber and Faber.

Larkin, Philip. (2001) *Further Requirements: Interviews, Broadcasts, Statements and Book Reviews 1952–85,* edited by Anthony Thwaite. London: Faber and Faber.

Levin, Harry (ed.). (1976) *The Portable James Joyce.* Harmondsworth: Penguin.

Lodge, David. (1977) *The Modes of Modern Writing: Metaphor, Metonymy, and the Typology of Modern Literature.* London: Edward Arnold.

Lodge, David. (1988) *Nice Work.* London: Secker and Warburg.

Longley, Edna. (1986) *Poetry Between the Wars.* Tarset: Bloodaxe.

Macan, Edward. (1997) *Rocking the Classics: English Progressive Rock and the Counterculture.* New York: Oxford University Press.

Marcus, Greil. (1975) *Mystery Train: Images of America in Rock'n'Roll Music.* London: Omnibus.

Marcus, Greil. (1989) *Lipstick Traces: A Secret History of the Twentieth Century.* London: Secker and Warburg.

Marcus, Greil. (1993) *In the Fascist Bathroom: Writings on Punk 1977–1992.* London: Viking.

Marcus, Greil (ed.). (1996) *Stranded: Rock and Roll for a Desert Island.* New York: Da Capo.

Marcus, Greil. (1997) *Invisible Republic: Bob Dylan's Basement Tapes.* London: Picador.

Marsh, Dave. (1989) *The Heart of Rock and Soul: The 1001 Greatest Singles Ever Made.* Harmondsworth: Penguin.

McRobbie, Angela. (1996) "Looking Back at New Times and Its Critics", in David Morley and Chen Kuan-Hsing (eds), *Stuart Hall: Critical Dialogues in Cultural Studies.* London and New York: Routledge, pp. 238–61.

Mellers, Wilfrid. (1973) *Twilight of the Gods: The Beatles in Retrospect.* London: Faber and Faber.

Mercer-Taylor, Peter. (1995) "Elvis Costello Opens His Mouth Almighty", *repercussions,* 4/1, pp. 26–52.

Middleton, Richard. (1972) *Pop Music and the Blues.* London: Victor Gollancz.

Moore, Allan F. (1993) *Rock: The Primary Text.* Buckingham: Open University Press.

Moore, Allan F. (1995) "The So-called 'Flattened Seventh' in Rock", *Popular Music,* 14/2, pp. 185–201.

Moore, Allan F. (ed.). (2003) *Analyzing Popular Music.* Cambridge: Cambridge University Press.

Morgan, Kenneth O. (2001) *Britain Since 1945: The People's Peace,* 3rd edn. Oxford: Oxford University Press.

Morton, Colin B. and Chuck Death. (1998) *Great Pop Things: The Real History of Rock'n'Roll from Elvis to Oasis.* Portland, OR: Verse Chorus Press.

Mulholland, Marc. (2002) *Northern Ireland: A Very Short Introduction.* Oxford: Oxford University Press.

Negus, Keith. (1999) *Music Genres and Corporate Cultures.* London and New York: Routledge.

Negus, Keith. (2005) Review of Larry David Smith, *Elvis Costello, Joni Mitchell, and the Torch Song Tradition, Popular Music,* 24/3, pp. 453–7.

Palmer, Robert. (1996) *Dancing in the Street: A Rock and Roll History.* London: BBC Books.

Parkyn, Geoff. (1984) *Elvis Costello: The Illustrated Disco/Biography.* London: Omnibus.

210 Bibliography

Pattenden, Mike. (1999) *Last Orders at the Liar's Bar: The Official Story of the Beautiful South*. London: Gollancz.

Pattison, Robert. (1987) *The Triumph of Vulgarity: Rock Music in the Mirror of Romanticism*. New York: Oxford University Press.

Paulin, Tom (ed.). (1986) *The Faber Book of Political Verse*. London: Faber and Faber.

Paulin, Tom. (1996) *Writing to the Moment: Selected Critical Essays 1980–1996*. London: Faber and Faber.

Perone, James E. (1998) *Elvis Costello: A Bio-bibliography*. Westport, CT, and London: Greenwood.

Piston, Walter. (1987) *Harmony*, revised and expanded by Mark de Voto. London: Victor Gollancz (first published 1941).

Preminger, Alex and T. V. F. Brogan (eds). (1993) *The New Princeton Encyclopaedia of Poetry and Poetics*. Princeton, NJ: Princeton University Press.

Reese, Krista. (1981) *EC: A Completely False Biography Based on Rumour, Innuendo and Lies*. London: Proteus.

Reynolds, Simon. (1990) *Blissed Out: The Raptures of Rock*. London: Serpent's Tail.

Reynolds, Simon. (1991) "Elvis Costello and Martin Amis: Prophets of Doom", *Arena*, Summer.*

Reynolds, Simon and Joy Press. (1995) *The Sex Revolts: Gender, Rebellion and Rock'n'Roll*. London: Serpent's Tail.

Ricks, Christopher. (1984) *The Force of Poetry*. Oxford: Oxford University Press.

Ricks, Christopher. (2002) *Allusion to the Poets*. Oxford: Oxford University Press.

Ricks, Christopher. (2003) *Dylan's Visions of Sin*. London: Viking.

Rosen, Charles. (1976) *The Classical Style: Haydn, Mozart, Beethoven* (rev. edn). London: Faber and Faber.

Rosen, Charles. (1995) *The Romantic Generation*. Cambridge, MA: Harvard University Press.

Russell, Tom, and Sylvia Tyson. (1995) *And Then I Wrote: The Songwriter Speaks*. Vancouver: Arsenal Pulp Press.

Sabin, Roger (ed.). (1999) *Punk Rock: So What? The Cultural Legacy of Punk*. London and New York: Routledge.

Sadie, Stanley (ed.). (2001) *The New Grove Dictionary of Music and Musicians*, 2nd edn. London: Macmillan (accessed via www.grovemusic.com).

Sakolsky, Ron and Fred Wei-han Ho (eds). (1995) *Sounding Off: Music as Subversion/Resistance/Revolution*. New York: Autonomedia.

Savage, Jon. (1996) *Time Travel: Pop, Media and Sexuality 1976–96*. London: Chatto and Windus.

Scott, Clive. (1988) *The Riches of Rhyme: Studies in French Verse*. Oxford: Clarendon Press.

Shepherd, John, David Horn, Dave Laing, Paul Oliver, and Peter Wicke (eds). (2003) *Continuum Encyclopaedia of Popular Music of the World, Volume One: Media Industry and Society.* London: Continuum.

Sheppard, David. (2000) *Elvis Costello* [The Music Makers]. London: Unanimous.

Smith, Larry David. (2004) *Elvis Costello, Joni Mitchell, and the Torch Song Tradition.* Westport, CT, and London: Praeger.

Springsteen, Bruce. (2003) *Songs.* London: Virgin.

St. Michael, Mick. (1986) *Elvis Costello: An Illustrated Biography.* London: Omnibus.

Staunton, Terry. (1989) Review of Elvis Costello, *Spike*, in *New Musical Express*, 11 February.*

Street, John. (1986) *Rebel Rock: The Politics of Popular Music.* Oxford: Basil Blackwell.

Street, John. (1997) *Politics and Popular Culture.* Cambridge: Polity.

Strong, Martin C. (2002) *The Great Rock Discography.* Edinburgh: Canongate.

Swiss, Thomas. (2005) "That's Me in the Spotlight: Rock Autobiographies", *Popular Music*, 24/2, pp. 287–94.

Thomas, Bruce. (2003) *The Big Wheel*, 2nd edn. London: Helter Skelter.

Thomson, Graeme. (2004) *Complicated Shadows: The Life and Music of Elvis Costello.* Edinburgh: Canongate.

Thurschwell, Pamela. (1999) "Elvis Costello as Cultural Icon and Cultural Critic", in Kevin J. H. Dettmar and William Richey (eds), *Reading Rock and Roll: Authenticity, Appropriation, Aesthetics.* New York: Columbia University Press, pp. 287–310.

Tosches, Nick. (2000) *The Nick Tosches Reader.* New York: Da Capo.

Tovey, Donald Francis. (1931) *A Companion to Beethoven's Pianoforte Sonatas.* London: Associated Boards of the Royal Schools of Music.

Tovey, Donald Francis. (1949) *Essays and Lectures on Music.* Oxford: Oxford University Press.

Ward, Ed, Geoffrey Stokes and Ken Tucker (eds). (1986) *Rock of Ages: The Rolling Stone History of Rock and Roll.* New York: Rolling Stone Press/Summit.

Webb, Jimmy. (1998) *Tunesmith: Inside the Art of Songwriting.* New York: Hyperion.

White, Timothy. (1983) "A Man Out of Time Beats the Clock", *Musician*, October.*

Wimsatt, William K., Jr. (1954) *The Verbal Icon.* Lexington: University of Kentucky Press.

Wimsatt, William K., Jr, and Cleanth Brooks. (1957) *Literary Criticism: A Short History.* New York: Vintage.

Woolrich, John. (1995) Reply to Andrew Clements, *Guardian*, 24 June, p. 28.

Wordsworth, William. (1984) *The Major Works*, edited by Stephen Gill. Oxford: Oxford University Press.

Zollo, Paul. (1997) *Songwriters on Songwriting* (expanded edn). New York: Da Capo.

Album Discography

Note: UK issue unless otherwise indicated.

My Aim Is True (Stiff, 1977)

This Year's Model (Radar, 1978)

Armed Forces (Radar, 1979)

Get Happy!! (F-Beat, 1980)

Ten Bloody Marys & Ten How's Your Fathers (F-Beat, 1980) (in USA *Taking Liberties*)*

Trust (F-Beat, 1981)

Almost Blue (F-Beat, 1981)*

Imperial Bedroom (F-Beat, 1982)

Punch The Clock (F-Beat, 1983)

Goodbye Cruel World (F-Beat, 1984)

The Best Of Elvis Costello: The Man (Telstar, 1985)*

King Of America (F-Beat, 1986)

Blood And Chocolate (Imp Demon, 1986)

Our Of Our Idiot (Demon, 1987)*

Girls Girls Girls (Demon, 1989)*

Spike (Warners, 1989)

GBH (Demon, 1991) (with Richard Harvey)

Mighty Like A Rose (Warners, 1991)

The Juliet Letters (Warners, 1993) (with the Brodsky String Quartet)

The First 2½ Years (Demon, 1993)*

The Very Best Of Elvis Costello (Demon, 1994)

Brutal Youth (Warners, 1994)

Deep Dead Blue (Warners, 1995) (with Bill Frisell)*

Kojak Variety (Warners, 1995)*

Jake's Progress (Demon Soundtracks, 1996) (with Richard Harvey)

Costello And Nieve (Warners, 1996)*

All This Useless Beauty (Warners, 1996)

Extreme Honey (Warners, 1997)*

Bespoke Songs, Lost Dogs, Detours And Rendezvous (Rhino, 1998)*

Painted From Memory (Mercury, 1998) (with Burt Bacharach)

Sweetest Punch (Universal, 1999) (with Bill Frisell)*

The Very Best Of Elvis Costello (Universal, 1999)*

For The Stars (Deutsche Grammophon, 2001) (with Anne Sofie von Otter)

When I Was Cruel (Island Def Jam, 2002)

Cruel Smile (Island Def Jam, 2002)*

North (Deutsche Grammophon, 2003)

The Delivery Man (Lost Highway, 2004)

Il Sogno (Deutsche Grammophon, 2004) (London Symphony Orchestra/Michael
Tilson Thomas)

The River In Reverse (Verve Forecast, 2006) (with Allen Toussaint)

My Flame Burns Blue (Deutsche Grammophon, 2006)*

Best Of Elvis Costello: The First Ten Years (UM3, 2007)*

Rock'n'Roll Music (UM3, 2007)*

* indicates compilations, retrospectives, concert performances, cover versions

Websites

www.elviscostello.info
www.maccaspan.com
www.robertchristgau.com
www.rockcritics.com
www.rocklistmusic.co.uk
www.rocksbackpages.com
www.youtube.com

Index

Page references in *italic* indicate illustrations.